Introducing Organisational Behaviour

Longman modular texts in business and economics

Series Editors
Geoff Black and Stuart Wall

Other titles in this series:

Business Information Technology: Systems, Theory and Practice
Geoffrey Elliott and Susan Starkings

The Macroeconomic Environment
Andrew Dunnett

Marketing
Elizabeth Hill and Terry O'Sullivan

Business Economics
Win Hornby, Bob Gammie and Stuart Wall

Management Accounting
David Wright

Financial Accounting
Christopher Waterston and Anne Britton

Introducing Human Resource Management
Margaret Foot and Caroline Hook

Quantitative Methods for Business and Economics
Glyn Burton, George Carrol and Stuart Wall

Introducing Organisational Behaviour

Jane Weightman

Cartoon illustrations by Rebecca Green

An imprint of Pearson Education

Harlow, England · London · New York · Reading, Massachusetts · San Francisco · Toronto · Don Mills, Ontario · Sydney
Tokyo · Singapore · Hong Kong · Seoul · Taipei · Cape Town · Madrid · Mexico City · Amsterdam · Munich · Paris · Milan

Pearson Education Limited
Edinburgh Gate
Harlow
Essex CM20 2JE
United Kingdom

and Associated Companies throughout the world

Visit us on the world wide web at:
http://www.pearsoned.co.uk

First published 1999

ISBN 0 582 35642 3

British Library Cataloging-in-Publication Data
A catalogue record for this book is available from the British Library

Library of Congress Cataloging-in-Publication Data
Weightman, Jane.
Introducing organisational behaviour / Jane Weightman ;
p. cm. -- (Longman modular texts in business and economics)
Includes bibliographical references and index.
ISBN 0-582-35642-3 (pa.)
1. Organizational behaviour. I. Title. II. Series.
HF58.7.W337 1999
158'.7--dc21 98-44044
CIP

10 9 8 7 6 5
07 06 05 04

Set in Stone Serif 9/12pt
Typeset by 30
Produced by Pearson Education Asia (Pte) Ltd
Printed in Great Britain by 4edge Ltd, Hockley, Essex.

Contents

Preface

This book is aimed at people who are studying organisational behaviour for the first time. This could be as a major part of their studies in management and business studies. It is more likely, however, that this will be as part of a mixed programme of studies where the main substance is not organisational behaviour, for example, leisure and tourism or textiles where some management studies are included. I have mostly concentrated on the main theories and models used to analyse organisations that experts in the field agree are worthy of consideration, the 'received wisdom' of the discipline. In addition to this I have tried to show some of the underlying disciplines and some practical implications of the models.

Throughout the book there are various devices. 'Pause for thought' is intended to get you to reflect on what you have just read. 'Did you know?' supplies additional pieces of information such as specific examples or extra quotations that are not central to understanding the chapter but may add interest. An 'Activity' is where you are asked to do something to give you experience of the issues. 'Exercises' are rather longer activities, often involving other people. 'Self-check questions' appear at the end of each chapter so you can check whether you took in the main points. 'Case studies' are a specific example of some aspect of the chapter. The figures include some cartoons by Rebecca Green who is an illustrator, coming, like you, to organisational behaviour for the first time. I hope you enjoy them.

Jane Weightman

CHAPTER **1**

Introduction to organisational behaviour

Objectives

When you have read this chapter you will be able to:

- Know how to use this book.
- Understand something of the difference between psychology and sociology.
- Realise that there are different strands of thinking which can be useful in analysing organisational behaviour.
- Understand some of the different schools of thought about organisational behaviour.
- Systematically observe someone at work.

Introduction

The human race survives and operates through organisation. Organisation is required to provide us with our motor cars and cultural amenities; our health care and education; our consumer goods and information services. For all these things we have to work together – to organise and to be organised. Organisational life is the setting in which most of us spend our working hours and at least part of our leisure. A day at the office may well be followed by an evening at a concert or a weekend at an activity centre.

The study of organisational behaviour is the study of what people do in organisations and why they do it. The purpose of studying organisational behaviour is not purely an academic exercise, it is also to help answer such questions as:

- Can I make a better contribution?
- Am I secure?
- How do I resolve this problem?
- How do I get things done?
- How do I meet my responsibilities?
- Why do people behave this way?
- Why is my undertaking organised differently from the one in which my neighbour works?
- How do I cope with this situation?
- Do I understand the structure properly?
- How do I understand what is going on around me?

By understanding what goes on around us we are better placed to behave appropriately to achieve our goals. In recent years there has been a reaction against very large scale, impersonal and bureaucratic organisations. But working together with others rather than working alone continues to be our conventional idea of a 'job'. The extraordinary achievements of people doing things on their own, like sailing around the world or long walks, are famed because of the courage and skill of individuals triumphing over formidable obstacles. But when Armstrong walked on the moon it was the triumph of thousands who had contributed to the cooperative venture of the NASA space programme.

Individuals will continue to make great contributions to society on their own, but the major achievements that are needed come from organisations; not only factories, offices, shops, hotels and other commercial undertakings but hospitals and research centres, government departments and charitable bodies, schools and colleges. There are many challenges to mankind that require an organised contribution for their resolution. We have to learn to handle problems such as atmospheric pollution and the shortage of energy; technological innovation and the obsolescence of traditional skills; poverty in the third world and the underemployed in the West. Few of these problems have a simple solution requiring no more than the political will, and few of them depend on the intuition or insight of an individual. Organised activity is needed both to produce the solutions and to implement them.

DID YOU KNOW?
The contemporary rock star tours with an entourage of dozens or hundreds of people, all of whom are needed to put together the eventual performance even though it seems as though only one individual is performing.

The different strands needed to analyse organisational behaviour

To study organisational behaviour we need to look at ideas and evidence from several traditions. First, there is material which originates in the social sciences: psychology, sociology, political theory and philosophy. These subject areas have developed individual specialisms in work organisation. You will find psychologists using the phrases 'organisational psychology' or 'organisational behaviour' in the titles of books. Sociologists and political theorists use phrases such as 'organisation analysis' and 'organisational theory'. Although this book has 'organisational behaviour' in the title I intend to use models from a variety of traditions not just psychology.

Second, there is material from what the Americans call 'management' specialists: ideas, research and practice that are devoid of any academic pedigree but look particularly at work organisation from the management perspective. This group includes various sorts of expert. It may be successful managers who have written autobiographies, for example John Harvey Jones (1994) former chairman of ICI, or Bill Gates (1996) who set up Microsoft. It can be systematic researchers of management, such as the study of core competencies in organisations by Prahalad and Hamel (1990). Or it may be management textbooks where assumptions are made about the nature of the management task and are written to help managers do their work more effectively from that perspective, see for example Handy (1985). Subsections of this group of material are people working with a personnel, training and development perspective which is now often called 'human resource management'. Each of these specialisms has a contribution to make to understanding organisational behaviour.

Figure 1.1 **Two ways of looking at things.**

This book tries to use material from a wide range of different disciplines. In the first part, which concentrates on the individual, there is a lot of material from a psychological perspective with its language of behaviours, motivation and feedback. Part 2 mostly uses the language of sociology to look at groups with an emphasis on such things as norms and roles. Part 3, which looks at the organisation as a whole, uses language from a variety of disciplines. From engineering comes the language of systems, structures and control. From politics the language of power, influence and authority. From management that of overall responsibility and from theology the language of vision, leadership and commitment. The study of organisational behaviour therefore involves a range of human language and analysis. It is also the case that there are always several different ways of looking at the same behaviour or issue. Sometimes these differing views are compatible but not always (see Figure 1.1).

What are the social sciences?

The two disciplines in social science that are most relevant to analysing organisational behaviour are psychology and sociology. Other disciplines normally included among the social sciences are economics, geography and political theory. They are not included in detail in this book. However, the idea of people as economically and politically active is important for understanding organisational life and is included in discussions throughout the book about the analysis of how things are done.

When I tell people I'm a psychologist they usually say something such as 'Oh I'd better be careful then as you can read my mind.' Fortunately this is not true. I cannot read people's minds. Another confusion is that psychology is the same as psychiatry. It is not. Psychiatry is concerned with particular accounts and treatments of people with mental illness. So what is psychology?

Psychology is normally defined as the study of behaviour. It may be animal or human behaviour. This study can include detailed descriptions of particular behaviours – for example, how we learn. It may also include some analysis to try to account for why these behaviours happen in the particular way they do. By looking at the underlying structures and hypothesising about the effects of previous experience and the environment in which it takes place we try to understand such questions as:

- Why do people choose to do different things?
- Why does someone reject this course of action when the previous person did not?
- Why do decisions change?

Psychology usually tries to account for the behaviour of individuals, but that includes what happens to them when they are in groups large and small.

A particular branch of psychology relevant to our needs is organisational psychology. People working in this area apply the findings and models of psychology generally to work organisations. They also do research into organisations to try to improve our understanding of them. As with all psychology there is particular emphasis on the effect on individuals and their effect on others. This includes such questions as:

- What do managers do?
- How do groups influence each other?
- How does change in people's behaviour happen most effectively?

I use several examples from this discipline throughout the book, particularly in Parts 1 and 2.

DID YOU KNOW?

Liam Hudson, a British psychologist, when asked why he become a psychologist (Cohen 1977 p. 151) replied: 'It was heavily overdetermined in my case. I think you could have looked at me at fifteen or sixteen and seen four or five over-riding reasons why I would end up as a psychologist. A preoccupation with people. I was looking recently at a journal I kept when I was fifteen, a very intimate, heart-felt journal. It has only three things in it – an account of the sports I played, which were almost endless, the amount of food I'd eaten and the people I'd spoken to by name. I think that kind of personal interest has obviously stayed with me.'

Sociology is concerned with the social, group and institutional aspects of human society. There is some overlap with all the other social sciences. What distinguishes sociology is a desire to understand the influences and agreed norms of the institutions of society that affect the behaviour of its members. Sociologists look for generic (general across groups) concepts and patterns that can help to explain social activities. They examine such questions as:

- What are the roles we play?
- What institutions are most dominant in society?
- Does the nature of the community affect the individual's choice of career?
- How do bureaucracies work?
- What distinguishes the professions from other groups of workers?
- Are there different sorts of conflict?
- What are the effects of different cultures?

These enquiries can then be used to analyse specific examples in work settings such as the role of a senior manager, the profession of accounting, the culture of the health service. Of all the social scientists, sociologists are the most interdisciplinary, sharing insights and ideas with economists, geographers, psychologists and political scientists as well as philosophical and religious writers. This interdisciplinary tradition is useful for analysing and understanding work organisations. The complexity and variety of the analytical tools that we need to make sense of the different aspects of working life are often reflected in one of sociology's concepts. This is particularly so when we try to understand a specific organisation as compared with another or the position of a particular group within the organisation. I have used insights and models from sociology throughout the book but particularly in Parts 2 and 3.

ACTIVITY **1.1**

If you were going to do research on issues facing universities you would start with some questions. You would then need to decide which tradition could best answer these questions. Then you would need to decide on an appropriate way of carrying out the study, the methodology. If you were to do this sort of research would psychology or sociology be your first choice of discipline for studying the following organisational issues in universities?

1 Training the newly-appointed lecturer.
2 The problem of amalgamating the tourism department with the hotel and catering section.
3 What does the dean, one of the senior academic managers, do?
4 The effect of increased student numbers on the library staff.
5 Can we resolve the conflict between the social committee in the hall of residence and representatives from the community?
6 What would motivate the porters so they will ensure the building is available for use into the evenings?

Other disciplines from social science that are also involved in studying organisational behaviour are economics when considering performance management, Chapter 9, and political science when considering power, Chapter 12. Some other disciplines are also influential, for example, history and cultural studies will tell us about the context of organisational behaviour, and engineering some of the control language that some management writers use.

Social scientists use all sorts of different methods to study behaviour. Some psychologists use biological methods to study the biological basis of behaviour. This sort of study seeks to determine the limits and the inherited components of behaviour. For example, how is memory stored in the brain? see Greenfield (1997). Other psychologists use a scientific framework but study behaviour. They set up carefully controlled experiments in the laboratory where everything is kept the same except one element, any differences in behaviour are then accounted for by variation in the one factor. As an example of this type of study one author tells us that any sort of additional attention to people at work improves their productivity on routine tasks (the so called 'Hawthorne effect' which was found in some early work in factories by psychologists, see page 10).

Yet other psychologists and sociologists study behaviour in its natural setting, trying to use systematic description and analysis to account for that behaviour. This might involve questionnaires, interviews or observation. Examples would be studies of stress in teachers or the behaviour of street gangs in country towns. Sociologists use interviews and observation to collect their data. Sometimes they use outsider, non-participant, observation; on other occasions the study is conducted by a member as participant observation. Unlike psychologists they rarely use controlled experiments preferring to study real situations.

You will notice throughout this book reference is made to some quite old writings. This is for two reasons: first, the academic tradition of referring to original material where possible; second the current state of social science. The development of any discipline is never even; sometimes there is a rapid increase in knowledge and theory, at other times progress is slower. The last decade or two has seen a marked change in confidence in psychology and sociology with an increase in the variety of views about what is going on. Two areas where there has been the most consensus about genuine development in psychology, for example, are physiological psychology where study of the brain's mechanisms is increasing our understanding, and developmental psychology with its analysis of how children develop. In other areas there is rather less sign of new fundamental agreed theories. Much of the introspection and self-analysis, see, for example, Kline (1989), is probably because the basic description and analysis of behaviour have been done and psychology and sociology are now looking at higher order models and integrations. Many are looking to applied areas such as studying the mentally ill, education and indeed organisational behaviour to help develop these higher order models using the basic research of older references as their starting points.

ACTIVITY **1.2**

Think of an organisational issue to study for which you would use each of the following methods.

- Observation by a participant – where the person is part of what is going on and makes notes later or surreptitiously.
- Non-participant observation – where the person stands around with a clipboard making notes of the observations made.
- Interview – a structured interview is where the questions are prepared; an unstructured interview is where the areas to be covered are listed but the interview is more like a conversation.
- Questionnaire – a structured list of questions that are asked either in the researcher's presence or not, and anonymously or not.

If you can't think of any issues go back to the questions on the first page of this chapter and use them to get started.

Specific models of organisational behaviour

Organising to achieve various outcomes has been part of human history since at least the time of the Egyptians and their pyramid-building enterprises. Many important insights into organisational behaviour can be found in very early writings about the Roman army, such as how to organise the men, or in books such as Machiavelli's sixteenth century *The Prince* on the politics of obligations. It is not my intention to go quite that far back here, although I would recommend a brief dip into Machiavelli, he was among the first to describe what leaders were really like rather than how they liked to be described and was excommunicated for his efforts. We could perhaps liken him to a whistle blower of today who gets sacked for publicly pointing out the shortcomings in an organisation. In more recent times there have been several different schools of thought about organisational behaviour that are important to understand as they examine different issues in organisational life and reflect a continuing difference of approach. Here is a brief summary of some of the main trends or schools of thought that initially were used by management specialists but also influenced the way more detached analysis of organisational behaviour took place. There are several more detailed accounts of these schools of thought available, see the Further reading section at the end of this chapter.

PAUSE FOR THOUGHT

Machiavelli's main points are:

- *Cohesive organisation. The prince should maintain cohesiveness of the organisation by binding his friends and those on whom he will depend. This will involve giving them rewards for their contribution and making sure that they know what the prince expects and what they can expect from him.*
- *Mass consent. However cohesive the power structure of the organisation the prince has to maintain the consent of the governed, as it is the source of his authority. Not only does it give him authority over the governed, it also gives him authority over his courtiers.*
- *Leadership. Cohesive organisation and mass consent can only be achieved if the prince is a leader and example setter for his people, being wise and tempering necessary justice with mercy.*
- *Toughness. There will be attempts to unseat the prince, so he must have the toughness to resist any such attempt and be ruthless with the instigators.*

Scientific management

An influential model of organisational behaviour at the beginning of the twentieth century was scientific management. This was the approach developed by F. W. Taylor to find the 'one best way' of working. Some of his key innovations – selection, training and job analysis – still form the basis of modern management and particularly human resource management or personnel management. His work is particularly associated with the emphasis on productivity that led to mass production and the development of the car assembly line of Ford.

Taylor is a figure of overwhelming importance in the development of management thinking and organisational behavioural analysis. He was an American working at the turn of the nineteenth century, as were other pioneers associated with scientific management: Henry Ford, Henry Gantt and the Gilbreths. The basic premise of this approach is that if you study what to do in sufficient detail you can optimise the performance of individuals by cutting out all the redundant effort and maximising the useful movements. For example, by looking at how someone skins and slices

DID YOU KNOW?

Gantt is most famous for the introduction of the Gantt chart which is a simple planning device where you start with the finishing point of the due date. You then work back with the estimated time for the various component tasks necessary for completion of the whole job to see where there are real periods of panic and when you need to get things done by if the task is to be finished on time. Figure 1.2 shows an example from a GP's office where they were introducing a Well Person Clinic.

white fish in a fish factory you can see that some workers are much more efficient than others. By analysing them 'scientifically', that is systematically, to see each movement they make of the fish, hands, body and knife you can arrive at a pattern to teach others to make them more efficient fish skinners and slicers. If this principle of careful analysis is then applied to the whole selection of staff and equipment you arrive at a 'scientifically' managed organisation.

This scientific management tradition is still widely seen in such devices as quality procedures, the design of control systems in factories and in the analysis of tasks for piece work. The difficulties of using only such a 'hard' mechanistic approach is that it takes very little account of individual differences. Not everyone works in the same way effectively. It also tends to dampen any initiative and creativity that the individual may offer the organisation. This approach can, however, be very useful for managers where there is a high turnover of staff, a very simple routine task or where the staff cannot be expected to be very motivated. The prime example of this approach in contemporary society is the McDonald's burger chain which has 'scientifically' analysed every aspect of their business from the raw materials and packaging, to training of staff and the ambience of their outlets. Clearly with a deal of commercial success. Another example is call centres, such as telephone banking and advice lines, where staff are under pressure to keep to quotas and have very little influence over their work. No wonder a 'burn out' after twelve months is considered normal.

Figure 1.2
A Gantt chart to set up a Well Person Clinic.

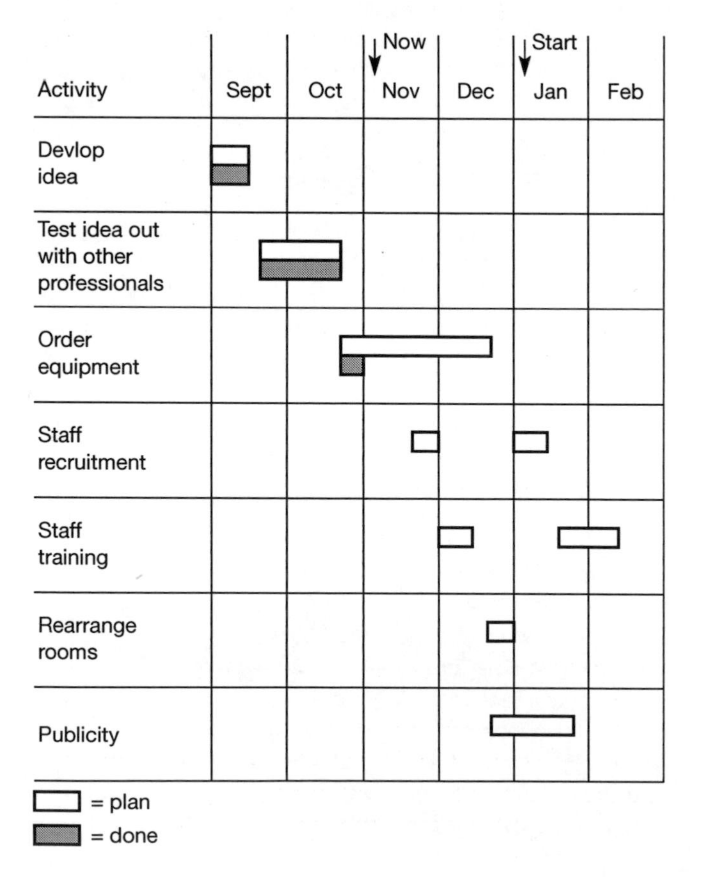

Bureaucracy

The German sociologist Weber was very influential on this school of thought by his analysis of bureaucracy. He argued that the market structure of Western societies required business organisations to be highly structured, or bureaucratic, with the following qualities:

- Role definition. The duties and responsibilities of organisation members are clearly defined.
- Hierarchy/authority. There is a clear chain of relationships with all the members knowing precisely to whom they are responsible and who is responsible to them.
- Rules and procedures. The organisation operates according to an elaborate system of rules determining the way in which each member should perform. Records should provide precedents to be followed so as to ensure consistency.
- Qualification for office. People are appointed to positions on the basis of merit that is formally attested and subject to systematic selection and training.
- Impartiality. Members of the organisation discharge their duties without heat or partiality, motivated by the prospect of moving up the hierarchy, as well as by a sense of duty.

This has proved to be a very accurate account of how many organisations have functioned, especially large and complex ones. But there is a tendency for rules to become an end in themselves and for personal initiative to be discouraged. Bureaucracy is perhaps best suited to managing the steady state, where a predictable service needs to be delivered at the point of use. There are still many examples around. Such as parts of the banking system (branches), parts of the public sector such as tax collection and parts of the voluntary sector such as charity telephone appeals. To realise how useful a bureaucracy can be consider the following questions. How could we know how to use a different branch from our own without a known procedure? Would we really want to negotiate every time we wanted cash?

The development of a theory of administrative management to deal with these large organisations came initially from the French theorist Fayol, who defined the five functions of management as planning, coordinating, organising, commanding and controlling. While Taylor's work was a model for supervision, Fayol produced a conceptual framework for management as a whole. Working in the same mode of thinking were such people as Mary Parker Follet and Lyndall Urwick. These basic concepts of management are still at the heart of much writing on the management of organisations, although there is a great deal of discussion about their appropriateness.

The human relations movement

A number of researchers set out to redress what they saw as an imbalance in the work of Taylor and Fayol, by taking greater account of the mind as well as the body of the individual worker. The most famous proponent of what came to be known as the human relations school of thought was Elton Mayo. He conducted experiments to demonstrate the limits of the precision of Taylor. From this perspective workers were no longer the extension of the machine, responsive only to financial incentives. Instead they were seen as individuals and members of a social group, with attitudes and behaviours that were the key to effectiveness.

Mayo and his colleagues conducted a series of experiments in an electrical company which demonstrated several aspects of behaviour at work:

- Work pacing. The pace at which people produce is one set informally by the work group.
- Recognition. Acknowledgement of an employee's contribution by those in authority tends to increase output, as do other forms of social approval.
- Social interaction. The opportunities provided by the working situation for social interaction between fellow workers, especially if they could select for interaction those with whom they were compatible, enhanced job satisfaction and sometimes influenced output.
- The Hawthorne effect. Regardless of what changes were made to the way the employees were treated, productivity went up as they seemed to enjoy the novelty of the situation and the extra attention – the so-called 'Hawthorne effect'.
- Grievances. Employees responded well to having someone to let off steam to by talking through problems they were having.
- Conforming. The pressure from work mates in the group was far more influential on behaviour than any incentives from management.

The importance of this work was to show the effect of work groups on behaviour. It also helped to generate new ideas about the nature of supervision to include some better communication and some personnel management. It was perhaps most important in recognising the critical nature of informal processes at work as well as the rational, scientific procedures that management prescribes. Criticisms of this work have usually been of its methodology and can be very technical.

Socio-technical systems and the contingency approach

Another school of thought about organisations is the systems approach which treats organisations as systems with inputs and outputs. One group within this are the British researchers at the Tavistock Institute of Human Relations (an offshoot of a famous psychiatric centre) who after the Second World War were charged with finding better ways for people to work productively. They were particularly interested in the changes that occurred when new technology was introduced. For example, in coal mining there used to be small groups working on a face who were very cohesive and supportive of each other with excellent coordination between shifts, see Trist (1963). When a new method of cutting coal, the longwall method, was introduced these socially cohesive groups broke down and coordination of effort was much more difficult.

This school of thought showed that there was an important relationship between the size of the enterprise, the nature of the work, the way it was organised and the nature of the work group. These were all important contributions to our understanding of organisational behaviour.

From this, and other, research there developed a group of theories about organisations which are grouped together as the 'contingency' approach. This basically says that there is no one ideal state of organisation but that the sort of ideal organisation is dependent, that is contingent, on the nature of the task to be done. This is currently the most popular approach and will appear again throughout this book when we look at different aspects and issues of organisational behaviour. I have, therefore, not described it in detail here as you will use it in a variety of contexts throughout the book.

The pursuit of excellence

Another school of analysis of organisations is exemplified by the management gurus of the 1980s and 1990s. The most influential book in the field of management in the 1980s was *In Search of Excellence* by the management expert Tom Peters and R.H. Waterman, a journalist who transcribed his findings into readable English. The book reports a study of 43 American companies that were excellently managed according to a range of criteria. Peters and Waterman concluded that the success of these companies was not due to anything more elaborate than being 'brilliant at the basics', and working hard at fundamental aspects of management. Peters and Waterman described eight attributes of the management style of their excellent companies as follows:

- Bias for action. A preference for doing something rather than waiting for further analysis.
- Keeping close to the customer.
- Autonomy and entrepreneurship. Breaking a corporation into small units, each thinking independently and competitively.
- Productivity through people. Enabling all employees to appreciate the importance of the personal participation and enabling them to share success.
- Hands on, value driven. Keeping everyone in touch with the main task of the business.
- Sticking to the knitting. Remaining in a line of business that the people are good at.
- Simple form, lean staff. Uncluttered organisation charts with the minimum number of levels in the hierarchy and few people at the upper levels.
- Simultaneous loose–tight properties. A climate in which there is dedication to the central values of the company combined with tolerance for all employees who accept the values.

The attractiveness of these ideas has been their simplicity and their realism, although the subsequent performance of some of the companies has not necessarily confirmed the unfailing accuracy of the diagnosis.

PAUSE FOR THOUGHT *In what ways are organisations you have experience of 'brilliant at the basics'?*

The influence of Peters and Waterman's work emphasised a whole school of thought looking at the development of excellence in organisations and led to an increasing emphasis on studies and models of strategy. The orientation was very much that of senior and top management but used researchers from a variety of traditions.

Unitarist or pluralist

Many would like to think that the history of thought on organisational behaviour is developing in an evolutionary manner. This has the attraction of integrating everything currently known, implying that the latest is the best. This is certainly the position of many management consultants who peddle their versions to various organisations. However, there seem to be fundamental differences in the basic assumptions of some schools of thought that have not been reconciled or integrated. This has been well described in a technical book by Burrell and Morgan (1979) who argue that some contrasting assumptions could never be reconciled. For example, a deep underlying assumption is whether we believe organisations can be one happy family, believing in the same ideals as a strong leader, such as Body Shop and Anita Roddick. Technically this is called the unitarist view. Or whether we believe that organisations are made up of people with a variety of views and beliefs that should all be heard, such as in most universities. Technically, this is called the pluralist view.

For those of us concerned with the practical business of analysing the behaviour of organisations as part of our working life it is perhaps best to be pragmatic and find the analysis that seems to make most sense of the particular problem presented at any one time.

Hard and soft approaches to organisational behaviour

As we have seen from the above review of models of organisational behaviour there are both hard and soft approaches: the 'hard' mechanistic approaches of scientific management and the 'soft' concerns of the human relations models. These are no longer seen as alternatives but rather as two sides of a coin and most effective operators will use a combination of both. Let us look at some of the modern practical implications of this in the ways managers behave.

The *hard* approaches to getting the right things done include the view that by carefully analysing the work we would then be able to specify exactly how things should be done and so become more efficient. This mechanistic approach has always had the appeal that if we only spent just a little more time and effort analysing things we would have a perfect system. Modern day examples are to be found in some exponents of the quality movement and competencies approach. The quality movement is enshrined in two standards, one British, BS5750, and one international, ISO 9000. For example, very detailed BS5750 or ISO 9000 quality standards can specify the exact nature of the memos which need sending if there is a complaint. The competency movement is an approach to recruiting, developing and rewarding staff that looks in detail at what they should do to meet the required performance level. Similarly competency lists have been seen to include such minute detail as, 'smile at the client when they first come to the reception desk'. An example of this 'hard' approach in nursing is the desire to break down the whole job of nursing into its component parts and get less skilled, and less well paid, people to do the more menial tasks. This approach expects people to comply with a carefully laid down analysis of what is required.

These hard approaches, where tasks are carefully specified, are useful where a high degree of conformity is required, where there are a lot of temporary or unskilled staff or where there is a major crisis to be dealt with. Their disadvantage is that the more prescriptive an approach the more people will work to rule and show no initiative as it is 'more than their job's worth'.

In contrast, the *soft* approach to management tends to put the emphasis on getting the right things for people to do. This includes an appreciation of individual styles and motivations. Here there is a great deal of discussion about empowering people to take control over their own work and to allow them to express their views on how things could be done better. The softer approach emphasises the fulfilment of individual talents. It is about developing people over a period of time and allowing them to make different contributions at different times in their career. Some of these softer approaches emphasise individualism and others the building of teams. But all encourage the individual to feel that what they are doing is worthwhile and worth making a commitment to. Some of this is expressed in very caring terms which makes those from the 'hard' approach feel very suspicious. An example is how some nursing homes allow individuals to express their personal service to the residents in a variety of different ways.

DID YOU KNOW?

The concept of competency is currently widely used in management circles. There is much academic debate about whether it refers to the observable, demonstrable behaviour or the underlying abilities which allow one to behave in this way. The concept is used in a wide and confusing way but has gained a lot of popularity for describing preferred outcomes at work.

These softer approaches, which emphasise autonomy and collegiality, are most appropriate where the full commitment of the people in the team is necessary, for example when the situation is novel, and when everyone needs to deliver the service. Such as when health visitors in clinics were faced with a new recommendation on the best way to put babies in their beds to prevent cot death, but no one knew quite which was the most effective way of communicating this to parents. Each health visitor was encouraged to use their own personal skills and judgement on how to convey this to parents.

There does seem to be some need for bringing together both these aspects of getting things done. One example of how this might be done is by trying to systematise some of these softer approaches so they can be evaluated alongside the traditional harder methods. One such way was some work I did with my colleague Royston Flude at Kelloggs plc using the MCI (Management Charter Initiative which is the NVQ body for management standards) list of competencies as our starting point. We (Weightman and Flude 1996) felt that the different competencies could fall into four distinct groups.

1 Managing activities which were about getting things done and the actions required by the business.
2 Managing the analysis of information and resources to solve problems and reach decisions which involved thinking.
3 Managing people and dealing with one's own and other people's feelings.

4. Managing the vision, values and assumptions that underpin the organisation. This involves understanding one's own values and expressing them in strategic ways.

The first two groups of competencies might be described as the hard approaches to getting the right things done and the latter two groups as the softer approaches. We found that teams needed all four groups of competencies and that the more senior a manager was the more of the second two groups of competencies he or she needed and the less of the first, although they often still had to supervise these competencies in others. The important point of this exercise was the emphasis on the need for different competencies within a team and that both hard and soft competencies are required for sustainable, excellent performance. This work was based upon the Motivational Driver Model (or FIN) developed by Royston Flude.

The importance of trying to develop both hard and soft competencies can be seen within almost any organisation. There are times when we need the analytical, hard, competencies of making the most of the resources available to us. At other times we have to deal with other people and our own feelings using the softer competencies. It may be that we personally take more easily to one group of competencies rather than the other. If we are to become useful members of a work organisation we do need to try to acquire at least a modicum of the whole range.

Positivism and phenomonology

The theoretical distinction between many models of organisations can often be made between the originators of those models, some of whom fall into a realist view of organisation, called positivists and others who believe in relativism and who are called phenomonologists.

- Positivism is the study of organisations using objective methods independent of a particular person's view. There is a belief that the organisation exists outside of the understanding of any one person. There really is an organisation. They are often associated with the 'hard ' approaches outlined above.
- Phenomenology is the study of organisations using a variety of individual perspectives. Here the belief is that there is no external truth, only the social world as constructed by the meanings and interpretations we put on our experiences. They are often associated with the softer approaches outlined above.

This book will try to give sufficient examples of work from both traditions so that later (see Chapter 11 on culture) we can refer to this typology again and see how different theories fit in.

Conclusion

This chapter has tried to give you an overview of some of the issues involved in analysing organisational behaviour and some of the differing perspectives involved. As you use this book keep asking yourself which point of view a particular model is taking and what might be the disadvantages and advantages of this view for the people involved in such an organisation. As you proceed you are likely to find that some perspectives and models feel instinctively more sympathetic to you. This will tell you something about how you understand the world but, of course, it does not mean it is the only reasonable understanding!

EXERCISE **1.1**

Try to arrange a morning observing a person at work, ideally, someone with some sort of management responsibility.

As you observe write down the following:

(a) What they are doing.
(b) Who they are with or whether they are alone.
(c) Who initiated the activity – themselves or another.
(d) Try to decide whether they are using mostly professional/technical skills [T] that they would have had training and experience in, administrative skills [A] that any moderately literate teenager could perform, or managerial skills [M] of influence and negotiation.

Start a new line every time that the person does something different or talks to someone different or changes the topic of conversation. I use the form given in Figure 1.3 when I am doing this and include [S] for social activities and [P] for personal activities.

When I am making these observations I am interested in the relative proportions of the day spent on each of the different sorts of work by managers. It varies considerably. I once had a senior manager who spent half the time while I was observing her on personal activities to do with fixing up a mortgage. I have no idea

Figure 1.3
Observation schedule. (© Derek Torrington, Jane Weightman, Basil Blackwell Ltd, 1989.)

sTAMp Document II: Record of time spent

Time	Activity	With	Initiated	sTAMp work	Notes

what she did when she wasn't being observed! For your purposes this is really an exercise in observation and how having something structured to do during observation makes you observe better than when you are just vaguely looking. But you could work out the percentage of time spent on the different sorts of activity and see whether it is what you would expect.

EXERCISE **1.2**

How to use this book.

1. Try looking up the following words in the index:
   communication
   group
   learning
   change

   How many different views were there of these words?
2. Work through the Activities in this chapter and then find the answers to them at the end of the book.
3. Do Exercises 1.1 and 1.2 and then find the answers to them at the end of the book.

Self-check questions

1. What is psychology the study of?
2. What do sociologists study?
3. What was Machiavelli famous for?
4. What is the main emphasis in scientific management?
5. Which qualities would you associate with a bureaucracy?
6. What is the Hawthorne effect?
7. What does contingency theory emphasise?
8. What did Peters and Waterman study in organisations?
9. Are there any examples of hard and soft approaches to organisational behaviour still in organisations? If so what are they?

CASE STUDY **1.1**

In all the other case studies in this book I give you a story and ask you to answer some questions, but this one is different. Below are several different kinds of places for eating out that are commonly found in Britain.

1. Which do you think has been organised along scientific management principles?
2. Which on administrative principles?
3. Which on a human relations basis?
4. Which on a socio-technical basis?

These are real examples rather than 'ideal' perfect types, so use your imagination. Models are analytical tools. You never come across perfect examples of social science principles in real life.

(a) A formal French restaurant with a Maître d'Hôtel overseeing the waiters and a formal system of chefs in the kitchen.

(b) A local café bar with lively, talkative, stylish waiters and a small number of owner cooks in the kitchen.
(c) McDonald's with uniform quality provided to a standard training.
(d) A cooperative wholefood café where everyone shares the profits.
(e) A large, bustling, efficient diner that is part of a chain owned by a large stock market quoted company. There are handheld computers that transfer the orders from the waiters to the kitchens where the staff cook to a formula laid down from head office some 200 miles away.

References

Burrel G. and Morgan G. (1979) *Sociological Paradigms and Organisational Analysis*. Heinemann, London.

Cohen D. (1977) *Psychologists on Psychology*. Ark, London.

Fayol H. (1949) *General and Industrial Management*. Pitman, London.

Gates B. (1996) *The Road Ahead*. Penguin, Harmondsworth.

Greenfield A. (1997) *The Human Brain*. Weidenfeld and Nicolson, London.

Handy C. (1985) *Understanding Organisations*. Penguin, Harmondsworth.

Harvey Jones J. (1994) *All Together Now*. Heinemann, London.

Kline P. (1989) *Psychology Exposed*. Routledge, London.

Machiavelli N. (1981) *The Prince*. Penguin, Harmondsworth.

Mayo E. The Hawthorne research is classically described in Roethlisberger F.J. and Dickson W.J. (1939) *Management and the Worker*. Harvard University Press, Cambridge, MA.

Morgan G. (1997) *Images of Organization*, 2nd edn. Sage Publications, Beverly Hills, CA.

Peters T.J. and Waterman R.H. (1982) *In Search of Excellence*. Harper and Row, London.

Prahalad C.K. and Hamel G. (1990) The core competence of the corporation. *Harvard Business Review*, May June, 79–91.

Taylor F.W. (1947) *Scientific Management*. Harper and Row, New York, NY. (This is an anthology of Taylor's work from 1903–1912.)

Trist E.L. (1963) *Organizational Choice*. Tavistock Publications, London.

Urwick L.F. (1973) *The Elements of Administration*. Pitman, London.

Weber M. (1964) *The Theory of Social and Economic Organisation*. Collier Macmillan, London.

Weightman J. and Flude R. (1996) Report for Kelloggs plc. Unpublished.

Further reading

Arnold J., Cooper C. and Robertson I. (1995) *Work Psychology*, 2nd edn. Pitman. These are well known psychologists from the school of management at UMIST in Manchester. They apply the material to organisations and this has become a standard text. (NB. It is always worth looking at something that has run to several editions as this means it is well accepted and you won't go too far wrong in using it.)

Corbett J.M. (1994) *Critical Cases in Organisational Behaviour.* Macmillan. For those who enjoy doing case studies this book is full of short cases with a few questions to start you using the analytical tools to understand particular organisational behaviours.

Gross R. (1996) *Psychology: The Science of Mind and Behaviour,* 3rd edn. Hodder and Stoughton. Again a standard student text for psychology students. It is not specifically applied to organisations but useful for material on motivation, perception and basic psychology.

Morgan G. (1997) *Images of Organization,* 2nd edn. Sage. A rather heavier academic text than Pugh (below), but excellent.

Pugh D.S. (1990) *Organisation Theory: Selected Readings,* 3rd edn. Penguin. This book has always been a very useful source for all the classic material on organisation analysis. Read this first for detail of particular models.

PART 1

The individual in the workplace

CHAPTER 2

Individual differences

Objectives

When you have read this chapter you will be able to:

- Describe some psychological models for analysing personalities.
- Understand some of the reasons for individual differences.
- Appreciate why we all perceive the world differently.
- Begin to use some of these models to look at individual behaviours in organisations.

Introduction

We often say to ourselves at work such things as 'Why can't I make any sense of Ross?' 'Why isn't Les more predictable?' 'Why can't Pat be more like me?' Imagine what would happen if we really could understand each other all the time, or predict each other's behaviour, or if we were all the same. It would take away a lot of the frustrations at work but it would also remove most of the fascination. It would be like working with robots, predictable but dull. The great delight of being part of the human race is that we are all different with a unique pattern of understandings and contributions to make.

Trying to understand some of these differences can help us to work better with each other in various ways. We learn to be more tolerant and so cooperate better. We are able to communicate more effectively and so understand better what others are doing. We know when someone else may be better suited to a particular task because they have specific abilities we do not have. But can we explain why we are so different?

Psychological models can help us to analyse why people are different and why they have different personalities. This is not just an academic exercise but can help in getting things done. By understanding the differences among those we work with we are more likely to put requests, demands and expectations in a way that is appropriate to them. When we are experiencing difficulties in influencing someone it can be helpful to have a range of analytical models to understand their behaviour and suggest alternative approaches. When we have a difficult piece of information to give to those who work with us we can think of different strategies and decide which is most likely to succeed with the particular individual, if we have some understanding of what sort of person they are.

Most of us already change our behaviour to suit the occasion instinctively but psychological models can help to systematise our knowledge and to suggest new approaches when everything else has failed.

PAUSE FOR THOUGHT

Two defending solicitors in a magistrates court were making the case for their clients. Mr Fish addressed the bench with a great deal of elaborate courtesy, jokes and smoothness. Ms Lacey addressed the bench in a hectoring style, with lots of histrionics and sighing.

Which would you react to most favourably if everything else was equal? Would another approach appeal to you more?

Working with individual differences

If we are going to work successfully with a variety of people we have to come to terms with the fact that there are quite wide ranges of people doing the same job. If we were all the same it would be very boring, but also detrimental to the organisation as there would not be a sufficient width of experience and opinion when we need to solve problems. Sometimes the differences between people will mean they can reach the same level of performance through different routes and reach the acceptable standard of performance. For example, some students work steadily throughout the weeks and months of study taking each weekend off; while others have periods of intense study with periods off at any time. Where the performance is satisfactory each can claim a success.

At other times the differences between people can be stimulating and innovative and lead to a better performance all round. Think, for example, of problem solving discussions and idea generating sessions where different ideas can lead to a new view that no one had at the beginning. By understanding, tolerating and celebrating the differences between people we are more likely to get a cooperative, productive effort from those we come into contact with. This does not mean we have to understand and tolerate all behaviour, indeed that would amount to indifference. So we need to try to influence some people to behave differently, but show some tolerance of individual differences, which is essential if we are to work with other people.

I have included here three concepts about individual differences to demonstrate how we can analyse the differences between people. Having analysed and understood the differences we might then want to change that person's behaviour at work. By understanding why they may behave differently we are more likely to be able to accept the difference. Alternatively we may need to find a convincing way of helping them to change rather than just saying 'I want you to be different'. The three concepts used to analyse individual differences I have given below are the nature/nurture debate, models of personality and perception.

Nature and nurture

One of the continuing debates in philosophy from Plato onwards which has been taken up by psychologists in the past hundred years has been the relative contribution of our inherited characteristics, nature, and our upbringing, nurture. This is not just an academic issue as it has practical implications involving the extent to which we can modify our own or anyone else's behaviour. If our ability to learn languages, acquire new skills and adopt new attitudes is all laid down by our inherited characteristics then how we grow up and whom we work with will not affect this ability. If, on the other hand, such abilities are influenced by the environment in which we develop it is important to look at what influences we are experiencing and what influence we are having on others.

Psychologists, sociologists and social anthropologists tend to focus on the effect of the environment on the child. This does not mean that they assume that the child is infinitely pliable, but they do assume that nurture plays an important part. If we look at some of their models we will see that each of the main psychological theorists about childhood operates with a different assumption about human nature and this would have implications in the analysis of organisational behaviour, as we will see later in the chapter.

- The Freudian model is a conflict model with an emphasis on how innate, antisocial impulses become restrained by society.
- Piaget's developmental model, very influential in education circles, is that the unfolding thought processes of the child enable it to make varying sense of its environment but that same environment can in turn affect the child's thought processes.
- Behaviourist psychologists take the most extreme view that behaviour is entirely shaped by the environment claiming to be able to train any child towards any goal.

PAUSE FOR THOUGHT

To what extent is intelligence the result of innate constitutional characteristics? To what extent is it due to environmental factors? If to these questions you add the question of whether ethnic groups vary in their intellectual capacity you begin to understand some of the emotional and political context of this debate. The difficulty of reaching any universally acceptable solution is because:

- *It is difficult to define the phenomenon; what do we mean by intelligence?*
- *It is difficult to set up a suitable experiment or observation; how could we separate nature and nurture?*
- *There are differences over what would be an acceptable statistical conclusion.*

Similar debates continue over the relative contributions of nature and nurture to language development and the differences between men and women.

The implications of this debate for organisations are apparent in such questions as: Should we only select school leavers with proven ability or do we take those who have lacked opportunities and expect them to learn once they have had the chances they need?

It is rare to meet anyone claiming everything is wholly nature or nurture nowadays but the important issue is that each of us has a unique combination of genes, unless we have an identical twin, and experience. Each of us is different and so is everyone we work with or will work with. So it is inappropriate to treat everyone in the same way but we do need to treat everyone equally!

Different models of why people have different personalities

We all need to understand other people so we can make friends, understand our families and influence each other. An important step in our understanding is the need to see things from the other person's point of view, an extremely difficult thing to do. To do this we have to analyse something of their personality. One way of doing this is to have some models to help us with our analysis. In other words, one way of understanding more about the nature of individual differences is looking at the theory of personality.

In everyday parlance we tend to use the term 'personality' to describe the impression a particular person makes upon others. It is the differences in our personalities that sum up the difference between you and me. Inevitably there are lots of theories about how, why and what our personalities are derived from. There is no one best theory of personality. The theory (or theories) that seem to account best for our own and other's behaviour will vary from time to time and place to place. We are likely to be attracted to theories of personality that fit our own personality! Our view of personality will also affect how we interact with people. It is well worth understanding what that view is so we can interpret the effect we may have on others and modify it where appropriate.

Some models for understanding individual differences of personality are given here, but there are plenty of others. Three main contrasting schools of thought on personality are those of the psychoanalysts, the behaviourists and the humanistic psychologists. Although what follows may appear as an historical review of theories of personality these three views are still the most influential in this area. Let us look at each in turn and see what insights they can offer on behaviour in organisations.

Psychoanalysis

The psychoanalysts are dominated by the theories of Sigmund Freud (1962), developed from his work in Vienna at the beginning of the twentieth century. Freud concluded that personality consisted of three separate parts. The 'ego' is made up of the individual drives that focus a person's particular nature. It will make people do different things from those around them and interpret the world differently. The 'superego' is learned from society. It represents the injunctions of parents, school and other important members of society about what is acceptable behaviour and what is not. The superego can have a modifying effect on the ego. This suggests that basic drives are modified by society. The 'id' is that part of the personality consisting of the basic, animal instincts that get us going and help us become involved with our surroundings.

Freud argues that personality develops through a series of traumatic stages when these three aspects of personality are in conflict. Trying to get them into some sort of harmony is the business of maturing. The classic stages described by Freud include the following.

- First, the early period of breast feeding with its implicit intimacy between mother and child which leads to anguish when the child is asked to give it up.
- Second, the anger felt by children over the external control implicit in toilet training.

- Third, the disapproval demonstrated by society of childhood sexuality.
- Fourth, the difficulties for all of us in learning to control anger and aggression in socially acceptable ways.

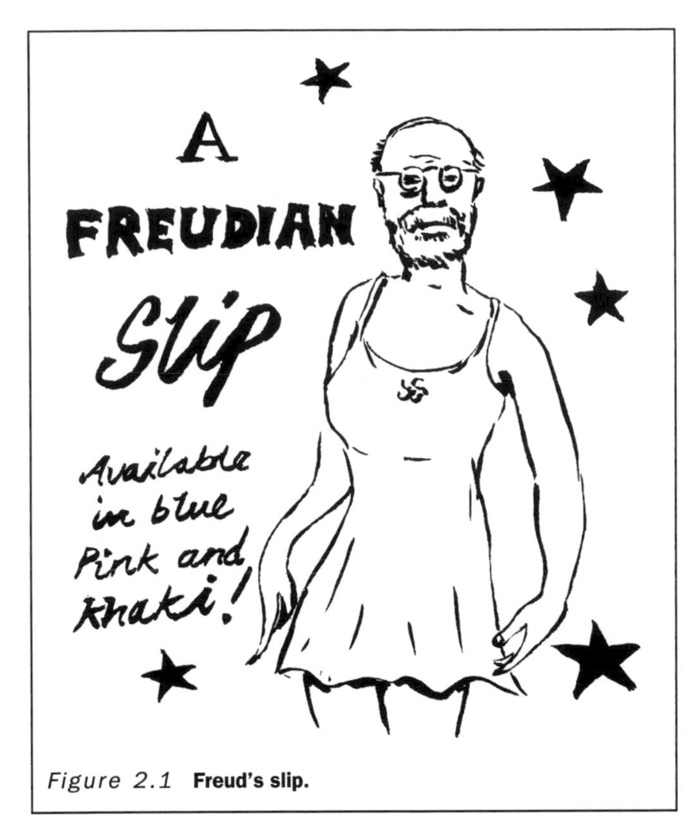

Figure 2.1 **Freud's slip.**

Freud argues that these traumas get pushed to the back of the mind but continue to affect our behaviour into adulthood. The most obvious example is what we call the Freudian slip, when we say something with a hidden meaning instead of what we intended. For example, using a favourite brother's name when talking to the less-preferred brother. Another example is the early experience of severe toilet training which is thought to result in an extreme need for order and tidiness in adult life.

As well as the general implications of analysing how we deal with anger and aggression another way in which a Freudian approach can be useful at work is his idea of defence mechanisms. These are devices we subconsciously use to defend ourselves from being psychologically undermined. We use these when we feel under stress and they give us relief. The most common defence mechanisms are:

- Fixation – where the individual becomes rigid and inflexible and sticks to the known procedure and behaviours.
- Rationalising things – where the individual covers up their behaviour and contributions with elaborate explanations.
- Regression – where the individual behaves in a less mature or childish way than is usual or required.
- Projection – where the individual attributes their own motives and feelings on to another where this is inappropriate.

ACTIVITY **2.1**

During this coming week see if you can identify any of the above defence mechanisms in your own behaviour or the behaviour of those around you. This should be a light-hearted activity not a critical one!

Perhaps Freud's greatest contribution to our understanding of behaviour in organisations is that we must consider the whole person and everything that has happened to them to understand their personality. The main criticisms of his theories are that they are based on a very small sample of Viennese bourgeois life in the early part of the twentieth century and that by placing so much emphasis on childhood it makes it difficult to see what we can do to change ourselves once we grow up. The nature of the theories makes them very difficult to test and collect data about.

DID YOU KNOW?

Dixon (1976) used Freudian analysis to look at the work of the people in the army. He demonstrated how military life attracts those who like regimentation and orderliness. This he regards as due to their early childhood experiences. With so many people in the military falling into this category there are not enough who can be flexible when the rules, regulations and procedures do not cover a particular circumstance. Dixon maintains that since those with potty training traumas tend to be drawn to military organisations there should be nothing surprising in the fact of military incompetence.

Eysenck was a British psychologist who did much to popularise the subject through books such as *Know Your Own IQ*. He was also responsible for the widespread use of the terms 'introverted' and 'extroverted', originally proposed by the Austrian psychiatrist Carl Jung. Eysenck's main suggestion is that we differ in our basic state of arousal, that is how much stimulation we require to 'get going'. Those with an introverted personality are naturally highly aroused so any extra stimulation sends them into a state of anxiety. By contrast extroverted people are in a low state of arousal and consequently need a lot of stimulation to get them going. This distinction suggests that introverted people will seek out quiet whereas extroverts will thrive in large noisy gatherings. Eysenck (1976) has proposed that there is a continuum from the most introverted to the most extroverted. He has also suggested that people differ on a dimension he calls neuroticism as opposed to stability, see Figure 2.2. Once we have a measure of an individual's score on each of the dimensions they can be pinpointed on Figure 2.2. Eysenck argued that a stable extrovert was quite a different personality from a neurotic introvert. The logical conclusion from this is that their behaviour at work would be quite different. The former could tolerate a more robust environment than the latter, while the environment which suited the neurotic introvert would probably bore the stable extrovert. Eysenck did a lot of research to support his theory but has been criticised both for the nature of some of the research and for his emphasis on the role of nature and genetics.

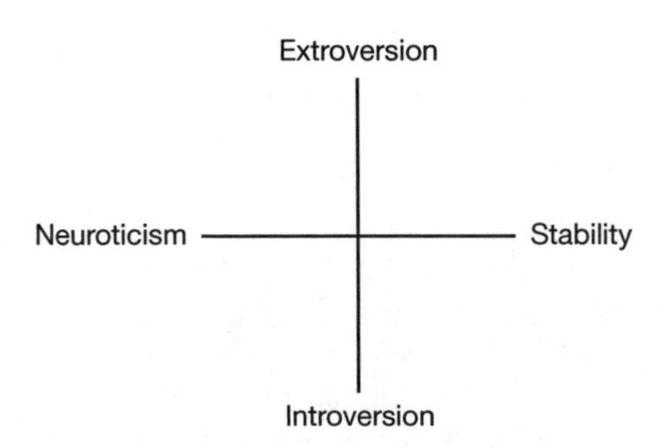

Figure 2.2
Eysenk's dimensions.

ACTIVITY 2.2

Below there is a list of jobs. Each of them requires some technical skills. Each of them also requires some personal skills. Thinking of these skills, which do you think would be more suited to an introvert? Which would be better suited to an extroverted personality?

Bar person	Trader on the foreign currency floor of a bank
Hotel receptionist	Computer programmer
Long distance truck driver	Teleworker at home
Research chemist	Museum guide
Nature reserve warden	Leisure centre manager

Do any of the jobs seem suitable to both types of personality?

The usefulness of psychoanalytic models for analysing organisational behaviour is in understanding that there may be deep-seated reasons for strange behaviour. The models are also useful in giving us some basic vocabulary to describe the differences between people. When analysing organisational behaviour, the difficulty in holding only a psychoanalytical view of personality is that there is such an emphasis on the early years. This gives the impression that nothing can be done later about people's personalities. This can lead to a feeling of hopelessness if someone does not fit in. However, much of our everyday understanding of personality has come from Freud and the other psychoanalysts.

Behaviourism

The behaviourists are dominated by the work of B.F. Skinner. His main point is that we learn through our experiences and that these experiences affect who and what we become. He explored (1953), with others, in minute detail how behaviour is learned (see Chapter 4 for further details). Skinner emphasises the external control of behaviour. We behave in the way we do because of our history of reinforcement (rewards). For behaviourists, a stimulus evokes a response from the individual which in turn evokes a reaction that may or may not be reinforcing to the individual. Where the response leads to a reinforcing reaction the individual is more likely to respond in that way in the future. For example, if every time we offer to wash up we are given a grateful hug we are more likely to offer again in the future, assuming we like hugs from that person; if we are told we are washing up in the wrong way, at the wrong time, we are unlikely to offer again, unless, of course, we like being told off!

By studying observable behaviour and the effect of different rewards, given at different times, the behaviourists have built up a detailed technology for specific learning. It has proved highly successful in teaching new skills. A lot of computer programs for teaching are based on this 'programmed' learning. The idea is to make the instructions as clear as possible: when the correct response is elicited a reward is given, it may well be 'well done' or something more concrete. The behaviourists have suggested that if we can find which reward, or reinforcement, each individual prefers, learning will take place more effectively. Reward is defined as that which the person will work for. The process of manipulating people's behaviour by adjusting the instructions, task and reward is called 'behaviour modification'.

There are clear implications here for analysing organisational behaviour. If personality is learned and dependent on the history of reinforcement, then managers can institute a suitable system of rewards to elicit the behaviours that are required to run an organisation effectively. The only task is to analyse the desired behaviours and reinforcements in enough detail and with enough accuracy for individuals to be motivated to behave appropriately. Luthans and Kreitner (1975), among others, develop this idea. They give reinforcement schedules, analysis of behaviour and the training necessary to enable managers to put it into effect. The application of their ideas does seem to improve productivity and can be seen in such training schedules as that of the McDonald's fast food chain.

The limitation on applying this approach comprehensively is the difficulty of including the idea of intrinsic rewards emphasised by Maslow, as I discuss in Chapter 3. This approach also suggests that workers are entirely dependent on managers getting the analysis right, whereas many people work in environments where some degree of self-control and personal responsibility is necessary. There are also ethical issues related to the degree of control and obedience we are prepared to accept at work. Very few of us have difficulty in accepting the use of behaviour modification techniques to teach a mentally handicapped child to feed themselves. But most of us would object to having the same techniques applied to us by a manager with complete control over us at work – assuming, of course, that someone was clever enough to analyse both the task and the rewards accurately enough to get us to comply.

ACTIVITY **2.3**

Have a look at a computer teaching program, for example, the one in the library showing you how to use the library or the Internet. Does it have any of the following behaviourist qualities?

- Are the instructions clear?
- Does it break things down into small chunks at a time?
- When you get something right does it provide some sort of reward?
- When you get something wrong does it make you go through the process again?

Humanistic psychology

Humanistic psychology has been very influential among organisational psychologists and the study of organisational behaviour. Unlike the other two schools of thought it is not dominated by one outstanding figure, this school of thought is really about ideals. It is more a description of what 'could' and 'should' be than an analysis of what is. The central belief is that each of us has within ourselves the capacity to develop in a healthy and creative way. The emphasis is on becoming an independent, mature adult who can take responsibility for our own actions. There may be distortions due to the vagaries of parents, schools or society but we can overcome these difficulties if we are prepared to take responsibility for ourselves.

Maslow is usually seen as the founding father of this school (see Chapter 3) with his ideas of the self-actualising personality. By putting his concept of the people who work for themselves, to see how far their abilities will take them, at the top of his hierarchy of needs Maslow is obviously advocating this as an ideal that we should aim for.

Carl Rogers (1967) has also been very influential. He describes a sequence of stages for an adult in becoming a fully functional person.

- First, is the need to be open to experience and move away from defensiveness.
- Second, is a tendency to live each moment more fully and in the present, rather than relating everything to the past.
- Third, the person increasingly trusts themselves physically, emotionally and mentally.
- Fourth, the ideal person takes responsibility for themselves and their actions.

To go through the stages Rogers advocates using other people as a resource to interact with. Only by sharing experiences and developing trust do we come to know and trust ourselves.

PAUSE FOR THOUGHT

The use of the word 'ideal' person in social science does not refer to the person we would most like to spend an evening or the rest of our life with. It is a technical term referring to a concept of the logical conclusion of the particular argument, theory or model.

Consultants working in organisations will often be operating from this particular standpoint. The enthusiasm for participation in decision making, ownership of ideas, autonomous work groups, and developing potential all fit within humanistic psychology. One particular application is the concept of stress and the analysis of sources of stress. The cure is dependent on this diagnosis but usually some increase in openness and trust is advocated with higher degrees of autonomy and self-management being associated with a healthier organisation.

The limits on using humanistic psychology are that not everyone shares the ideals. Given the unproven nature of some of the basic tenants it can be difficult to persuade non-believers of the benefits of the proposed changes.

Other theories of personality

One group of theories that has been widely used by people studying organisational behaviour rejects the idea of motivation and single stages in personality development and emphasises the individual's conceptualisation of their world. Kelly (1955) introduced the idea that each of us constructs our own world. We each see things differently and interpret things differently using our own dimensions and models. This means we each construe the world differently. One dimension he uses is the process of 'attribution' by which we make sense of our world by making assumptions, or attributions, of what is causing things to happen. By having these attributions we hope to be able to predict and control social events. Each of us will have different attributions and so perceive the world differently. By enacting many roles and engaging in continuous change we have constantly to practise this process of construction. Kelly's theory is called personal construct theory. Various devices based on Kelly's original device of the repertory grid have been developed to discover what 'constructs' each of us is most likely to use. One simple one is demonstrated in Activity 2.4.

ACTIVITY **2.4**

You need eight pieces of paper or card. On each write an example of (a) or (b). You need four examples of each.

(a) Write a description of something you do that is important.
(b) Write a description of something you do that is time consuming or frequent.

When you have eight shuffle them and take three at a time. Write down the ways in which two of them are similar and the other is different. Do this with several different groups of three cards.

The words you have written down will tell you something about how you construct – that is make sense of – the world. Another person will have a different set of words. (NB. This can be a very useful device when you are trying to find out about someone else's work and how they make sense of it. I use it in research as an opening device when I know very little, if anything, about the subject).

A related group of concepts are the social learning theories. These deal with the learning of behaviour and particularly the learning of maladaptive behaviours, see, for example, Bandura (1977). They emphasise dysfunctional (that is unhelpful) expectancies or self-concepts. Expectancies can be dysfunctional in a variety of ways. If we wrongly expect a painful outcome we are likely to avoid the situation. If this is a wrong expectation we may miss out on the good times. For example, if you fear that closeness will bring pain you are likely to act in a hostile way which leads to rejection by others, which in turn confirms the expectation that closeness will bring pain. Dysfunctional self-evaluation can be exemplified in the person who has no standards of self-reward, so is bored and dependent on external pleasures. It can also be seen in the person who has set over-severe standards for themselves which lead to self-punishment and depression. All these can be a problem at work. The recommended therapy from this point of view is modelling, guided participation and desensitisation.

Various models of personality are used in organisations for assessing the personalities of people wanting to join the organisation. Psychometric tests, that is systematic tests, have an increasing popularity in the assessment of personality. In psychology circles there is much debate about this as the reliability of the tests and the ethics of assessing something as personal and private as one's character are not clear cut. On the other hand the personality of a candidate is inevitably assessed at interview with a view to seeing whether the candidate will fit in with the workgroup. Might it not as well be done by a systematic test rather than guesswork? A widely used test is the Occupational Personality Questionnaire (OPQ) developed by the British consultancy company Saville and Holdsworth. The various forms have thirty scales of personality attribute covering such things

DID YOU KNOW?

One of the difficulties of selecting staff on the basis of their personalities is there is a real risk of cloning and of there not being sufficient variety of people to present different arguments and deal with all possible situations.

'"One of us" is a phrase that epitomizes the Thatcher era. Originally it referred to an exclusive clan: "Is he one of us?" the prime minister would fiercely enquire about anyone who was put up for the jobs she had to fill. Only those who passed the test were admitted to the band of partisans with whom she hoped to revolutionize Britain.' (Hugo Young 1989)

as persuasive, active, modest and critical. An individual profile of these attributes can then be compared with the desired qualities of the person specification for a particular job.

Perception

Another useful concept in trying to understand individual differences is what psychologists call perception. *Perception* is the term used to describe the process of selecting, organising and interpreting incoming stimuli. We all do it differently and so perceive a different real world. The real world is so stable and familiar to us it seems curious to discuss the way we perceive it. But this familiarity and stability of the world has more to do with our own mental processes than the actual sensory input which is constantly changing. Because we organise the incoming message into our stable view of the world we make it seem stable to us. But your stable world is a different one from mine.

There are several reasons why people may perceive the same situation differently.

- Physical sensitivity. Human organs are only sensitive to a limited range of things. For example, none of us can see x-rays. Some people are more or less sensitive than others, for example, partial sight or hearing makes a difference to the stimulus received. We differ in our visual and auditory acuity.
- Selective attention. We notice some things and not others. For example, at a party we can concentrate on one conversation and ignore others; we focus on what is important to us. If, however, someone mentions our name we usually hear it, even in a conversation we are not part of.
- Categorisation. We categorise the cues as they come in. The incoming stimuli are fitted into one of our existing categories such as concepts, ideas and associations built up in our memory as a result of experience. This process may well be influenced by language. We fit things into our existing pattern of understanding.
- Limits on our capacity. We can only deal with a limited amount at any one time. The limit is set not just by how much is coming in but also by the ease of categorising the stimulation. The time we feel most overwhelmed at work is when lots of difficult communications are coming to us. The office party, when there are probably just as many communications, is nothing like as daunting as the communications are easier to categorise and it is easier to decide what action to take.
- The environment. Our expectations and the context will determine the kinds of categorisation we will apply. If we are expecting to see our colleague at the airport it is surprising how often we misidentify someone else before we meet the right person. Whereas if we meet the same person in the supermarket it may take us a little while to remember their name.
- Individuality. Our attitudes and personality will influence what we perceive. They generate expectations. A prejudiced person sees the behaviour of those they are prejudiced against in a negative way, whatever actually happens. A friendly act will be seen as false, a casual attitude as sloppy, a remote stance as difficult and so on. This in turn will affect the behaviour of the perceiver and you get the beginnings of a vicious circle.

ACTIVITY **2.5**

Using Figure 2.3 get two friends to draw the figures shown after looking at the figures for 30 seconds.

Tell one of them that the figures are:

(a) Curtains at a window.
(b) A pine tree.
(c) A crescent moon.

Tell the other that they are:

(a) A diamond in a rectangle.
(b) A trowel.
(c) The letter C.

Does there seem to be any effect from the words on the drawings? Eysenck (1976) found there was. If there is a difference this might indicate the influence of language and labelling on our perception.

Figure 2.3
Effects of words on perception.

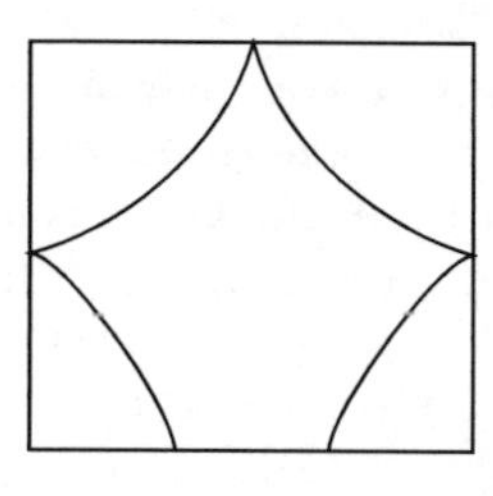
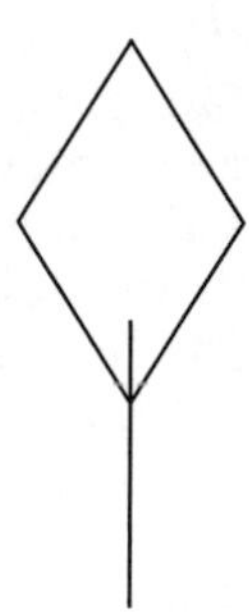

The act of perceiving is a constructive process where we try to make sense of our environment by trying to make it fit our experience. The real world is different for each of us as we perceive it differently. At work with people you undoubtedly will be faced by people perceiving things differently from yourself. Sometimes this will be because of a different job perspective and access to information. Sometimes because of the amount of time and commitment we have given to the topic. Resolving the difference where necessary is usually achieved by discussion to unravel the basis of the different perceptions.

Stereotyping

In trying to understand other people we all instinctively use a short-cut method known as stereotyping. This is an essential aspect of dealing with others but can also be a straightjacket if we do not use it carefully. If you have lost your way in a foreign city and decide to ask for directions you do not ask the first person you see; you pick out someone from the surrounding crowd who looks to you a potential source of good information. You probably look for someone who is not in a hurry, neither too young nor too old, appearing intelligent and sympathetic. You have a working stereotype of who would be an appropriate person to ask.

At work we carry round in our heads a series of stereotypes which influence all our dealings with other people. For example;

- Don't trust anyone under 30.
- All Dutch people like bureaucracy.
- All accountants are dull.
- All Conservatives believe in the rights of a manager to manage.
- Women do not want too much responsibility at work.
- Older people work more slowly.
- Once a thief, always a thief.

There is seldom time in all working situations to abandon stereotyping as a way of approaching matters. Especially in emergencies, where some sort of working hypothesis is needed immediately. The danger of stereotyping is that people are not treated and understood as individuals but as categories. This is unreasonable to them and can be unlawful. Stereotyping also discourages the use of all the talents available to an organisation. If we label someone as only being capable of one level of performance we may never know what else they may excel at. And this is to say nothing of how demotivating it can be for an individual who is constrained by the labels others have applied to them. Just think of the experiences of those labelled as being in the less academic groups at school – they often find it difficult to get into any mainstream activities.

Stereotyping also limits the ability of those who use it too much to work with others to the full extent of their abilities. A special form of this is the halo effect where individuals are judged according to an imaginary halo. For instance, someone who is never late may be pointed out as an excellent member of staff even though the quality of their work is poor. Stereotyping often occurs between departments in organisations, for example the marketing department is regarded as superficial while production is seen as earnest and harassed.

Stereotyping can lead to prejudice and discrimination. There are various Acts of Parliament which make discrimination illegal, see Box 13.4 for a checklist on equal opportunity legislation. An organisation develops through the will of those who make it up. If there are people who feel they do not have fair opportunities in the organisation they will have little commitment to making things successful. See Chapter 13 (page 225) for further discussion of this.

PAUSE FOR THOUGHT

If we want to improve our ability to perceive others accurately it helps if:

- *We know our selves – by asking ourselves what is important and not important to us; by knowing what we are attracted and not attracted to; by understanding our attitudes and prejudices and understanding our assumptions about people.*
- *We understand the effect we are having on others – through the nature of our communications and how they are received; through the way in which we present ourselves; through the way in which we perform and how we integrate with others.*

- *We are sensitive to the differences between people – in that we do not overreact to a particular physical attribute; that we focus on the content of what is said rather than the way it is said and that we concentrate on the performance not on how it is done.*

Conclusion

We have examined several different models for analysing individual differences. We will each differ in which models we find most attractive and convincing. None of them is wholly right and each of the models can be useful in particular circumstances. That is, they are contingent on the environment. In practice they can be useful in unravelling things when there is a problem.

EXERCISE **2.1**

Get in a group of six to eight people. The better you know each other the more fun this can be!

(a) One person in each group is selected to be the 'psychiatrist'. This person then goes out of the room.
(b) The other members of the group sit in a circle and adopt the identity of the person on their left/right/opposite, whatever you agree.
(c) The 'psychiatrist' comes back into the room, and is told that he or she has to find out who everyone is, and that the group are all suffering from the same delusion. The psychiatrist can ask anyone any question.
(d) After 10–15 minutes, stop the game and explain to the psychiatrist what has been happening.
(e) Discuss how each member of the group has been interpreted by the person on their right/left/opposite.
(f) Have you learnt anything about how you perceive different personalities? Which questions were most fruitful?

EXERCISE **2.2**

Get into a small group with four or five other people. You need to do this exercise quickly, without really thinking, otherwise the point will be lost. If you deliberate too long you will not get your perceptions but some much more considered, polite response.

1. Write down the following:
   - Five or six words to describe yourself.
   - Five or six words to describe each of the others present.
   - The name of an animal to describe yourself.
   - The name of an animal to describe each of those present.
2. Now compare results.

This is meant to be relatively light hearted so don't get too serious!

What does this tell you about the different ways in which others perceive you? What does it tell you about the differences in the way you all perceive and understand each other?

(NB. A similar exercise can be done when analysing people's jobs by asking those who work for, with and more senior to them, to write down the responsibilities of the job. This is known as a role analysis using a 360 degree analysis (see Chapter 4 for a further description).

Self-check questions

1 We are all different because of differences in our inherited genes and our experience. What two words are used to describe this balance?
2 What are the main features, in one sentence, of the psychoanalytic model, the behaviourist model and the humanistic psychology model of personality?
3 Describe six ways that can account for how we perceive things differently.
4 What are the problems associated with stereotyping at work?

CASE STUDY **2.1**

Courtney and Peter are brothers in their late forties. They were brought up in a small market town where their father owned and ran the main pharmacy shop. Both went to the local secondary school and did well at 'A' levels. Courtney chose to go to the nearest university to study pharmacy and then went to work in a pharmacy near the university. After two years he returned to the family shop and has remained there ever since. When his father died he took over the shop and business. Peter did not go to university but joined British Airways as a cabin steward and has spent his life travelling the world and is now a senior steward. He never returns to the market town he grew up in. The two brothers do not see each other.

Questions to answer:

1 What sort of questions would a Freudian ask to account for this difference?
2 What about a behaviourist?
3 And a humanistic psychologist?

References

Bandura A. (1977) *Social Learning Theory*. Prentice Hall, Hemel Hempstead.
Dixon N.F. (1976) *On the Psychology of Military Incompetence*. Jonathan Cape, London.
Eysenk H.J. (1976) *The Measurement of Personality*. MTP Press, Lancaster.
Freud S. (1962) *Two Short Accounts of Psychoanalysis*. Penguin, Harmondsworth.
Kelly G. (1955) *The Psychology of Personal Constructs*. Norton, NY.
Luthans F. and Kreitner R. (1975) *Organizational Behaviour Modification*. Scott Foreman, Glenville, IL.
Rogers C. (1967) *On Becoming a Person*. Constable, London.
Skinner B.F. (1953) *Science and Human Behaviour*. Macmillan Free Press, New York, NY.
Young H. (1989) *One of Us*. Macmillan, London.

Further reading

Any good introduction to psychology: for example, the Gross or Arnold books mentioned in Chapter 1 both have good chapters on personality, perception and individual differences.

Hayes N. (1994) *Foundations of Psychology*. Nelson. She is a well-established author of introductory books on psychology. I find her very readable and sensible.

Hardy M. and Heyes S. (1994) *Beginning Psychology*, 4th edn. Oxford University Press. A widely available simple introductory book written by the pioneers of 'A' level psychology.

CHAPTER 3

Motivation and attitudes to work

Objectives

When you have read this chapter you will be able to:

- List a hierarchy of needs which affect people's motivation.
- Give examples of things at work which demotivate people and others that are a positive motivation.
- Distinguish different individual attitudes to work.
- Understand some of the reasons why individuals differ in their attitude to work.

Introduction

In common parlance we often say things like 'Jo is motivated by money' or 'Les really enjoys competition'. The assumption is that we can see motivation. The reality is that we can only hypothesise that someone is motivated by some particular thing by looking at their behaviour and seeing if there is anything different when the particular 'thing' is involved. Motivation is not something we can feel, smell, hear or see; we can only see the consequences of someone's inner motivation. Motivation is a drive within a person to try to achieve a goal to meet a want or need.

We use the words 'motivation', 'wants', 'needs' and 'motives' freely both at work and elsewhere. We talk of Pat having the motivation to get on. We talk to Jan about wanting promotion. We listen when Chee says he needs the project. We discuss with Jo other people's motives for doing things. All these attributes have to be deduced from their behaviour. We are in reality guessing at what motivates people from the way they behave in different circumstances. There seems little doubt that beyond the very basic needs of food, shelter and safety our wants are culturally determined. For example, in the developed Western cultures we tend to emphasise individuality and achievement whereas in many Eastern cultures there is an emphasis on the family and group achievements, and fitting in and being accepted is valued highly. This affects what people are motivated to work for. How stable these culturally determined motivations are, how varied and whether they can be influenced is the subject of much academic debate and really too theoretical for our requirements here.

Our task is to examine the motivation of people at work. For managers this understanding is important if they are responsible for people working satisfactorily. For individuals the understanding is important if they are to understand their own and other people's behaviour at work. Motivating people at work is not just a case of pressing the right button to switch them on, no matter that some managers feel this is how it should be. Indeed managers cannot technically motivate people as it is an internal state that directs people towards certain goals or objectives. The management task is to ensure that each individual's motivation is engaged by checking that they are willing to work, to a standard, for the rewards offered. It is important to understand this distinction as many managers treat everyone in the same way and try to manipulate people by trying to 'motivate' them. A better way is to try to understand the needs and objectives of those who work for or with you and arrive at some sort of equitable arrangement that their needs as well as the organisation's needs will be met.

This is sometimes enshrined in the phrase the employment, or psychological, contract (Schein 1978, see Chapter 14 for further discussion of this). This contract involves a series of expectations between the individual member and the organisation. These expectations are not defined formally and the individual and the organisation may not be conscious of the contract but the relationship is affected by the expectations. This means taking into account individual differences in how they interpret the rewards offered. For example, we will all differ in our interests, attitudes and needs. That will affect how we react to different aspects of the job, such as its degree of autonomy, variety and amount of work to be done. We will also react differently to the work environment of peers and supervision and the organisational climate. We all have different reasons for going to work and we want different things from work. Some of us are looking for totally involving jobs that offer opportunities for responsibility and recognition, for example becoming general managers. Others are looking for a little more money and the freedom to get on with things away form work. That is, we have different *attitudes to work*.

Understanding the motivation of people at work means admitting that different things will have different values to different people. This suggests that we need to understand that those who work with us may not have the same orientation to work as ourselves. To paraphrase Mills (1956):

> Work may be a mere source of livelihood, or the most significant part of one's inner life; it may be experienced as hard draft, or as an exuberant expression of self; as a bounden duty, or as a development of man's universal nature. Neither love nor hatred of work is inherent in man, or inherent in any given line of work.

An example of the different approaches to work can be seen when some people opt for part-time, temporary or contract work, so-called periphery work. Others opt for permanent, full-time work, so-called core work. This can be an expression of a different set of priorities as well as the available opportunities.

ACTIVITY **3.1**

List three reasons why you are doing this course. Include a mixture of internal (personal) and external (pressure from outside) reasons for doing it.

Now get three other people in your group to do the same thing. Compare the results to see where you agree and disagree about the 'motivations' for doing this course.

Maslow's model of motivation

Psychologists have studied the behaviour of animals and humans to try to find out what things people will work for – what gives pleasure and what inhibits behaviour. There have been very precise and detailed studies of animals learning new skills and of the difference a suitable reward can make. The word 'motivation' is used technically in these studies to describe the hidden, inner drive or need to seek that reward. Different models have been developed to account for the variation in motivation across time with the same person and between different people.

The most famous model of the variation in motivation across time, for the same person and between people is that of Maslow (1954), see Figure 3.1. He grouped needs into a hierarchy of five stages. The first two he called primary needs, concerned with our basic physical requirements. The latter three stages he calls secondary needs, which are learned, psychological needs which only come into play when the primary needs are satisfied and are more culturally determined. For example, if we are hungry or physically exhausted we are less

Figure 3.1
Maslow's hierarchy of human needs.

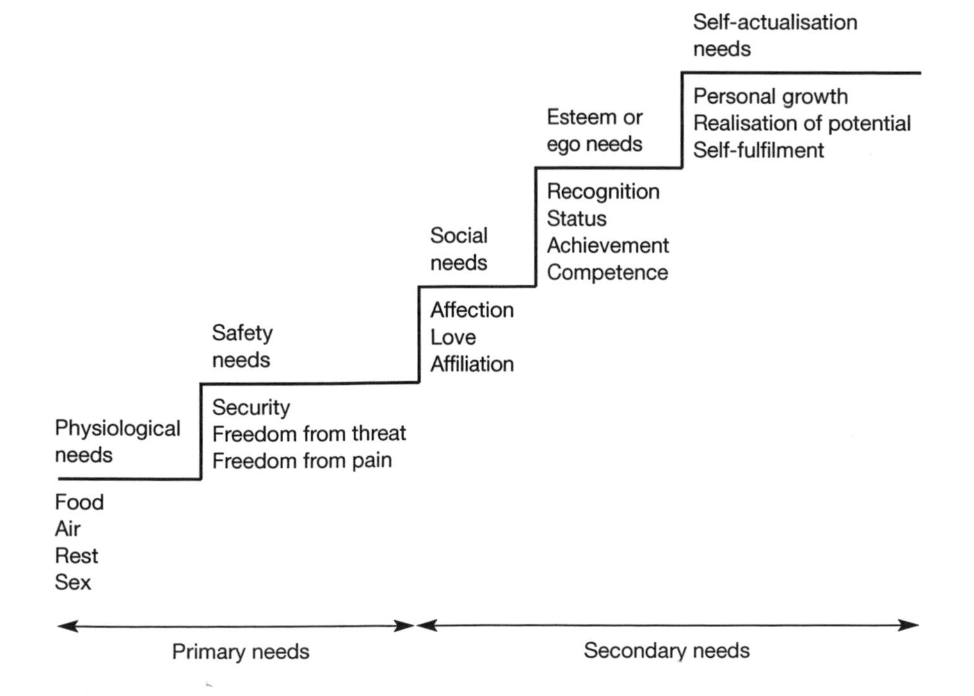

concerned about being free from pain or secure. He also points out that once a primary need is satisfied it loses its potency and is no longer a motivator. So in our example, once the hunger or exhaustion is satisfied the person will be less motivated by food and rest and will be more motivated to seek safety. By contrast, Maslow argues secondary needs continue to motivate and we seek more of them even when we have experienced some satisfaction of this need.

At work, at least in the developed world, most of us have our primary needs satisfied by regular periods of rest and food with sufficient shelter to protect us from the climate. Just think of the fuss we make when the heating or airconditioning is not working. In analysing the behaviour in Western organisations we are mostly concerned with the motivation based on secondary needs. Many organisations recognise that social contact and belonging to a group can be helpful to get the work done especially to relieve a tedious task. For example, in one head office I visited, notices had to go out to 20,000 pensioners. The manager in charge decided that the whole department, including himself, should spend the last half hour of the day, for a week, putting the papers in the envelopes as they sat round a big table. He could, of course, have hired temporary staff or given it to the most junior staff. He saw the opportunity to get the task done efficiently by bringing everyone together. They certainly all seemed motivated by the social gathering and chatter as they did the task. The importance of groups at work is dealt with in detail in Chapter 7.

Maslow's next level, esteem needs, are met at work through all sorts of status distinctions, for example size of room, company car, having a secretary, use of telephone for overseas calls or not. Many organisations are now trying to reduce these distinctions by having, for example, only one dining room or style of uniform. This is usually to reduce the number of spurious symbols of esteem rather than to remove symbols of esteem all together. Not many organisations give everyone the same pay and conditions of employment! Often those in senior positions have more autonomy in how they organise their time. Not many senior staff are happy to give over complete control of their diaries to the e-mail.

At the top of Maslow's hierarchy is self-actualisation. This term is applied to a person who is motivated by the urge for self-fulfilment. That is, trying to become everything they have the potential to become. The idea of self-actualisation has been particularly developed by humanistic psychologists, mentioned in the introduction. This view has been very influential in work organisations as management consultants, organisation developers and advisors on change have pursued these ideals. There is some individual variation in the degree to which self-actualisation can be a motivator. First, it is a learnt, culturally determined, need. Second, the other needs must be satisfied first.

ACTIVITY **3.2**

As an indication of how some of the studies of motivation are put to practical use consider their application in the sophisticated lifestyle distinctions exploited by advertising agencies, marketing people and the retail industry. For example, have a look at the advertisements in three different magazines such as a Sunday colour magazine, a teen magazine and a TV listing magazine.

➤ Can you find any that are appealing to the individual's desire to belong?

- Can you find any that are appealing to a desire for esteem?
- Are there any appealing to self-actualisation?

You can also try the same exercise when looking at shops or restaurants.

ACTIVITY 3.3

Think back to something you have done recently in which you were really involved. This might have been a social activity, a sporting experience, doing something solitary, to do with your studies or a family event.

1. Describe the event objectively with the 'who, what and where'.
2. Now describe your feelings during the event.
3. Using Maslow's hierarchy of needs which of your needs do you think were being satisfied?
4. Would you have felt the same if you were really exhausted? Hungry? Frightened for your safety?

Maslow's model is a general model of human motivation. How well suited is Maslow's hierarchy in the work situation? Although it was not devised for looking at motivation at work it has become very popular. It is useful as an indicator of individual differences. Its main strength is in listing what might motivate people. Steers and Porter (1991, p. 35) suggest various organisational factors which could be used to satisfy different needs:

- Physiological
  - pay
  - pleasant work conditions
  - dining facilities
- Safety
  - Health and Safety well monitored
  - company benefits
  - job security
- Social
  - cohesive work group
  - friendly supervision
  - professional associations
- Esteem
  - social recognition
  - job title
  - high status job
  - feedback from job itself
- Self-actualisation
  - challenging job
  - opportunities for creativity
  - achievement in work
  - advancement in the organisation

The difficulty with using a Maslow approach to motivation at work is that many people will not wish to satisfy all their motivations at work. This implies that the motivating factors at work will not be equal for different people, even where they apparently have the same motives.

Alderfer (1972) developed Maslow's theory for work by suggesting that there were three groups of needs:

- **E**xistence needs to do with survival.
- **R**elatedness needs to do with social belonging.
- **G**rowth needs to do with individual development.

He called this the ERG theory and he argued that organisations and their managers need to address all three of these but where growth is not possible at work the other two needs must be addressed more powerfully. This suggests that where growth cannot be met more emphasis on the existence needs through money and strong social actions for relatedness will help to keep people satisfied.

Herzberg's theory of motivation at work

Herzberg (1968) developed Maslow's model with particular reference to people at work. He described the lower order needs as having the potential to dissatisfy if they are not met but once they are met more of them will not increase motivation. These he called the *hygiene factors* – if managers do not get them right there will be complaints and people will be demotivated, if they are right no one will comment or notice, just like the effect of hygiene in the kitchen. In contrast to the hygiene factors, are the *satisfiers*. People will work for these and want more of them. These satisfiers tend to be intrinsic to the person. The list of satisfiers are more culturally determined than the hygiene factors, so your group may have slightly different ones from those listed in Box 3.1. Herzberg's model has been particularly useful in drawing attention to the way jobs are designed so that jobs are enriched and the quality of life at work can be improved. These concepts of job enrichment and job design are explained further in Chapter 9.

DID YOU KNOW?

Some of these findings about motivation can be seen in modern concerns about what makes people contribute their best at work. For example, one survey found the following job features that are said to make people work hard.

- *Psychological safety*
  - *Support – authority and backed by boss*
  - *Role clarity – what is expected and to what standard*
  - *Recognition – praise*
- *Meaningfulness*
  - *Self-expression – express self*
  - *Contribution – make a difference*
  - *Challenge – feel stretched*

The phrases 'psychological safety' and 'meaningfulness' are similar, although not identical, to Herzberg's hygiene factors and satisfiers. (The full article can be found in Leigh T. and Brown S. 1996. Journal of Applied Psychology *August.)*

ACTIVITY 3.4

Look around your place of study and ask the following questions:

- Which of Herzberg's hygiene factors are currently causing a problem for you?
- What could be done about it?

Box 3.1
Herzberg's theory of motivation

Hygiene Factors

Company policy and administration
Supervision
Working conditions
Salary
Relationship with peers
Personal life
Relationship with subordinates
Status
Security

Satisfiers

Achievement
Recognition
Work itself
Responsibility
Advancement
Growth

How is behaviour driven by our needs?

The Maslow and Herzberg theories given above are both concerned with what motivates an individual, that is, the content of motivation. If we start looking at the process of motivation we find that how behaviour is initiated, directed and maintained are also important areas of study.

A theory which adds an important dimension to the models of Maslow and Herzberg is the *force field theory* of Lewin. Lewin (1952) emphasises that individuals operate in a field of forces that represent subjective perceptions about the environment, the importance of a goal and the psychological distance of the goal. Lewin uses it to try to account for the difference of motivation in people at different times. For example, you and I might both want to meet the Prime Minister. I see the circumstances as far too difficult; the goal of seeing him is not compelling enough to overcome the psychological distance to make any effort to see him worthwhile. You, however, may be in more favourable circumstances; you may want to see him enough to overcome the psychological distance between him and you. So you will be more motivated to try and meet the Prime Minister than I am.

An additional view about motivation is called *expectancy theory*, see, for example, Vroom and Deci (1974). This is the influence on our motivation of our expectancy of the success of our actions. The more likely we think it is that we will be successful the more effort we will put in and vice versa. For example, if I feel that when I go to the library I will find the books and access to computers that I want I am more likely to put the effort into going than if I expect to find all the resources 'out' or 'booked'. My expectancy of success influences my motivation to go to the library. Another concept that Vroom and Deci use is 'valence' which is the degree of preference an individual attaches to a particular outcome; this can be positive, negative or indifferent. The theory then makes the motivation of the individual a result of expectancy and the valency attached to the outcome or the equation $M = E \times V$.

One influence on expectancy is the perceived equitability of the results. This is people's feelings about how fairly treated they have been in comparison with others, see Adams (1979) for further discussion on this. This is based on exchange theory where people expect certain outcomes in exchange for certain contributions. For example, if in seminars/tutorials two of us are always contributing to the discussion and have always done the reading when the others have not we may begin to feel very demotivated and begin to make less effort.

Motivation and work behaviour

Some people feel that with the increasing use of automation and the advent of computers the most tedious jobs have now disappeared. Consequently motivation at work is no longer an issue for individuals or the managers responsible for organisations. However, even if we accept the premise which is arguable, our expectations as consumers about standards of service from service industries, the public sector and other organisations make it important that staff are well motivated at work. To say nothing of the humanitarian argument that people should be doing something they want to do! Motivation at work remains an important part of analysing the behaviour of people at work so we can improve the work that we do and improve the working life of those employed in organisations.

Steers and Porter (1987, p. 21) indicate some of the more important variables which influence people's motivation and work (see Box 3.2). These variables give us a helpful checklist for looking at some of the reasons for poor performance in organisations. There can be a problem with any one of the variables.

PAUSE FOR THOUGHT

When someone is thought to be performing badly at work the first task is to establish that there is a gap between the desired and the actual performance. The second task is to find out why. The Steers and Porter checklist could help analyse this. Once you have a reason, strategies for change are easier to think up. These may include redesigning the job as it is a problem job not a problem person.

Attitudes to work

There are several important questions about work and people's motivation, such as: what is the meaning of work for individuals? Does work have the same importance for us all? Clearly not. Is there some inevitable connection between certain work conditions and experiences and particular attitudes and feelings? What do we mean by job satisfaction? Is it the same for us all?

Box 3.2
Steers and Porter's checklist of influences on motivation at work

1 Individual characteristics
- Interests
- Attitudes towards
  - self
  - job
  - aspects of the work situation
- Needs such as
  - security
  - social
  - achievement

2 Job characteristics
- Types of intrinsic rewards
- Degree of autonomy
- Amount of direct performance feedback
- Degree of variety in tasks
- Work environment characteristics such as
  - peers
  - supervisor(s)

3 Organisational actions such as
- Reward practices
- System-wide rewards
- Individual rewards
- Organisational climate

Most studies in this field have been done on manual labour in manufacturing workplaces. This is partly because this group of people are easy to study, as they have less to hide, and partly because they have been seen as a problem by management. By studying the effect of work and the differing attitudes to work it is hoped that better working practices can be developed for the benefit of the organisation and the workers.

However, it is clear that the technology used by workers will constrain the way in which their work can be organised. Whether a work process is done sequentially with everyone adding their little bit or whether each individual can do the whole task will influence how work is organised. The sheer physical scale of an operation and the noise generated during production will influence how things are organised. Whether the technology is required in the same place for several years or is constantly on the move will determine how things are organised. All of these in turn will influence the attitude and behaviour of the workers. For example, some technologies like printing allow social groupings at work. Others such as car assembly are much more difficult to organise in social groups at a reasonable cost. Some tasks such as shutting down oil wells are by definition always happening somewhere different from the previous occasion. Workers engaged in these different tasks will have different attitudes and behaviours, on average as a group, from groups engaged in the other activities.

The classic study which introduced the concept of 'orientation to work' was that of Goldthorpe *et al* (1969) who examined the attitude and behaviour of assembly line workers at the Vauxhall plant in Luton. They found that different workers had different wants and expectations of work, that is, work had a different meaning for them. They distinguished three main orientations to work:

- An instrumental approach to work meant work is a means to an end outside the work situation. Work is a means of acquiring the income to support a valued way of life.
- A bureaucratic orientation describes people who sought to give services to a company over a long time in return for a career that saw some promotion and increases in salary, security and pay.
- A solidaristic orientation characterised those people who in addition to an economic orientation also valued group loyalty to their mates.

This research work suggests that not everyone is seeking self-actualisation through work; maybe they are resigned to being unable to do so. It is a useful counterpoint to the assumptions made by Maslow and Herzberg. Discussing the meaning of, and attitude to, work involves our basic assumptions about morals, power, equality, the rights of individuals and so on, all of which have a political aspect to them. This makes research in this area very difficult as different interpretations can be put on the same findings. In addition there is the thorny problem of exactly what do we mean by job satisfaction and the meaning of work?

ACTIVITY **3.5**

Try to list three different attitudes to work that supermarket checkout people might have. Which of these would you expect to take full-time, permanent, committed, so-called 'core' work? Which would you expect to work on Sundays at 'time-and-a-half' pay? What do you think the difference would be in how the people were supervised?

Can people's attitude to work be changed?

If people have different attitudes to work how important is this? What do we mean by attitude? Can those attitudes be changed? The most widely quoted definition of attitude in psychology is Allport's (1954, p. 45):

> A mental and neural state of readiness, organized through experience, exerting a directive or dynamic influence upon the individual's response to all objects and situations with which it is related.

Krech and Crutchfield (1948, p. 173) have a similar definition:

> An attitude can be defined as an enduring organisation of motivational, emotional, perceptual and cognitive processes with respect to some aspect of the individual's world.

These two classic definitions state or imply that attitudes have the following characteristics:

- They are related to an object – some aspect of the individual's world.
- They are part of the general way the individual experiences and reacts to this world.
- They are relatively enduring.
- They imply evaluation and feeling.

Katz and Kahn (1978) suggest that attitudes and motivation are intertwined. Depending on the person's motives an attitude can provide the following:

- Knowledge – attitudes give a base or framework for classifying and interpreting new information.
- Expression – attitudes enable us to indicate what our values are, what self-concept we have and which group values we have adopted.
- Instrumental – depending on our past experiences of rewards and negative experiences we will hold differing attitudes to people and experiences.
- Ego-defensive – attitudes may be held to protect us from an undesirable truth or reality.

Most social scientists agree that attitudes are a complex, multidimensional concept that have an emotional and a cognitive aspect to them. For this reason attitudes can be difficult to change. Some of the techniques that are used to try to change attitudes are:

- The rational approach – as we experience and assimilate material in accordance with our expectations, attitudes and motivation (see Chapter 2 on perception) it is not surprising that a straightforward, rational approach which merely presents the good reasons why we should change our attitudes and beliefs rarely has much success.
- Social influence – social pressure is likely to have more influence but only where the communicator has credibility and seems an attractive model.
- Emotional approach – emotionally toned communications tend to be more influential than straightforward rational explanations as long as the emotion is appropriate and does not raise emotion to a level of anxiety.

PAUSE FOR THOUGHT

One area where attitudes are expressed publicly is in general elections. In the 1997 general election one of the strategies used by the Labour party, who won, was an appeal to the emotions rather than to spell out specific, rational arguments. Do you think they were wise to do so?

Alienation

An important concept that can help explain people's motivation at work is alienation (see Figure 3.2). This concept, used in sociology and elsewhere, was originally formulated by Marx to analyse the effect of capitalism on people. Marx referred to people's detachment, estrangement and loss of control over their lives in capitalist society. Alienation is about the separation of people. It is applied to the way we feel cut off from important decisions, people or outcomes.

Figure 3.2 **Alienation**

The concept can be applied to work organisations. The work we do can feel alien and oppressive. It is thought that it is the way work is organised that leads to this alienation rather than particular work processes. Individuals can also be alienated from other people because the relationships have become calculating, self-interested and untrusting. This is demonstrated when individuals have become so alienated from others that they are able to behave callously towards others without a sense of embarrassment. Examples can be found in some city dealing rooms where the drive to make a profitable deal means ignoring a colleague who is clearly in distress. People can also be alienated from the product of their labours when the end product is not seen or is remote from their control. Alienation can happen when people are not involved in the original decision about what the work should be. The classic example of alienation is seen in large-scale manufacturing, such as car plants (see Beynon 1973), compared with traditional crafts such as pottery where the workers can see the results of their labour and are less likely to be alienated.

People are alienated from their own labour when they are unable to derive satisfaction from work because they are controlled by others and so are meeting someone else's requirements and standards as opposed to their own. An example is when two building societies merge and the workers from one society has to adopt the procedures, standards and requirements of the other. The individual operators can feel alienated.

Marx argues that alienation is an objective state. We may feel dissatisfied with our job but not necessarily alienated. We may feel satisfied with our job but are alienated at the same time as we may be excluded from something much more rewarding. An example may be seen in those managers who have been made redundant and have developed alternative activities which they then find more worthwhile than their former employment making them wonder why they had not done this earlier. Before redundancy they were in a state of being alienated.

It is an ideal world where everyone is highly motivated and doing exactly what they would choose to do. We may not achieve this ideal but that does not mean not trying to improve things. There are real dangers if the organisation of work does not give sufficient consideration to the needs of the individuals working in the organisation. If work is organised so that we are cut off from important decisions, people and outcomes we can feel the work we do is alien and oppressive, that is, we are alienated. Blauner (1963) argues that alienation consists of four conditions or states: powerlessness, meaninglessness, isolation and self-estrangement.

- Powerlessness comes when people feel controlled by others.
- Meaninglessness is felt when people do not understand the coordination or

purpose of their work.
- Isolation is where people do not feel they belong.
- Self-estrangement is when people do not feel involved with their own work.

All of these can happen to people at all levels of the organisation and are particularly likely to be found in periods of reorganisation. It can be very difficult to find ways of reorientating people once they have become alienated. So it is worth learning to recognise the early signs so that something can be done to make people feel more valued. Attempts to pre-empt these elements of alienation found within organisations include trying to empower staff, setting reasonable objectives, valuing staff and engendering commitment. These concepts are all dealt with elsewhere in this book.

PAUSE FOR THOUGHT

Is anyone on your course showing the signs of being alienated from their work – teaching or non-teaching staff, students? For example:

- *Feelings of loneliness, exclusion, rejection.*
- *Actions seeming mechanical, uncommitted.*
- *Behaviour not bound by rules.*

Conclusion

This chapter has been about motivation at work. I hope it has persuaded you that this is not just a mechanical process where you press button A and everyone is 'motivated'. However, you can help another to be motivated if you carefully analyse what is in it for them, from their perspective.

EXERCISE 3.1

A headteacher was concerned that the school staff were not working well as a team. There seemed to be several factions vying for dominance in discussions about resources. At lunchtime there were quite a lot of staff sitting in their own classrooms rather than contributing to the rest of the school. When asked why they did not get involved a frequent response was, 'where should we meet?'

What would you do about this situation?

(a) Read Box 3.3 'A staffroom'.
(b) Using your understanding about motivation and attitudes to work answer the following questions.
   1 What would you do to make people feel valued?
   2 What about the staffroom?
   3 What about the coffee facilities?
   4 What would you do about the staffroom in Box 3.3?
   5 Imagine that you had a budget of £1,000. How would you spend it given the following prices?

Chairs – £50 each	Curtains – £100	Carpet – £200
Kettle – £40	Fridge – £200	Bookcase – £50
Coffee machine – £200	Employing someone – £4 per hour	

   6 What else would you do?

Box 3.3

A staffroom

Not only is the present staffroom a sad little place – it is in the wrong place! It is situated in the far left-hand corner of the school, up some stairs above the main administration block; about as far away as you can get from the main teaching areas.

It occupies a space about 4m by 3.5m in which there is just room for six shabby armchairs, a 3m upholstered bench, a narrow worktop, some lockers, the staff pigeon-holes and, in the centre, two coffee tables piled high with back copies of the *Times Educational Supplement*, school journey brochures and assorted flotsam and jetsam. Noticeboards which cover two walls carry general information and notices from the National Union of Teachers and the National Association of Schoolmasters/Union of Women Teachers. These are kept reasonably tidy. On the worktop is the staff telephone and a series of racks designed to carry the school report folders. In the corner is a small sink containing some mugs which do not seem to have been washed for about five years (which also happens to be the last time the place was used for drinking tea or coffee).

Five years ago the staffroom was three times as big since it incorporated the room next door. At that time the space occupied by the present room was the Quiet/Marking room, off the main staffroom and separated by a moveable screen. Five years ago the consultative committee (the main staff forum) voted the bulk of the staffroom out of existence to become a keyboard skills room. At that time no one could find a substantive reason for keeping it because few teachers, besides the smokers, actually used it. The school is socially compartmentalised not because the staffroom is small and smokey but because most departments have a convenient cubbyhole which they can call their own. Most staff only come to the staffroom to collect their mail and peruse the noticeboards. This is partly because it is too far to travel to the staffroom for the single break of the day. Tales are told of the nice dinner lady who 'got the hump' and withdrew her kettle which she used to make tea and coffee for the staff. Following this walkout the staff tried for a time to organise their own tea and coffee facilities. Apparently the effort failed because nobody was prepared to collect money for the materials.

Self-check questions

1. What are the five levels in Maslow's hierarchy of needs?
2. What is the difference between Herzberg's hygiene factors and the satisfiers?
3. What might influence different attitudes to work?
4. What are the four signs of alienation at work according to Blauner?
5. Why is motivation not something that is 'done' to people?

CASE STUDY **3.1**

Can the workers do better?

At Ken Lewis's sheet metal working firm in Sandy, Bedfordshire, the staff decide their own salaries and hours of work, set their own budgets and double as salesmen, cost accountants and quality control inspectors. Mr Lewis, managing director of Dutton Engineering (Woodside) Ltd, says 'I don't think I've made a decision for two years, I've not had to sack anybody and I've only had to discipline one chap and as it happens he brought in a £300,000 contract the other week'.

The 28 staff work in teams of seven and decide their own work patterns and when to take a long weekend to go fishing instead of slaving over a hot press. There are no workers' committees or trade unions and overtime is an alien concept. The average salary is £16,500 but at the end of every month 20 per cent of the profit is shared amongst the staff.

The business benefits claimed are:

- The sales per employee are twice the industry average.
- Paperwork has been reduced by 70 per cent.
- Lead times have been cut from six weeks to eight hours.
- Reject rate is down to a fraction of a decimal point.
- A £250,000 overdraft has been turned into a positive bank balance.

Mr Lewis says 'It's just common bloody sense. Too much British management is devoid of common sense. I am a happy man and so is everyone else because people's quality of life has gone up. We work smart, not hard.'

(Reported in *The Independent*, 24 July 1997, p. 1)

Answer the following questions after reading the above description.

1. What do you think is motivating the people at this works? Use the Steers and Porter checklist in Box 3.2. to help you.
2. What attitude to work would you need to work at Duttons?
3. Can you think of anyone who would not want to work there?
4. Could this model work in other places?
5. What about different size companies?
6. What about different sorts of activity?

Mr Lewis, the MD, is publishing a book on his experiences called *How to Transform your Company and Enjoy It*.

References

Adams J.S. (1979) *Injustice in Social Exchange in Steers and Porter: Motivation and Work Behaviour*, 2nd edn, pp. 107–24. McGraw Hill, London.

Alderfer C.P. (1972) *Existence, Relatedness and Growth.* Free Press, New York, NY.

Allport G.W. (1954) The historical background in modern social psychology. In Lindzey G. (Ed.) *Handbook of Social Psychology*. Addison-Wesley, Reading, MA.

Beynon H. (1973) *Working for Ford.* Penguin, Harmondsworth.

Blauner R. (1963) *Alienation and Freedom: the Factory Worker and his Industry.* University of Chicago Press, Chicago, IL.

Goldthorpe J.H., Lockwood D., Bechhofer F. and Platt J. (1969) *The Affluent Worker in the Class Struggle*. Cambridge University Press, Cambridge.
Herzberg F. (1968) One more time: How do you motivate employees? *Harvard Business Review*, Jan/Feb.
Katz D. and Kahn R. (1978) *The Social Psychology of Organizations*, 2nd edn. Wiley, New York, NY.
Krech D. and Crutchfield R.S. (1948) *Theory and Problems of Social Psychology*. McGraw Hill, New York, NY.
Lewin K. (1952) *Field Theory in Social Science*. Tavistock Publications, London.
Maslow A.H. (1954) *Motivation and Personality*. Harper and Row, New York, NY.
Mills C.W. (1956) *White Collar: the American Middle Classes*. Oxford University Press, New York, NY.
Schein, E. (1978) *Career Dynamics: Matching Individual and Organisational Needs*. Addison-Wesley, Reading, MA.
Steers R.M. and Porter L.W. (Eds) (1987) *Motivation and Work Behaviour*, 4th edn. McGraw Hill, London.
Steers R.M. and Porter L.W. (Eds) (1991) *Motivation and Work Behaviour*, 5th edn. McGraw Hill, London.
Vroom V. and Deci E. (1974) *Management and Motivation*. Penguin, Harmondsworth.

Further reading

Coupland D. (1995) *Microserfs*. Flamingo, London. Very amusing novel about the choices, motivations and life of computer geeks.

Maitland I. (1995) *Motivating People*. IPD, London. Short (56 pages), practical booklet.

Steers and Porter (1991), mentioned above, the latest edition – this book is an academic text with various articles exploring some of the issues associated with understanding motivation and its application to the work environment.

CHAPTER 4

The learning process

Objectives

When you have read this chapter you should be able to:

- ➤ Describe different models of how we learn.
- ➤ Distinguish five types of learning.
- ➤ Understand individual learning styles.
- ➤ Use role analysis.

Introduction

If there is one common issue that people at work have to deal with it is change. Where change is involved so is learning. It may be a new skill we have to acquire, such as a new telephone system or process. We may have to get to know new people when their company and ours are amalgamated. Perhaps we have to learn the details of the new organisation structure so that we can follow the correct procedure for informing people about a forthcoming meeting. Whatever changes are happening they require us to learn something. The specific organisational issues of dealing with change are dealt with in Chapter 14 whereas this chapter deals with how the individual learns. Chapter 10 deals with the way organisations formally and systematically try to encourage particular sorts of learning to increase the performance of individuals and groups within the organisation. The central importance of learning to the analysis of organisational behaviour can be seen by the fact that there are three chapters, one in each part of this book, dealing with the subject from different perspectives.

Another important aspect of learning in organisations is called experience. Experience is a crucial part of authority, expertise and effective work. It is seen in the gradual learning of better ways of getting things done that someone who has been in their job some time takes for granted, and incidentally is often overlooked when jobs are being reorganised. A more formal sort of learning in organisations is when people systematically set out to learn a different way of doing something by going on a course or to a conference. A further way of learning is the process of being coached by someone else to improve already competent behaviour such as chairing meetings. All these examples of learning involve a change in knowledge, skills or attitude. Change in behaviour can come about through formal training which is dealt with in Chapter 10, through the demands of organisational change which is dealt with in Chapter 14 or by more informal processes. Most learning in organisations, and elsewhere, takes place informally and is the subject of this chapter.

How people learn

As well as the purely academic pleasure of trying to understand how people function there are many practical reasons for trying to understand how people learn. Before we can start learning systematically or help someone else to do so we need to know how people learn. It might enable us to reduce the time it takes us to learn something. When difficulties arise we can start analysing where the problem lies and so do something about it. If organisations are to compete in an ever-changing world they need to assist people to learn the new ways of operation so that they can retain their jobs and contribute to the new processes. Similarly individuals need to understand how they learn best so they can adapt to a variety of environments and people. So, what models about learning are there? It will come as no surprise that their are several different models of how people learn.

Behaviourist theory

Behaviourists are interested in studying observable, measurable behaviour. Many of these studies have been of how we learn. The two classic studies are those of Pavlov and Skinner.

The Russian scientist Pavlov (1927) demonstrated how reflexes could be trained to a new stimulus. He used dogs and found he could get them to salivate when a bell was rung as this was associated with a plate of food. The dog learned that the bell meant food and so had become 'conditioned' to salivate. Anyone who has a cat will recognise the pattern, my cats come whenever they hear a tin or the fridge door being opened! This association of S(timulus) and R(esponse) is called 'classical conditioning' or S–R learning. The responses fade if the connection is not maintained. We probably have various physiological responses, such as raised blood pressure, to specific situations, such as visits to the dentist, that are classical conditioning.

Skinner's (1965) model was more complex. He experimented with rewards and punishment and their effects on animal learning. For example, by rewarding pigeons with corn when they showed suitable behaviour he was able to teach them to play ping pong. He showed that a response would be learned when it was rewarded, or technically 'reinforced'. This is called operant conditioning. He found that learning took place more quickly by using rewards for positive behaviours rather than by punishing inappropriate behaviours. His maxim is that for effective learning to take place you need a regime of 80 per cent rewards.

This behaviourist, or behaviour modification, approach has led to many examples of programmed learning such as using praise to reinforce people working and the use of computer assisted learning. The important concept to remember about behaviour modification is that learning only takes place if the individual is prepared to work for the reward offered. This model is now felt to be too simplistic for the complexities of applied social systems such as organisations but it is worth remembering as it emphasises the importance of feedback or knowledge of results without which learning is unlikely to be effective.

Experimental psychology

A model that has been very influential in education circles and with adult training is the model of Gagne. This summarises the findings of various experimental psychologists who have studied the behaviour of individuals in an experimental setting to understand the details of how we learn. In the sense that they studied behaviour systematically they are behaviourists but not in the strict sense of Skinner's approach. Gagne (1975) has identified a chain of eight events that occur whichever sort of learning is taking place. These are, in order:

1. Motivation. The learner has to want to learn and want to learn this particular thing or the final product of this type of learning. For example, a student of hotel and catering may be highly motivated to become a manager of a hotel and so is motivated to learn about organisational behaviour.
2. Perception. The matter to be learned has to be distinguished from others. This involves identifying a clear objective. At first it is difficult because one has not learned the different categories in the area. With time one learns more and more detailed ways of classifying the matter to be learned. For example, at the beginning of this course you will wonder where to start and what it is essential to learn. After a few weeks or months many of the terms become familiar and identifiable topics that need learning become clear.
3. Acquisition. What has to be learned is related to the familiar, so that it makes sense. For example, in this book I have tried to give examples from work settings to help to make sense of a new area of study. You can help yourself by recalling your own examples from your own experience.
4. Retention. The two-stage process of human learning comprises first, short-term memory where items are stored, before being transferred permanently to the long-term memory. Not everything needs to go to the long-term memory. For example, the anecdotes and jokes that aid the process of understanding at the time do not need to go to the long-term memory.
5. Recall. This is the ability to summon things up from memory when required. There are different levels. Recognition is where we know we have seen the item before and it takes less time to familiarise ourselves with it but we could not have relied on memory alone. Recall is where we can generate the memory of our own accord. For example, at the end of your course you may be able to recognise some of the material in this book as vaguely familiar: it may just seem 'common sense'. Some other bits you could recall from memory without the book because you have learnt them more thoroughly.

6. Generalisation. This is the ability to apply the learning in situations other than the specific one in which it was learned. For example, learning about motivation on this course as it applies to work may be generalised to thinking about motivation at the sports club or in the family.
7. Performance. This is where what has been learned is done. It is the test of learning. The organisational behaviour student takes the exam, writes the essay or tries to use the materials from the course in a work environment.
8. Feedback on performance. This is where the learner finds out whether the performance is satisfactory or not. Sometimes it will be obvious because of the quality of the performance, particularly with physical skill learning such as car driving. But some feedback from the coach or trainer can help to distinguish more subtle levels of satisfaction or analyse what went wrong, how it could be avoided, what needs more practice, what to do next and so on.

Learning can fail because of problems at any of these stages. The model is useful as a practical checklist when helping others prepare for learning or when giving feedback at the end of some session of learning. It is also a useful model for analysing more informal methods of learning such as why some get the message at meetings and others do not.

PAUSE FOR THOUGHT

Count the Fs in the following passage.

> *Finished files are the result of years of scientific study combined with the experience of years.* (New Scientist *28 June 1997, p. 93)*

How many did you see? On first reading most people see three, however, there are six. Try spelling the words out. Once you have seen this you will never say three Fs again. You have learnt something.

Experiential learning

Another useful model of how people learn is that of Kolb *et al* (1974). Figure 4.1 shows their experiential learning model. All the stages are necessary, in their view, if learning is to take place.

Figure 4.1
Kolb's learning model.

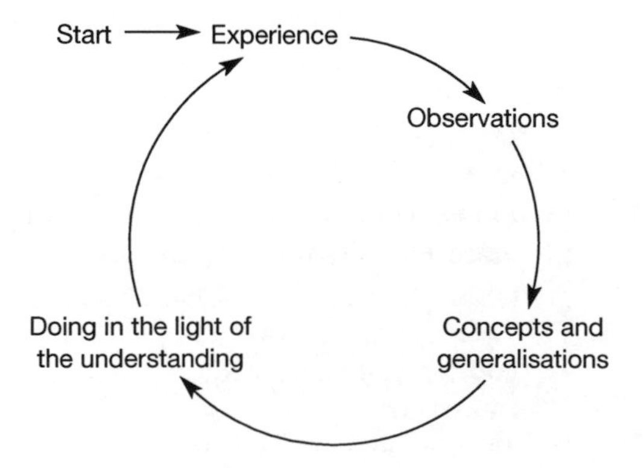

The model suggests that learning is a cycle of the following stages:

1 Concrete experience, that is, involving doing. For example, getting a student on a work placement to develop particular skills.
2 Observation and reflective analysis of the experience, that is, using listening and looking. This is most useful if done from many perspectives: in our example discussing the placement with someone from the work organisation, the course tutor and friends with similar experience.
3 Generalisation on the basis of experience, or doing some thinking. These generalisations use abstract concepts to integrate the observations into the theories we have about the world. For example, discussing with others what they would have done in the circumstances of the work placement.
4 Experimentation in future action based on the generalisation, or doing something similar. The application of ideas requires active experimentation. In our example the next time work is experienced, either on placement or for real, possible actions could be discussed and carried out.
5 New experience derived from this experimentation. In our example getting the student to do another work placement.
6 Initiation of new learning cycle.

If you can imagine a spiral of these experiential learning cycles you can see how a model of continual improvement and learning could be developed with the learner becoming increasingly confident and ambitious in their performance and analysis. This model of learning is very popular in higher education and is why there is an increasing emphasis in student texts on trying to get you to actually do something so the cycle can actually start. There is good theoretical evidence that by using different senses and actually doing something the person is more engaged in the learning process rather than by passively reading or listening which is the more difficult, but not impossible, way to learn. This model is further developed in the next section.

PAUSE FOR THOUGHT

It is claimed that the average rate of retention when learning new material is:

- *10 per cent of what is read.*
- *20 per cent of what is heard.*
- *30 per cent of what is seen.*
- *50 per cent of what is seen and heard.*
- *70 per cent of what the trainee says.*
- *90 per cent of what the trainee says and does.*

(Foot and Hook 1996, p. 180.)

ACTIVITY **4.1**

Use Kolb's model to analyse your own learning. Use one of the practical sessions in your course, for example an exercise, role play, case study or visit.

- Which part of the activity did you find most interesting?
- Which was most difficult?
- Which part seemed irrelevant and time consuming?

Now can you relate these findings to the Kolb cycle?

Individual differences

So far we have generalised that everyone learns things in the same sort of way. This may be generally true but there are also individual differences in how we learn effectively and in how we prefer to learn. We are all aware that people differ in the speed with which they learn new things and that some learn physical skills quickly and theoretical material slowly compared with others and vice versa. However, there is also some evidence that individuals differ in their preferred method of learning whatever the subject matter.

Kolb *et al* (1991) further developed their model of a learning cycle described earlier, see Figure 4.1, to suggest that the learning process is driven by individual needs and goals. So learning styles become highly individual in both direction and process. For example, a mathematician may come to place great emphasis on abstract concepts whereas a poet may value concrete experience more highly. A manager may be primarily concerned with the active application of concepts whereas a naturalist may develop observational skills highly. Each of us will develop a personal style that has some weak points and some strong points. We may leap into experiences and fail to observe the lessons to be derived from these experiences. We may form concepts but fail to test their validity. In some areas our objectives may give us clear guidelines, in others we wander aimlessly.

Let us try to systematise this understanding a little. There are two main dimensions in the Kolb model of learning styles: a concrete–abstract dimension, 1 and 3 in the cycle, and an active–reflective dimension, 4 and 2 in the cycle. By making a grid of the four main learning processes on these two dimensions Kolb arrived at a grid of four basic learning styles, see Figure 4.2.

Figure 4.2
Kolb's learning styles.

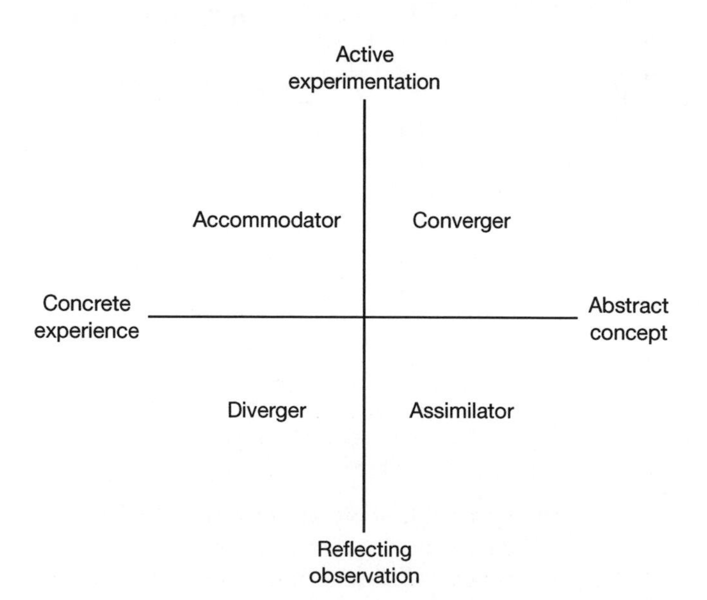

Kolb's four basic learning styles are:

- The convergent style. The main strength of this style is problem solving, decision making and practical application of ideas. People with this style do best where there is a single answer or solution. They prefer technical rather than social and interpersonal issues.
- The divergent style. This is the opposite of the convergent style. The great strength is in imaginative ability and awareness of meaning and values. People with this style look at concrete issues from a variety of ways. They are able to organise these into a pattern, or 'Gestalt'. This style is characteristic of arts people, counsellors and personnel people.
- The assimilation style. The great strengths here are the ability to create abstract models and assimilate diverse material into an explanation. There is less concern with people and more with ideas. People with this style tend to be researchers and planners.
- The accommodation style. This is the opposite of assimilation and people here are good at doing things and carrying out plans. They are quick to adapt if the plan does not quite work and get on with it. People with this style are most common in business and are likely to be in marketing and sales.

A variation on this learning style model is that of Honey and Mumford (1992), two British writers. They have used Kolb's model in a slightly different way by emphasising the particular stages of the cycle that individuals favour.

- Activists who use concrete experience involve themselves fully and without bias in new experiences. They tend to act first and consider the consequences afterwards.
- Reflectors who use observation and reflection and who like to sit back and ponder experiences are thoughtful and cautious.
- Theorists who form abstract concepts integrate things into logically sound theories. They tend to be perfectionists who do not give up till everything is fitted into a rational scheme.
- Pragmatists who rely on generalisations actively seek out new ideas to see if they will work in practice. They like to get on with things and like a challenge.

DID YOU KNOW?

'Gestalt' is a useful social science word for seeing the pattern. Originally it was used in psychology but has become more widely known. A Gestalt can be of a simple recognition of a pattern of visual material or it can be as complex as understanding the feeling of the population over something such as the death of Diana, Princess of Wales.

Whichever model of learning styles is adopted they are both useful in throwing some light on how people learn from experience and showing that there are individual differences. This means that those responsible for learning, training and development of people must ensure that there are sufficient different learning experiences to be had to suit different people. It is also suggested that the more we understand our own learning style the more likely we are to be able to learn effectively. Just because a method works for a friend does not necessarily mean you are dumb if it does not work for you!

ACTIVITY **4.2**

Using the models of either Kolb or Honey and Mumford what sort of learner do you think you are? What are likely to be the weaknesses of this? Any ideas on how to overcome them?

Types of learning

So far we have been looking at how people learn. This has attracted a good deal of attention, not only from school teachers but also from people involved in adult training. Another area that has been investigated is whether different sorts of learning material need different methods to optimise the learning. If we accept some of the generalisations of the previous section on how people learn, can we fine-tune them to suit different situations?

Traditionally a distinction is drawn between cognitive (intellectual) learning, learning skills and developing attitudes. Each of these is thought to be not only a different objective but also to require a different learning process. The distinction has been refined for practical use in adult learning by the Industrial Training Research Unit (ITRU 1976). They took the work of the Belbins to develop the CRAMP taxonomy. CRAMP divides learning into five types:

- **C**omprehension. This involves learning theoretical subject matter. It is knowing how, why and when things happen. This type of learning is best done through methods that treat the whole subject as an entity, rather than splitting it up into bits and taking one at a time. This is usually achieved by lecture, seminar, discussion, film or video. Clarity of presentation is critical so that the main points are distinguished from the supporting evidence. An example of such a learning type would be the learning of mathematics.
- **R**eflex learning. This is acquiring skilled movements or perceptual abilities. As well as knowing what to do, speed and coordination are at a premium. This requires practice and constant repetition. This is best approached by breaking the task into small steps and simplifying each step so that it can be easily learned. Even a simple piece of behaviour can actually be very complicated. Breaking a task into smaller steps is called 'task analysis' by behaviourist psychologists. If we get smaller steps right we have the opportunity to be 'rewarded'. If the steps are too big success is unlikely and there is no opportunity for reward and so learning does not take place readily. An example would be using a new piece of equipment, machining materials, inspecting of goods for quality problems or typing.
- **A**ttitude development. This enables people to change their attitudes and social skills. It is perhaps the most difficult sort of learning to achieve. Group methods that centre on the people knowing themselves seem the most effective as attitudes are very difficult to influence in other ways. One example would be a customer care course where the attitude of staff is explored by getting them to discuss their behaviour after doing an exercise such as 'finding the treasure' in a park. It is hoped that this will lead them to a better understanding of themselves and that through such self-knowledge they will be in a better position to change their behaviour towards customers.

- **M**emory training. This is learning information by heart. It is very similar to reflex learning, where each bit is taken one at a time. All sorts of jingles and mnemonics can be helpful here. You will frequently see in student texts mnemonics such as C-R-A-M-P. Obvious examples are actors learning their lines in a play or medical students learning the names of the bones in the body.
- **P**rocedural learning. This is similar to memory training but the items do not need to be memorised, only understood and their location known. This requires less practice. Examples are a lawyer's knowledge of the statutes or an engineer's knowledge of how to shut a plant down for maintenance. Neither would need to know by heart what to do but both would need to know where to look and to understand what they found. You have probably by now learnt to use your academic library. If you came to visit another you would know more or less how to use it but would probably need a few minutes to orientate yourself and find the references that you needed.

In practice most learning situations require more than one of these types but the categorisation is a helpful means of sorting out which would be the most appropriate way to learn something. For example, in professional exams there are some things that need to be learned by heart, other ideas that one needs to have some understanding of and yet others where procedural learning would be most appropriate. Whereas doing some reflex learning and learning to type might make the whole exam a great deal easier! The most effective learners are those who can classify their needs and do not waste time memorising everything.

ACTIVITY **4.3**

What types of learning would be most effective if you wanted to do the following:

- Use a CD-Rom to seek references for an assignment.
- Become influential in a political party.
- Really understand organisational behaviour.
- Understand a balance sheet in a company's annual report.

Role theory

So far we have very much been looking at learning from a psychologist's point of view. The sociologist's perspective on learning is to concentrate on how and why people come to belong to a group, that is, the need to belong and why. Sociologists seek to understand the reasons behind the behaviours studied by psychologists. Only by explaining the person's understandings of the situation and the method they use to organise their attitudes and knowledge, that is, their orientation, will we fully understand social relationships. That is, we need to understand the meanings of actions. Why do people want to learn particular things? Why and how do they become part of the group? Which things help and what hinders membership?

One very useful concept in understanding these sorts of question is that of role. The term 'role' describes some of the effects of the continuing process of social learning. In our various roles there are pressures to learn appropriate behaviours, values and understandings so that we conform to the differing groups we belong, or wish to belong, to. This concept is used very similarly to the use of the word in drama; it describes the social interaction rather than the specific person. Role playing is action in conformity with a set of social rules. These social rules will be based on the expectations and obligations based on the social or cultural values of that particular setting. Roles do not exist in any personal sense although any one person may have a unique set of roles to play. These personal collections of roles can in some circumstances have expectations that do not agree; this leads to role conflict and a choice has to be made between them. For example, your lecturers may have formal expectations that require them to be teachers, writers, counsellors, researchers and administrators; they will have to choose which is the most important when time is short.

ACTIVITY **4.4**

Think of three situations when you have experienced role conflict. For example, out with a friend when your granny comes over; being a student and a partner; working in a bar when your parent comes in.

How did you resolve the conflict? What were the consequences of your action?

The different roles we play are often defined by the institutions we belong to, such as families, communities, religions. These institutions set norms. That is, they set expectations and obligations that go to make up the role. Organisations are one such institution that set norms for various roles. These roles in turn make up the structure of the organisation or institution.

The commonly used concepts used to describe social learning, or socialisation, and roles are given below with some explanations:

- Role – set of expectations and obligations to act in specific ways in particular settings.
- Status – an actor's position in a social structure which limits the roles to be played.
- Social structure – the organisation of roles, statuses and social institutions into a determinate pattern.
- Institution – well-established orientations, values and norms in stable patterns.
- Norm – the normal standards of behaviour which a role is expected to conform to.
- Primary group – small, intimate group such as family, gang, close workmates. An important source of norms and values for the individual members.
- Reference group – social groups who provide the norms for people who want to belong to them.
- Significant other – this is a role model that the individual initially imitates to become part of the group that is 'socialised'.
- Generalised other – this is where the individual takes into account the other roles within the group and makes their own adaptation to this.

This gives us the conceptual framework to look at various social relationships and how we adapt to them. It is a different way of looking at learning from psychology.

ACTIVITY **4.5**

Look at the list of concepts about social learning above. Try to find an example of each from your life before coming to university and one from your first few days at university.

- Are there big differences in them?
- Are there any sources of conflict?

Induction and socialisation

One of the most obvious organisational behaviours that this learning theory and role analysis can be applied to is the newcomer to the organisation and their socialisation into, that is, their becoming part of, the organisation. This process is called induction by personnel specialists who deal with the formal introduction of people into organisations. They make sure that the newcomer is given information about specific rules such as health and safety, dress codes, security and that their supervisor ensures that they know what work is expected of them in terms of quantity and quality. These are the formal descriptions of norms and roles.

As well as the induction of the newcomer there is also the more informal socialisation which deals with aspects of coming to belong to the group. Chapter 7 deals in detail with how a group forms and how individuals relate to each other in the group. But it is worth remembering that a great deal of learning that takes place at work takes place in the informal setting of the group where members nudge each other into behaving in particular ways. For example, there will be norms about dress codes that are subtle variations on the formal rules, these need learning. There will be norms of how to speak to each other, what sorts of breaks to have and when to go home. All will need learning.

DID YOU KNOW?

In the Hawthorne experiments, already referred to in Chapter 1, group pressures were stronger than financial rewards. The group developed its own pattern of norms that were:

- *Not to be a rate buster – not to produce at too high a rate compared with others.*
- *Not to be a chiseller – not to produce at too low a rate compared with others.*
- *Not to be a squealer – not to say anything to supervisors or management that might harm other members of the group.*
- *Not to be officious – those with authority, for example, inspectors should not take advantage of their seniority.*

PAUSE FOR THOUGHT

Temps working in a variety of offices are often the most expert observers of the different norms applying in quite similar work environments. For example, supply teachers in secondary schools often have a blacklist of schools they never want to go to because of the culture of ignoring strangers, whereas they are happy to go to ones that ensure they know where the coffee room, lavatory and assistance are.

Encouraging lifelong learning or lifetime personal development

So far in this chapter we have been looking at social science models of learning generally. Let us now look more specifically at what is going on in work organisations. Increasingly organisations, professional bodies and the government are emphasising the need for individuals to develop and learn throughout their lives so they can cope with the increasing speed of change at work. The argument is made that the more learning that is undertaken by an individual, the easier it becomes and the more confident the individual will be in facing new changes and moving from one employer to another now that lifetime employment with one employer is rare. This emphasis on lifetime personal development is enshrined in two formal developments.

- Continuous Professional Development (CPD). Many professional bodies, but not all, are emphasising CPD and expect their members to fulfill a minimum training requirement every year to maintain membership. Some of this CPD experience is credit bearing leading to further qualifications and higher ranking within the profession.
- Investors In People (IIP). This is a government backed initiative to encourage organisations to train and develop their staff. Where suitable systems of identifying training and development needs and carrying out the required programmes of training and development take place organisations are entitled to a certificate as 'investors in people'. It has proved popular with organisations both in the private and public sectors.

See Chapter 10 for further discussion of these developments.

There is a parallel emphasis on the learning organisation which is able to encourage individuals to take on change and new tasks by a process of continuous learning. This is further discussed in Chapter 14.

Another aspect of encouraging lifetime personal development is managing individual careers. Managers have to learn to manage talent and this includes developing staff so that they build careers to suit themselves. This is increasingly important if Kanter's (1989) comments about security of employment coming from being employable rather than from being employed by a particular employer are true. All of us need opportunities to develop skills and a reputation. This involves ensuring that people get a variety of opportunities and experiences. As Handy (1989, p. 104) puts it, managers have to be:

> teacher, counsellor and friend, as much or more than he or she is commander, inspector and judge.

However, if we rely on our bosses to do this we are sometimes going to be disappointed so we might more usefully develop the habit of learning and developing ourselves.

My colleague Valmai Bowden, looking at the careers of bench scientists has pointed out that this nurturing of people's careers can be compared to parenting. Some managers are very strict and dogmatic, 'do like me', others are more facilitating and encourage self-direction and assessment. Those who are lucky enough to have good 'parenting' are likely to develop into the confident, learning, self-developing individuals who are likely to have rewarding careers. Those who feel ignored and rejected can become embittered. Maybe this facilitating of people's careers is at the heart of the relationship between managers and the managed in the new empowered climate.

Conclusion

This chapter has emphasised models of different learning styles, objectives and roles concerned with the individual. By now you should be aware that learning is not just a simple mechanical process. This concern with learning and the different models that can be used to analyse learning has now been applied to the whole organisation and the idea of a 'learning organisation' has been the subject of much interest over the past few years. This concept is dealt with in Chapter 14. The issue of learning is currently at the heart of a lot of discussion on organisational behaviour and so reoccurs in two further chapters in this book, Chapters 10 and 14.

EXERCISE **4.1**

1 Identify a learning situation that you have recently faced, for example, acquiring computing skills, sporting skills, driving ability, sports technique.

How did you go about it? What were the steps involved? What was the outcome?

2 What was the best group learning you ever experienced? What was good about it?

What was the worst group learning experience you ever had? Why was that?

What does this suggest you need for a useful group learning task? Think about both the content (knowledge, skills and attitudes) and process (the way you learn).

3 If you are in a seminar group, get into small groups of five or six and have a discussion about what you can offer each other to meet some of the wants described at the end of the last question.

EXERCISE **4.2**

1 Using the material on roles given earlier, go and do a role analysis of someone you know. Ideally this would be someone at work, about their work roles, for example, a nurse, lecturer, manager or sales person.

2 To do a role analysis you interview several different people about what the person doing that job would be expected to do.

Remember it is not whether the individual actually carries out these expectations satisfactorily, it is what would be expected of anyone doing that job.

I would start by asking the person in the job. Then anyone who comes into contact with them, for example, colleagues, bosses, those working for them, customers/clients, and any others.

3 When you have collected the material start analysing:

- Where there is consensus about the role.
- Where there is conflict.
- Whether there is role overload.
- Whether there is role underload.

Can you distinguish any formal/informal norms that differ?

Self-check questions

1. What is the difference between classical and operant conditioning?
2. What are the two different ways of summoning things from memory?
3. What is Kolb's cycle? Describe it.
4. Describe four different learning styles.
5. What does CRAMP stand for?
6. What do we mean by 'role'?
7. What is socialisation?
8. Why is it important to keep on developing oneself throughout a career?

CASE STUDY **4.1**

Nicholas is at the end of his first year at university studying law. He has a summer vacation job for ten weeks working in a prestigious law firm in the city centre. They want him to collate the responses from a questionnaire to their clients and write a report on the findings. This in turn will be professionally published and publicised using a PR firm.

What do you think Nicholas might learn from his summer job that he would not learn at university?

Figure 4.3 **What are the norms?**

References

Foot M. and Hook C. (1996) *Introducing Human Resource Management.* Longman, London.

Gagne R.M. (1975) *Essentials of Learning for Instruction.* Holt Reinehart and Winston, New York, NY.

Handy C. (1989) *The Age of Unreason.* Business Books, London.

Honey P. and Mumford A. (1992) *A Manual of Learning Styles,* 3rd edn. Honey, 10 Linden Avenue, Maidenhead.

Industrial Training Unit Research Unit (1976) Choose an effective style; a self-instructional approach to the teaching of skills. Cambridge ITRU, based on E. and R.M. Belbin (1972) *Problems in Adult Retraining.* Heinemann, London.

Kanter R.M. (1989) *When Giants Learn to Dance.* Simon and Schuster, London.

Kolb D.A., Rubin I.M. and McIntyre J.M. (1974) *Organizational Psychology: An Experimental Approach to Organizational Behavior.* Prentice Hall, Englewood Cliffs, NJ.

Kolb D.A., Rubin I.M. and Osland J. (1991) *Organizational Behaviour: An Experiential Approach,* 5th edn. Prentice Hall, London.

Pavlov I. (1927) *Conditioned Reflexes.* Oxford University Press, Oxford.

Skinner B.F. (1965) *Science and Human Behaviour.* Free Press, New York, NY.

Further reading

The chapters on learning in either of the Kolb *et al* books given above will give you more details of Kolb's view. I particularly like the 1991 book as it has all sorts of things to do including an exercise on finding out your own learning style.

Again any good introductory psychology book will have a chapter on learning such as the two books mentioned in Chapter 1.

For more on roles look at any introductory text on sociology.

CHAPTER 5

Communication

Objectives

When you have read this chapter you should be able to:

- Distinguish what are the purposes of a particular communication.
- Describe the chain of communication.
- Distinguish between Berne's different transactions.
- Organise a presentation.

Introduction

With the expansion of Higher Education in the latter part of the 1990s concern was expressed as to whether what was being offered to students was suitable. Various investigations were made, one was to find out what employers were looking for from recent graduates. When the views of employers were sought on what were the most important skills that graduates needed when they were recruited, see Harvey (1997), communication skills was at the top of the list. The next two most important skills were team working and interpersonal skills. This emphasis on communication is at the heart of organisational behaviour and cannot be over-emphasised. Indeed communication is very often blamed for all sorts of organisational ills, see, for example, Figure 6.2 on page 96. However, communication can mean a great number of different behaviours. The three basic questions to ask are: what is the subject matter, to whom is the communication directed and, how does the communication take place?

Communication can be to a wide range of audiences. Communication at work can be with just one person, with immediate colleagues, the larger department, the whole organisation, the customers or clients, to the community as a whole, with politicians, with fellow professionals or with overseas contacts and agents. The content of the communication may vary from the friendly conversation, to the sympathetic arm round the shoulder, to a formal disciplinary hearing. Communication can be anywhere along the following ranges:

- Formal–informal.
- Verbal–non-verbal.
- Written/electronic–face-to-face.

What all these different forms of communication have in common is that communication only takes place when the listener or audience has received the message sent. It is not sufficient for the sender to have sent the message. This

DID YOU KNOW?

'Nobody ever tells me anything.'
'The customers always seem to know before us.'
'Oh no! Not more bumph in my in-tray.'
'I'm sorry ... I didn't know about it.'
'Well you really should have. It was in your in-tray last week.'

I have heard people saying all these things in organisations. No matter how well a communication system looks on paper it is bound to fail sometimes – we are, after all, only human!

chapter is about using different psychological models to analyse communication at work. They come from a variety of perspectives and approach different parts of the communication behaviour in organisations. Other useful models for analysing communication come from social psychology, sociology and political perspectives and are discussed in Chapter 7 on group behaviour and Chapter 12 on the politics of organisations.

The purpose of communication

In all human interactions there are two major ingredients – content and process. The first deals with the subject matter or the task upon which the group is working. In most interactions, the focus of attention of people is the content. The second ingredient, process, is concerned with what is happening between and to the group members while the group is working. Usually very little attention is paid to the process, even when it is the major cause of ineffective group communication and action. Group processes include a whole range of things such as participation, styles of influence, norms, decision making procedures and many others. Studying the way in which people act in groups is important because their behaviour will communicate a variety of messages, both about the content of their communication and through the way they convey information about their feelings towards the message. These aspects of group interaction are dealt with later in this book, see Chapters 7 and 12, but a mention is made here of some of the concepts to emphasise that 'communication' is a complex interaction, and a variety of analytical devices to look at both the content and process of communication are appropriately included.

Let us now concentrate on the content of communication. In our everyday life we communicate for a variety of different reasons. For example:

- Communicating to achieve or obtain something.
- Communicating to try to get someone to behave differently.
- Communicating to find out something.
- Communicating to express our feelings.
- Communicating to enjoy the companionship.
- Communicating to sort out a problem.
- Communicating for interest.
- Communicating because the situation demands it.

ACTIVITY **5.1**

Think back over yesterday. Rough out a schedule of what you did. How much of your time was spent in contact with another person or persons? What purposes did these communications serve?

Try the list above.

Communication across the whole department, section or organisation

Much of the communication in organisations will serve similar functions to those listed above. However, communication in organisations is not just one-to-one but it is also sometimes with the whole work group. There are four main areas about which there needs to be communication within organisations, according to Greenbaum (1974).

- To ensure that everyone knows about and is using a particular method, standard or procedure. That is, something about *regulation* needs communicating.
- To change some aspect of how the work is done such as how to reduce waste, introduce some new software on the PCs or change the ordering system. So, some sort of *innovation* has to be communicated.
- To try to raise morale and develop a feeling of identity within the group by such devices as using jokes and planning an outing. That is, communicating about *integration.*
- Communication of factual *information* that people need to proceed efficiently with their work.

Each of these four main types of communication, regulation, innovation, integration and information, can be achieved in different ways. This could be through speaking with people, writing to them or including a non-verbal aspect to the communication, see Greenbaum (1974) for more extensive discussion of this.

For most purposes we probably make an automatic choice as to the appropriate way to communicate particular messages. There is certainly local custom and practice about the 'way we say things round here'. However, sometimes it is worth trying a different way, particularly when communication does not seem to be quite as effective as you would like. Box 5.1, based on Greenbaum's model for auditing organisations' communication, gives some of the different ways people in organisations communicate and may give you some suggestions if you are having problems. I have just given examples in Box 5.1 as it is surprising how very different organisations are in the way they communicate the four fundamental aspects of organisational life.

DID YOU KNOW?

Public Relations, or PR as it is commonly called, is concerned with how organisations communicate with people within the organisation and without. This might involve taking journalists on a trip to see a product in practice, such as the PR company for a seed producer taking agricultural journalists to look at sample fields in June. It might involve writing articles for magazines, producing in-house newspapers for staff communication or holding drinks parties for people to meet and discuss informally developments within the organisation. PR agencies would claim they are ensuring that the people who might want the service or product or need to understand some new venture are properly communicated with. Others sometimes feel that PR is trying to spin exaggerations and half-truths to persuade people to do things differently. But it is certainly true that PR people are consummate communicators!

Box 5.1
Communicating with the whole work group.

Regulation

Speaking	Departmental meetings
	Directions and requests
	Catching everyone at break-times and change of shift
Writing	Agenda for meeting
	Job descriptions
	Performance standards
	Memos
	E-mail
Non-verbal	Gesture
	Pauses and silences

Innovation

Speaking	Problem-solving meetings
	Conversations
	Team briefings
	Brainstorming
Writing	Reports on visits and courses
	Suggestions schemes
	E-mail
	Journals
Non-verbal	Seating arrangements
	Laughter

Integration

Speaking	Saying hello
	Coffee breaks
	Ritual of acknowledging birthdays
Writing	Letters of congratulation on passing courses
	House style stationery
	E-mail
	Report forms in house style
Non-verbal	Eye contact in the corridor
	State of staffroom
	Staff socials

Information

Speaking	Training sessions
	Mass meeting
	Change-over time for shifts
Writing	Memos
	Noticeboard
	E-mail
	Handbooks
	Bulletins and newsletters
Non-verbal	Demonstrate what needs doing
	Having an example

ACTIVITY **5.2**

Use the headings in Box 5.1 as a template, see if you can find examples of each category of communication either at your place of work or within the university you are studying at.

- Were any of the categories particularly easy to find?
- Were any particularly difficult?
- How do you communicate about integration?
- Compare your experience with someone in another part of the same organisation or another organisation altogether. What are the main differences?

ACTIVITY **5.3**

Using Box 5.1 as a guideline, which of the following areas would you communicate using verbal, written or non-verbal methods, or a combination of these methods?

- Changed safety regulations.
- A new procedure for claiming travel expenses.
- Proposals for merging two departments.
- A change to the holiday arrangements.
- Information regarding a particular member of staff or student.

The communication chain

Whatever the purpose of the communication it is a two-way process, complete only when the message is received and understood, even if the understanding is not exactly what was intended. Both the sender and the receiver of a message have an active part to play. This reciprocal process is sometimes described as the *communication* or *speech chain* and uses systems or information theory terms to describe the process. For effective communication to take place each of the following six stages needs to be operating well (see Figure 5.1):

- Encoding.
- Transmitting.
- Environment.
- Receiving.
- Decoding.
- Feedback.

Problems of communication may occur at any or all of these different phases in the chain. Where we consistently have problems communicating with another it can be worthwhile sitting down and analysing where in this chain we think the problem may lie.

When we want to be effective communicators we need to consider not only our own performance but also that of the people we are trying to communicate with, and the likely effect upon them of what we are saying and how we are saying it. Understanding other people is difficult because we all have a different set of operating assumptions, see Chapter 2 for discussion of individual differences, with which to conduct our lives. If we do not recognise this diversity, communication becomes at best awkward and at worst non-existent.

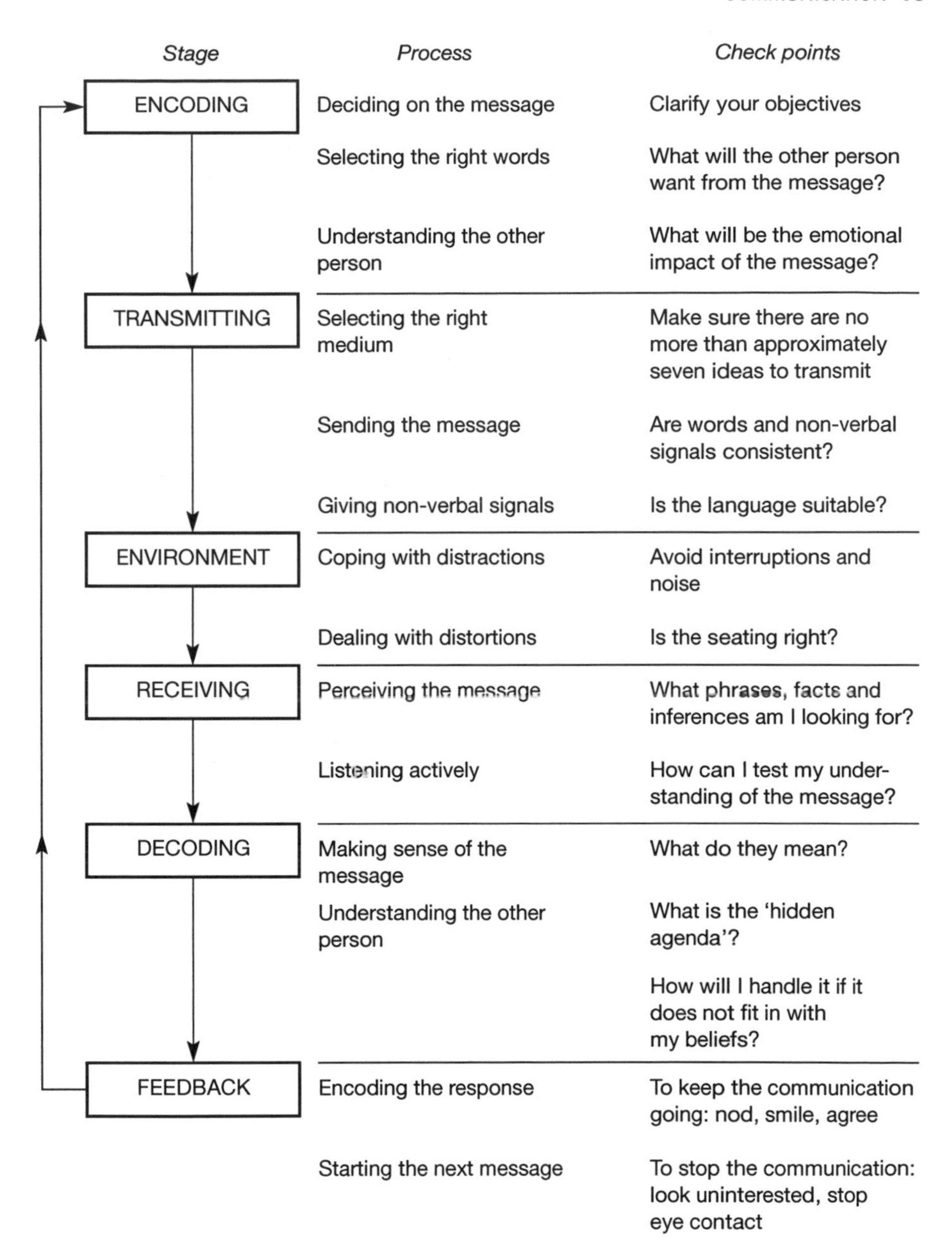

Figure 5.1
The basic communications model or speech chain.

PAUSE FOR THOUGHT

A special aspect of the environment in which we communicate is the non-verbal signals we give out. I have not included a great deal about how we communicate non-verbally here so consider the following sayings:

- *'The audience were on the edge of their seats.'*
- *'She gave me the cold shoulder.'*
- *'He remained poker-faced throughout.'*
- *'Speech is silver; silence is golden.'*
- *'She is down in the mouth today.'*

- *'He is all ears.'*
- *'She is a stuck-up person.'*
- *'He is on his high horse.'*
- *'Her face lit up.'*

What do these suggest to you about effective and non-verbal communication?

Factors other than those involved in the direct communication can also affect the outcome of a conversation or meeting. Physical things such as noise and temperature are obvious factors. The position of the furniture can also play a part. Seating a group so they can all see each other increases interaction – think of how seminars and training sessions vary if you are seated in a circle rather than in rows. Having a table between participants increases the formality but gives them quite literally something to hold onto if it is a tense situation. Interruptions from the telephone or keeping an 'open door' can disrupt communication.

Difficulties in communication can occur because:

- The purpose of the communication is unclear.
- There are problems in sending the message.
- There are problems in receiving the message.
- Outside physical factors intervene.

Where effective communication is critical each stage needs to be considered so as to pre-empt any possible problems.

The usefulness of this model is in emphasising the different stages of the communication and the equal worth that is given to both sender and receiver.

ACTIVITY **5.4**

What differences would you expect in the communication chain for the following sorts of communication?

1. Communicating to achieve or obtain something.
2. Communicating to try to get someone to behave differently.
3. Communicating to find out something.
4. Communicating your feelings.
5. Communicating to enjoy the companionship.
6. Communicating to sort out a problem.
7. Communicating for interest.
8. Communicating because the situation demands it.

Using transactional analysis

Another approach to analysing communication difficulties has been the psychiatric and therapeutic models of counselling. One that has had a lot of popularity is a simple device by Berne (1966) who suggests that we interact with each other with different behaviours which can be described as *parent*, *adult* or *child*. The 'parent' is one of authority and superiority and a person behaving in this way is typically dominant and scolding. It is the ego state in

Figure 5.2 **Childlike communication.**

which all our value judgements are stored and the state of a person every time they behave like their parents. The 'child' state contains all the unpredictability of tantrum and charm, obedience and defiance, tears and laughter, sulks and joy (see Figure 5.2). The parent acts in a way they were taught; the child acts in the way they feel, impulsive and uncensored. The 'adult' state is objective and rational. No matter what prejudices or emotions were communicated by parents, someone behaving in an adult way deals objectively with reality, analysing situations as realistically as possible, processing information, estimating probabilities and making decisions. The adult state is not prejudiced by the values of the parent nor by the natural urges of the child. These labels have nothing to do with age nor do we fit into only one of these categories; all of us have all three states and spend each day moving from one to the other.

As we each have all three sorts of behaviour and can bring any one of them to a communication, this means that when we communicate with each other all combinations are possible. The most frequent types of transaction are: complementary, crossed and ulterior (see Figure 5.3).

- A complementary transaction is appropriate and expected and follows the natural order of relationships.
- Crossed transactions are those where an opening statement elicits an inappropriate response.
- Ulterior transactions are more complex as they always involve more than two ego states. The most common is where a real message is disguised under an explicit and more socially acceptable message.

In most situations at work the ideal transaction is adult–adult, but any complementary transaction is better than any crossed one. If any two people are both in child mode and start shouting at each other they are not going to resolve their differences but will probably cope better than if one of them starts being a parent! You might find it useful to use this transactional analysis format when communication is getting nowhere, feels too emotional or when the relationship is awkward. By clarifying how you are tripping each other up you might stand more chance of understanding how to change the way you respond.

Figure 5.3
Transactions.

COMPLEMENTARY TRANSACTIONS

Member of staff:

'Will we be working overtime on Saturday?'

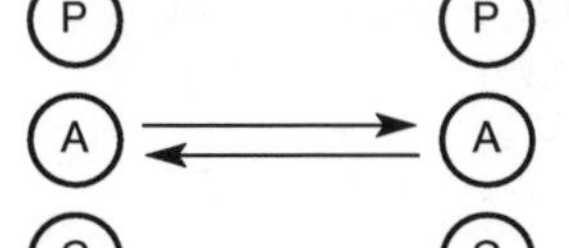

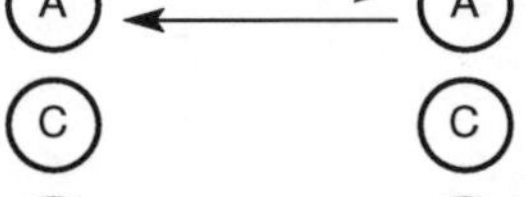

Manager:

'As far as I know at the moment, yes we will.'

Member of staff:

'I've got a splitting headache. Do you think I could go home?'

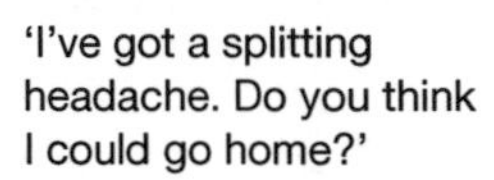

Manager:

'Yes, you get home to bed. It'll be all right.'

CROSSED TRANSACTIONS

Member of staff:

'I haven't had my copy of the new handbook. Have you got a spare?'

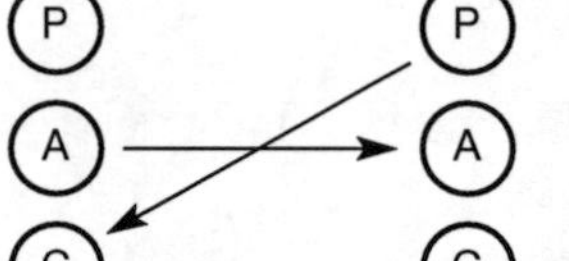

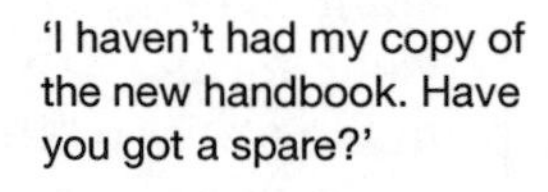

Manager:

'Surely you can see I'm busy. Can't you pick one up at the office on your way home?'

Manager:

'According to the rota, it's your turn to stay behind and clean up.'

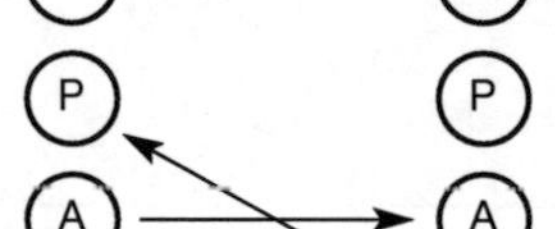

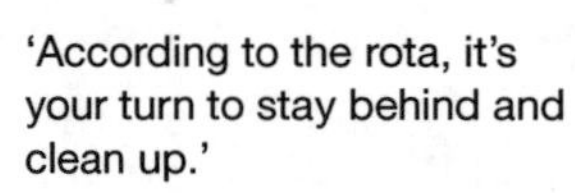

Member of staff:

'Oh no. I'm going out tonight. Can't you get someone else to do it?'

ULTERIOR TRANSACTIONS

Manager:

'They have an interesting vacancy in PR, but I'm not sure you're ready for it .'

('Go on. Pick up the challenge.')

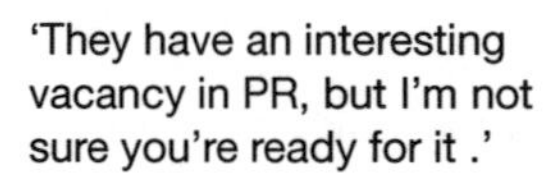

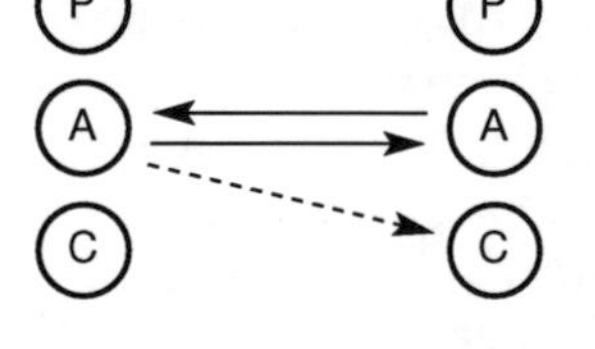

Member of staff:

'No, I suppose I had better get a bit more experience before I try for a move.'

Manager:

'They have an interesting vacancy in PR, but I'm not sure you're ready for it .'

('Go on. Pick up the challenge.')

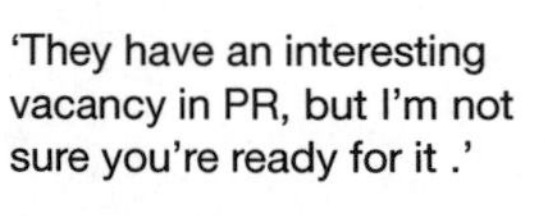

Member of staff:

'Why not? I think I stand as good a chance as anybody else, and I'd certainly like to give it a try.'

Key
A = adult C = child P = parent

ACTIVITY **5.5**

Next time you find yourself having an awkward conversation with someone analyse it afterwards using Berne's model and see if it makes any more sense.

Can you think of colleagues who frequently behave in parent, child or adult mode? Do you have particular difficulties with any of these?

Effective communication

Communication failure happens when someone is unable to transmit the desired message to another. This can happen in three main ways:

- Ineffective sending.
- Ineffective reception.
- A mismatch between the communicators.

What can we do about it?

There are various strategies that can help in developing good communication skills. One is the use of competencies. Many organisations now have lists of communication skills required for different posts and the appropriate training courses to go with them. For example, Box 5.2 gives the communication competencies expected at different levels in a section of the civil service. A similar list for managers in the National Health Service is given in Box 5.3. A rather different orientation on communication competency is given in Box 10.1 on page 164 of those skills required of secondary school heads of department.

One specific area of effective communication that is often required in organisations is that of making a presentation or case for something. This may be reporting the results of a project, making a bid for funding for a project, trying to sell something to a customer or client or trying to persuade a group of people towards a particular outcome. Whatever the purpose there are some basic ground rules for presentations that are summarised in Box 5.4. It is perhaps worth noting that the same model can be quite helpful for essay writing as well!

DID YOU KNOW?

How do you find out what is going on?

- *Bill and Ben. Often the reply to this question is something like: 'Oh, I generally ask, Bill, or Ben; they usually seem to know what's going on'. Here we have the growth of an informal network of cars and mouthpieces of management or the Bill and Ben system.*
- *Noisy plumbing. In other cases the answer is something like: 'Oh, my head of department sometimes tells me if they think it's something I need to know. Isn't that the way it's supposed to work?' Indeed it is, but it does not work very reliably. With these bureaucratic 'cascade' systems, much depends on the people controlling the taps at each level. All too often the staff on the ground floor are without water or else it arrives over filtered or even polluted.*
- *Just a minute! One method of finding out what is going on is through the minutes of meetings. Traditionally minutes are issued only to those who attended the meeting or who sent apologies for absence. But another view is to regard minutes as a form of communication as well as a record. Several organisations send them to everyone. Those that are interested read them, the others will throw them away.*
- *The legibility test. Sometimes minutes are hastily written up by hand along with the agenda just before the next meeting. The document looks like some weird psychological test. This is photocopied and distributed at the meeting. Is it any surprise that the meeting gets off to a rather spotty start?*

(From Torrington and Weightman (1989) pp. 106–7)

Box 5.2

Communication and representational skills expected at different levels in a section of the civil service.

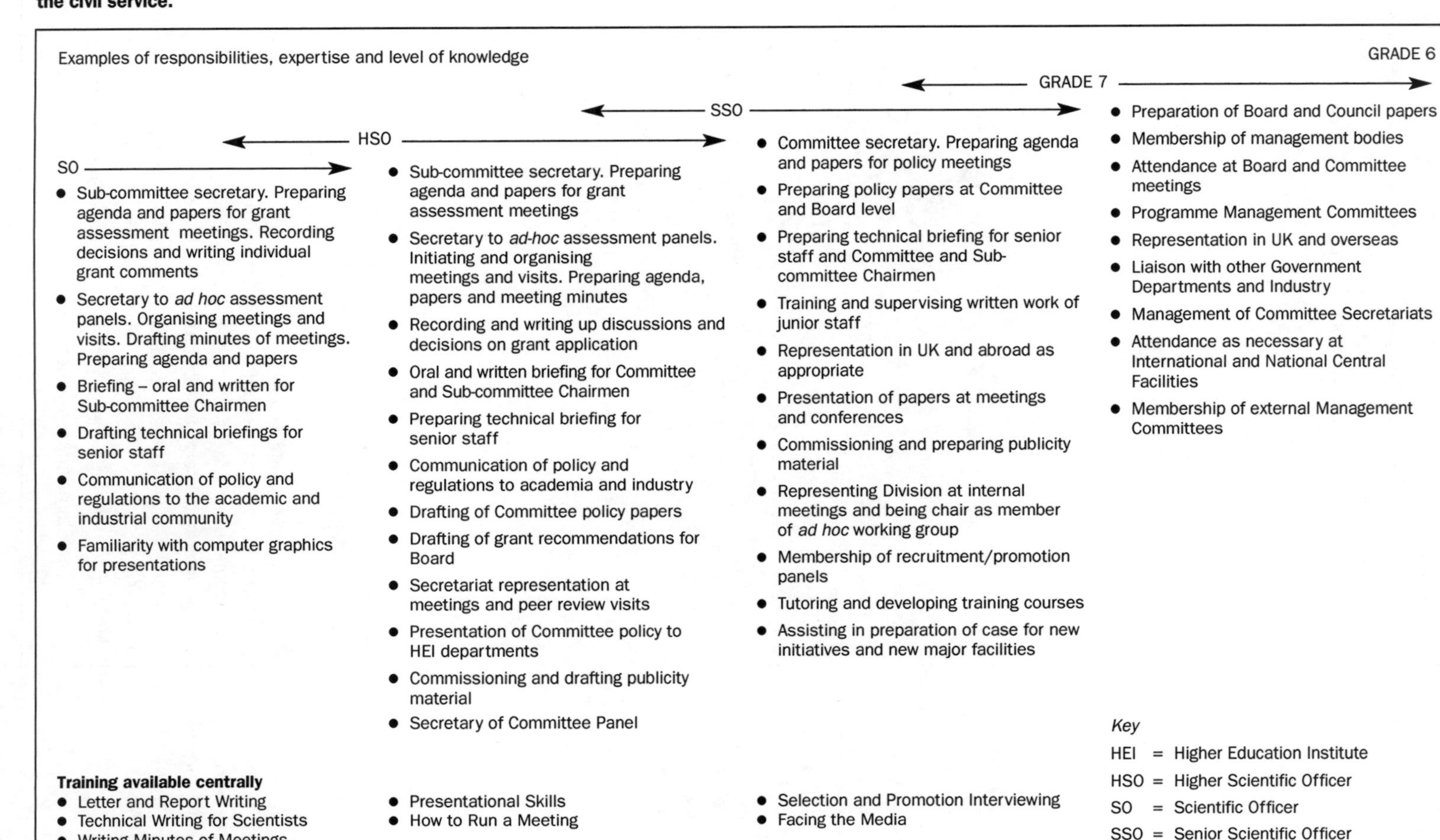

Examples of responsibilities, expertise and level of knowledge

SO →

- Sub-committee secretary. Preparing agenda and papers for grant assessment meetings. Recording decisions and writing individual grant comments
- Secretary to *ad hoc* assessment panels. Organising meetings and visits. Drafting minutes of meetings. Preparing agenda and papers
- Briefing – oral and written for Sub-committee Chairmen
- Drafting technical briefings for senior staff
- Communication of policy and regulations to the academic and industrial community
- Familiarity with computer graphics for presentations

← HSO →

- Sub-committee secretary. Preparing agenda and papers for grant assessment meetings
- Secretary to *ad-hoc* assessment panels. Initiating and organising meetings and visits. Preparing agenda, papers and meeting minutes
- Recording and writing up discussions and decisions on grant application
- Oral and written briefing for Committee and Sub-committee Chairmen
- Preparing technical briefing for senior staff
- Communication of policy and regulations to academia and industry
- Drafting of Committee policy papers
- Drafting of grant recommendations for Board
- Secretariat representation at meetings and peer review visits
- Presentation of Committee policy to HEI departments
- Commissioning and drafting publicity material
- Secretary of Committee Panel

← SSO →

- Committee secretary. Preparing agenda and papers for policy meetings
- Preparing policy papers at Committee and Board level
- Preparing technical briefing for senior staff and Committee and Sub-committee Chairmen
- Training and supervising written work of junior staff
- Representation in UK and abroad as appropriate
- Presentation of papers at meetings and conferences
- Commissioning and preparing publicity material
- Representing Division at internal meetings and being chair as member of *ad hoc* working group
- Membership of recruitment/promotion panels
- Tutoring and developing training courses
- Assisting in preparation of case for new initiatives and new major facilities

← GRADE 7 →

GRADE 6

- Preparation of Board and Council papers
- Membership of management bodies
- Attendance at Board and Committee meetings
- Programme Management Committees
- Representation in UK and overseas
- Liaison with other Government Departments and Industry
- Management of Committee Secretariats
- Attendance as necessary at International and National Central Facilities
- Membership of external Management Committees

Training available centrally

- Letter and Report Writing
- Technical Writing for Scientists
- Writing Minutes of Meetings
- Interactive Skills
- Presentational Skills
- How to Run a Meeting
- Selection and Promotion Interviewing
- Facing the Media

Key

HEI = Higher Education Institute
HSO = Higher Scientific Officer
SO = Scientific Officer
SSO = Senior Scientific Officer

Box 5.3
Management competencies expected in the National Health Service.

- **Organise people**
  - establish an appropriate organisational structure in their own department
  - define responsibilities clearly
  - establish accountability and reporting requirements
- **Lead people**
  - motivate people
  - harness their energies and efforts to get things done
  - harmonise their personal and organisational objectives
  - act appropriately to improve their performance
  - reward people in appropriate ways
- **Develop people**
  - identify people's needs for growth and development
  - assess their job performances accurately and systematically
  - appraise them sensitively and constructively
  - provide them with suitable opportunities for development
  - counsel them
  - coach them
  - train them
  - support them
- **Communicate with people**
  - inform people (notify, report, tell, teach)
  - influence people (persuade, convince)
  - seek information from people
    - accurately and succinctly in writing
      through correspondence
      reports
      papers
    - confidently and effectively in speech
      through briefings
      presentations
      negotiations
      interviews
      counselling
      teaching
- **Exercise discipline**
  - set (or adopt) standards of behaviour and performance
  - monitor individual performances against those standards
  - take appropriate action when deviations occur
  - follow diciplinary interviews systematically
  - conduct disciplinary interviews effectively
- **Handle conflict**
  - deal sensitively and appropriately with grievances
  - identify accurately the causes of grievances and conflict
  - seek to harmonise where possible

Box 5.4
Making your case. (Based on the video *Making your Case* by Video Arts.)

- **Preparation**
  - ➤ Why are you making this presentation?
  - ➤ What are you going to say?
  - ➤ Whom are you saying it to?
  - ➤ Where will you be saying it?
  - ➤ How will you say it?
- **The structure**
  1 Preface
  2 Position
  3 Problem
  4 Possibilities
  5 Proposal
  6 Postscript
- **The technique**
  - ➤ Delivery – beware mumbling, hesitancy, gabbling, catch phrases, poor eye contact, mannerisms and dropping voice
  - ➤ Language – use short words and sentences
  - ➤ Visuals – for explanation and persuasion
  - ➤ Detail – better too little than too much
  - ➤ Feedback – ask them
- **Summary and questions**
  - ➤ Look at original objective
  - ➤ Summarise, recommend, propose next step, thank and ask for questions

Conclusion

This chapter has emphasised psychological models of communication with the emphasis on individual communication and what can be done to improve personal performance. This needs putting in the social context of the group and the organisation. Every social system has its own pressures on communication as we will see in Chapter 7 on groups and Chapter 12 on politics. The whole nature of organisational communication is linked to issues of empowerment, performance management and accountability that are currently much discussed in management circles and which are discussed later in this book. The central nature of communication to human behaviour inevitably means it is critical to understanding organisational behaviour. All the underlying disciplines of psychology, sociology and politics have important things to add to our understanding of communication.

EXERCISE 5.1

In your seminar or tutorial group get each member to give a three minute presentation. Use Box 5.4 to help you structure it.

I would suggest giving yourselves a week's preparation time but it can be done with just ten minutes preparation and be just as effective. (At least everyone turns up!) I would allow each person to choose their own topic but if you want some suggestions of topics here are some:

1. Take one of the headings from this book.
2. How my perception of the Prime Minister is different from yours.

3 Why you should visit my home town.
4 The reasons for taking up .(some sport, hobby, pastime, food, drink etc.).
5 Why it is absolutley not on to do .(as above plus various specific behaviours).

Afterwards discuss which of the parts of the structure were well done.

Self-check questions

1 What are the four main purposes of communication within organisations?
2 What do we mean by the communication chain?
3 What are Berne's parent, adult and child?

CASE STUDY 5.1

The following letters, among others, were on the desk of a headteacher of a small primary school on 17 September. The head was the only teacher without a class and she had a secretary three mornings a week, but not on this day. I have changed the names to make them anonymous but they are the real experience of one headteacher!

How would you respond to these letters?

Letter 5.1

27 The Avenue
Anytown

31 August

Dear Miss Head.
Thank you so much for your help in getting our daughter into the secondary school of our choice. Your assistance during the appeal process was so very helpful. If there is anything that we can do to help in the future do please let us know.

Yours most gratefully
Mr and Mrs Heaven

Letter 5.2

3 The High
Anytown

15.9

Dear Headteacher,
Please will you make sure the children from your school do not come into my sweet shop ever again.

Yours
Miss Steak

Letter 5.3

Dear Miss
Our Jimmy has gone down with the measles and will not be in school for two weeks.
....

Letter 5.4

113 Main Street
Anytown

16.9

Dear Headteacher
I would like to resign my post teaching year 3 at the end of this term.

Yours sincerely
J. Campbell

Letter 5.5

Department for Education and Employment
Whitehall
London SW1

31st August

Dear Headteacher,
I enclose a copy of the new regulations and a copy of the monitoring form.
Please will you return it by 18th September.

Yours sincerely
pp The Minister

Letter 5.6

20 Wellington Rd
Anytown

15 Sept.

Dear Mary,
I am resigning from the governors after the outrageous attitude of yourself and the chair at the last meeting towards the parents who attended. I know they are not supposed to speak but it was an important issue. I do not think you should have thrown them out of the meeting.

Yours sincerely
June Blunt

PS I have enjoyed my ten years as a parent governor.

Letter 5.7

7 Acacia Avenue
Anytown

16.9

Dear Headteacher,
Yesterday I was standing outside the leisure centre when a bus full of school children disgorged onto the footpath and blocked the way for at least five minutes. I believe they were from your school going swimming.

My wife has difficulty walking and was hesitant to push past and yet no-one made a gap for us.

What are you teaching children today!

Yours outraged
Arthur Capp

References

Berne E. (1966) *Games People Play*. Andre Deutsch, London.

Greenbaum H.W. (1974) The audit of organizational communications. *Academy of Management Journal*, 739–54.

Harvey L. (1997) Report to Association of Graduate Recruiters. Warwick University 7–9 July.

Making your Case. (1982) Video Arts, Dunbarton House, 68 Oxford Street, London W1N 0LH.

Torrington D. and Weightman J. (1989) *Management and Organisation in Secondary Schools*. Blackwell, Oxford.

Further reading

Torrington D. (1991) *Management Face to Face*. Prentice Hall, Hemel Hempstead. This is a delightful, small book by my colleague. In it there is a lot of useful material about how to communicate with individuals at work. He is particularly good on how to listen and question people.

Katz D. and Kahn R.L. (1978) Communication, feedback, processes and evaluation research. Chapter 14 in *The Social Psychology of Organizations*, 2nd edn, Wiley, New York, NY. Most libraries have an edition of this title. The chapter is particularly useful on the social context of communication in organisations.

CHAPTER 6

Managing oneself to optimise performance

Objectives

When you have read this chapter you will be able to:

- ➤ Describe some of the issues facing individuals at work.
- ➤ Prioritise your time better.
- ➤ Understand some differences between management jobs.
- ➤ Draw a mind map.
- ➤ Have a better understanding of what is meant by stress.

Introduction

To conclude Part 1 of the book, which deals with the individual in the workplace, this chapter gets a bit more personal. It looks at questions such as: What is it like to be an individual in the workplace? What are some of the current issues facing people at work? How can one optimise one's own performance? There are several reasons for doing this. First, it makes some sense to show that all this study of organisation behaviour is not entirely an academic exercise but really should be related to the real working world. Second, there are such changes in the work environment that individuals will increasingly have to take responsibility for their own development and welfare rather than relying on their seniors to look out for them, so you might as well start here. Third, there is an area of work which is relevant to the study of organisation behaviour which is presented as advice, self-help, counselling. These are very soft approaches to analysing organisation behaviour that are particularly aimed at the individual's survival and development.

This chapter starts by looking at the reality of the working world, the role of managers and some of the issues facing working individuals and ends with some specific areas of self-help that might be relevant to you managing to optimise your own performance.

Changes in the culture of large organisations and their management

There have been major changes and reorientations in the working world and their associated organisations over the past two decades. These have led to various changes in the way staff are managed and the behaviour of those working in organisations. Large organisations in the past few years have increasingly been concentrating on factors such as:

- Being less centralised.
- Handling their staff in a more individualistic way.
- Offering less permanent employment.
- Dealing with rapid changes.
- Managing with fewer layers of managers.

This has been associated with two trends. One is accountability and the other is empowerment.

The trend to measure and make accountable every decision and use of resource is seen in all sorts of management information systems and quality audits such as ISO 9000. This desire to control everything is understandable as managers feel under more and more pressure from political masters or shareholders to account for the business. Increasingly people are asked to justify any action, decision or resource use with evidence that it is the right thing to do. Again this is understandable as we see ourselves as becoming an increasingly litigious nation and a 'blame culture'. There is a widespread feeling in many organisations that the public now blames not thanks. This is summed up by someone working in the Health Service who said to me, 'In the past we used to get chocolates and flowers, now we only get the blame if they do not recover'.

However, not everything worth doing is clear cut, sometimes we have to act on experienced judgement and trust ourselves to do the right thing and take a risk. Otherwise we will spend all our time justifying and auditing and not enough time doing things. As someone said to me 'No pig got fat by being measured'.

The second trend is the advocation of 'empowered' managers and the development of the people who work for them. One of the main developments in management strategy in the 1990s was the shortening of lines of communication and command and the associated attempts to empower line managers. The focus of this has been the individual manager, with a department, function or office to run. Theoretically this manager has been empowered to deliver all that is required, without being dependent on the personnel department or some other specialist function for assistance. Hyman and Cunningham (1996) in their research on empowerment list the traditional people responsibilities of line managers as:

- Changing work practice.
- Disciplining subordinates.
- Dealing with absenteeism.
- Dealing with disputes.

This compares with their list of empowering responsibilities of line managers which include:

- Recruiting people.
- Advising and counselling staff.
- Communicating with staff.
- Conducting appraisals.
- Training staff.

- Leading meetings.
- Communicating upwards.
- Dealing with staff suggestions.
- Ensuring high quality.

Inevitably a good idea has run ahead of the ability to deliver. At its best empowerment genuinely allows individuals to develop and contribute their best work. On the other hand all too often individual managers feel they have not been empowered, they have simply had responsibility dumped on them, without the training, time, resources or skills to meet their obligations. Those responding to the manager may also feel disappointed. Some managers respond to the new opportunities with enthusiasm and effectiveness; others are unhappy with their broadened role and are grudging in the way they discharge their people management responsibilities. I would argue that the empowered line manager needs some initial training and support in how to manage people and the individual working in an organisation needs some understanding of how to manage him/herself and so survive to do a good job. This is the basis for this chapter.

Working out strategy, operations and administration jobs

It is worth taking a little closer look at what managers do as they are often seen as responsible for a lot of the behaviour we want to analyse in organisations. Also, many of the readers of this book will become, if they are not already, managers. There are all sorts of different management jobs in any organisation.

The basic tasks of management are:

- Strategy. This means scanning the horizon for what is coming up, sifting to decide what is critical and making appropriate plans. This might include new legislation that is coming along, which new technical developments are appearing, what new ideas about the business are developing and what new competitors are being launched. All these would require the organisation to devise some way of dealing with them, that is, establishing the tactics for facing the future. This may include short-term objectives and longer-term plans that would reorientate the organisation.
- Operations. This involves keeping things going day by day and dealing with the difference between plan and reality. This is the everyday business of keeping work flowing despite illness, buses running late, deliveries not happening just-in-time and the irrational customer shouting abuse. It often requires exceptional personal and social skills on the part of those who have this sort of general management job.
- Administration. This is looking after procedures and policies so that not everything has to be reinvented every day. Policies are the declared intentions of an organisation about how things should be done. For example, organisations will have a Health and Safety policy about the way people should work that will include the legal requirement but usually have some specific aspects unique to the particular organisation. These policies are put into practice through procedures which are the description of how to do things. The Health and Safety policy, for instance, would be delivered

through specific procedures for such things as handling particular materials, procedures for dealing with fires, procedures for checking the wiring and so on.

Different management jobs have these in very different proportions. There can be different balances at different times in a career, for different positions in the hierarchy and for different sized organisations. We, Weightman, Butler and Griffin (1989), found all of these types of job in our study of management competencies for a Health Authority.

Strategic jobs are often about managing the managers. It is not the day-to-day contingencies but dealing with a major problem which has no 'by the book' answer. Job holders tend to have particular areas to promote within the institution and are involved in promoting change. They are constantly scanning to see what new trends, demands or initiatives are coming along that need replying to, implementing or capitalising on. Jobs of this sort are closely involved with policy making and getting decisions both made and implemented. People with these jobs feel they have the autonomy to get things done. Few are strategic all the time, as most have operations, administrative or professional work to do. Being strategic is determining the expansion of production or the service, dealing with outside bodies when the organisation is questioned and dealing with competitive negotiations and tendering. Areas such as discipline, recruitment and selection and day-to-day budgetary control are often left to other managers. Jobs in this group are about understanding and influencing a wide group of people. Examples of job titles bearing responsibilities of this kind are: chief executive, managing director, head of service, general manager.

Operation jobs are really the other side of the coin to the strategic jobs. Operation jobs are about keeping the show on the road. These people make it work day-by-day, hour-by-hour. The usefulness of these jobs is in dealing with the differences between plan and reality. The day-to-day problems need someone to handle them. There are all sorts of uncertainties, such as staff absences, transport breakdowns, supply problems, boilers leaking, delivery difficulties, patients getting confused, system failures. All of these need attention quickly and many job holders in this group see their work as managing people. They are often engaged in recruiting, disciplining and working out rotas. Additionally, they may be dealing with the stress of those in their sections by being available for a 'chat', and so reducing staff absences and turnover. This management of people cannot be divorced from other aspects of operations such as dealing with difficulties, resources and budgets. If all the emphasis is on managing people there is a danger of losing touch with what really needs doing. It is getting the balance between managing the staff and managing the tasks that is the clever art of operations jobs.

For people with jobs in this group there are two main people issues. First, there is the tension between how much autonomy to give to the staff and the degree of central control. For example, who should decide such things as rotas, resources, how the work is done, training. Second, is whether the job is interpreted as mostly about nurturing relationships of high trust and consensus or mostly about dealing with different groups whose interests conflict. Decisions on these two issues will effect the nature of the organisation climate of the department and how people work together. For example, a high trust, autonomous group will work in a collegial way with each other whereas a centralised group where conflict has to be managed is more likely to go for formal prescriptions of the work to be done. Whichever style is adopted these operations job holders are seen as one of the main audiences for this book. Examples of job titles for this group are: head of section or department, district specialist, plant manager, service manager.

Administration managers are in jobs where they need to know the procedures or how a system works and try to get staff to use it. This often involves being able to communicate with various people at various positions in the hierarchy and being a very good organiser. These jobs are about organisation maintenance, not just the administrative tasks. It is also about keeping things going by looking after the housekeeping; such things as preparing agendas, writing reports, preparing contracts, attending meetings and producing minutes would all figure largely for people with these types of job. Administration jobs are primarily about systems, procedures and monitoring – mutually agreed and laid down by other people. These job holders are not primarily involved in initiating procedures but in putting them into practice and using them. Above all job holders in this group need to know the minutiae of the systems they are using. This often involves experience and good contacts with other people to make them workable. For example, some of the people we met were responsible for servicing meetings; this required them to know exactly who to invite, who to consult over the agenda and minutes and where the most appropriate venue for the meetings was. However, they were not personally involved in the decision taking of these meetings although they were present. Examples of job titles are: health promotions officer, commissioning officer, personnel officer, coordinator.

ACTIVITY **6.1**

Can you think of two jobs for each of the classifications:

- Strategic.
- Operational.
- Administration.

If everything else fails can you find examples of these sorts of job in your university or a hospital, or a large retail organisation or school?

What is the role of the manager in supporting staff

The current thinking about the role of managers concerns the need to combine traditional skills, such as analytical thinking and a financial approach with the ability to listen well, give useful feedback and serve as coach and mentor to staff in order to enhance their satisfaction with and performance in the job. By implication all that needs to be done is that accountability systems have to be developed to support managers: standards are set, training arranged, feedback on achievements is given and individual assessment and possible rewards are given. In this approach there is emphasis on the use of a Human Resource Management (HRM) approach to more systematically obtain, deploy and pay the workforce whose performance determines the success of the organisation. For example, the Royal Bank of Scotland (Rick 1996) has established a framework for all Human Resource policies and practices with the idea of creating a high performing and capable organisation. The Royal Bank of Scotland model includes the following, some of which are discussed in this book in more detail:

- Job and organisation design – see Chapter 13.
- Selecting for success using a competency-based approach.
- Continuously managing performance using appraisal and coaching as a key responsibility for all managers and supervisors – see Chapter 9.
- Developing individual capability with individually agreed development plans – see Chapter 10.
- Business and resource planning.
- Rewarding performance with clear performance standards and rewards – see Chapter 9.

The idea behind these trends in management is to improve standards. No doubt they can all be very useful and enhance the effectiveness of any organisation. Unfortunately they have been used alongside a cost cutting environment in many organisations and so are seen negatively by some when 'best practice' is interpreted as 'most competitive', rather than in any other way. Another irony is that these newer approaches usually mean devolving responsibilities for staff to line managers at a time when substantial numbers of these very same managers are facing redundancy. I would argue that the negative overtones of some of the newer management methods have more to do with the environment in which they have been introduced. The techniques themselves can in reality be about improving the organisation of work for all of us.

ACTIVITY **6.2**

Look up the words used in the Royal Bank of Scotland model in the index of this book, or one on HRM, then write a sentence about each of them.

Particular issues facing managers

As well as specific issues about managing staff many individuals who are managers have particular issues to face. These will vary from time-to-time and place-to-place. The study of organisational behaviour is thought to be useful for analysing some of these. Here are some that are current at the end of the 1990s.

Professionals who accidentally become managers. Many professional people do not choose to become managers but are given responsibility to manage their section. This can lead to individuals being uncommitted to being a manager, unclear about what the role involves, unsure of the management skills required and unwilling to change. Udall and Hiltrop (1996) use the delightful analogy to describe this dilemma as leaving the secure island of one's profession to cross the swamp of uncertainty to a new island of expertise.

Managing cooperation in a newly competitive environment. There is a tendency where markets are new for a very competitive approach to be taken. For example, in newly privatised areas, where some element of competition is introduced into the public sector, or where charities suddenly find themselves competing. This is often because of a misplaced feeling that competition means no cooperation, whereas the reality is that there has to be some cooperation to keep things going. For example, many large commercial organisations belong to local 'salary clubs' where information about terms and conditions are exchanged. Most commercial organisations in established markets try to build cooperative partnerships with their long-term suppliers and customers. This is done by such things as including them in discussions at an early stage, trying to give notice of changes of demand or supply and dealing with their customers' problems.

Felt fairness. For many British people there is a desire to treat people fairly. Indeed K. Morgan (1993) in his edited history of Britain claims that a desire for fairness is the overriding characteristic of this country. An example is the National Health Service (NHS) which has traditionally imbued in its members a desire to treat patients fairly and equally at the point of treatment. There has also been a tradition in the NHS of everyone feeling that they have similarly poor pay and conditions but as 'we are all in the same boat it's not so bad'. This sense of equality is beginning to be eroded by quite large differences in pay awards. For example, in 1996 the government set pay norms, based on review bodies, of 6 per cent to doctors and 2 per cent for nurses. This when interpreted as cash means 6 per cent of a lot compared with 2 per cent of less, which can feel unfair. If these felt unfairnesses are not managed they can begin to undermine morale and consequently commitment to the joint enterprise. Other examples include over-managing people, when people see others with greater autonomy, they may feel unfairness; and the misuse of the small privileges at work such as rotas, breaks and types of work can all feel unfair.

Working with colleagues in different professions and organisations. To deliver a full service in many organisations we need to cooperate with, and manage, people with different professional qualifications. This can lead to misunderstandings when their orientation can be quite different from our own. It can be particularly difficult if managers try to exert control over professionals, who will resist. A more productive relationship between professionals and those who manage them is likely to occur if some mutual respect and trust can be established. This may require some clarifying of values and assumptions. Scholes (1994, p. 6) suggests that independently minded, self-motivated, self-regulating professionals may respect leadership but are often resistant to being managed (see Chapter 8 for further discussion of leadership).

Managing people in the newly privatised sector. For many people, moving from working in a large public setting to one of the smaller privatised settings has been a surprise. Some of the terms and conditions of work are very different from their previous experience, for the better and the worse. Some acknowledgement that this transition needs managing helps staff, particularly where the whole group has made the change. This will include the need to deal with the change cycle of anger and grief before individuals are able to deal with the change itself. The new setting also needs to be articulated clearly and frequently in ways that can be understood – not everyone speaks 'management' or indeed wants to speak 'management' (see Chapter 14 on change).

Managing those who are left. After any period of rapid change in organisations, particularly where there have been redundancies or a lot of people leaving, the major management task is to ensure that those who are left do not become too demoralised by the events that have taken place. Where those who are left find themselves doing more and more work and feeling less and less valued they can resent those who left and those who manage them (see Chapter 14 on change).

ACTIVITY **6.3**

Look through this week's news and identify an item which involves changes for an organisation. There is always at least one!

Now think what behaviours might need to be analysed because of this change. Areas to look at include:

- Cooperation and commitment of the staff.
- Skills required.
- Size of work teams.
- Communication with customers.

See if you can generate at least five different areas.

The move to a portfolio career

One implication of the issues discussed earlier in this chapter is that individuals need to look out for themselves. One major change in the work environment that some have made is the move away from working for one large organisation, with a career of internal promotion and development, towards having a portfolio of projects from a variety of different sources. The pressures for this to happen are various:

- Technology. For example, Bill Gates (1996) reckons that soon over 50 per cent of us will be working from home because of the advances in the Internet, computing, mobile phones. The IT and telecommunication revolution could mean that office working is increasingly unnecessary. Do you know whether the person answering your queries about your direct banking service is sitting in an office in Stockport or sitting in her garden?
- Security. Many people feel more secure with a part-time contract and a portfolio of other projects. Then, if one contract falls through they are not completely bereft. Whereas if a so-called permanent, full-time job goes the individual has to start all over again. Some mortgage lenders are now beginning to acknowledge this too. They prefer to lend to those in portfolio employment rather than to those in full-time employment.
- Trust. With the enormous reorganisations and reengineering of organisations in the early 1990s, when many people lost their jobs and large groups of middle-class people found themselves unemployed for the first time, the faith in organisations to look after the loyal employee was broken. Where organisations show a lack of commitment to their workers, these workers will show a commensurate lack of commitment in return.
- Flexibility. Organisations desire to have a flexible workforce so that when there is a lot of work they can have the people to assist on the project but when there is less work they are not responsible for those people.

The move towards portfolio work has also been associated with the development of more small organisations. This has led to an examination of the future and the possibilities for different structures. For example, G. Morgan (1993) suggests that we are leaving the age of organised structures and moving into a period when self-organisation will be the most important attribute to have. Looser organisations and different forms of control will mean that issues such as growth, team work, decentralising, franchising and subcontracting will become key areas for understanding organisational behaviour (see also Chapter 15 for discussion of these topics).

One way of analysing what is happening is expressed as organisations having a core staff of permanent, well-trained and cherished staff with a periphery staff of contractors, part-timers and temporary workers when required.

One particularly influential model of this is Handy's (1989) concept of the 'shamrock' organisation, see Figure 6.1 He describes an organisation that is made up of three distinct groups of people who are managed and paid differently.

- The professional core who are well-qualified professionals and technicians with essential skills and experience that the organisation depends on. They have the knowledge that is the organisation. They are likely to be committed to and dependent on the organisation. They are well paid and have training and development through the organisation.
- The contractual fringe are individuals and other organisations who provide services and do non-essential work. The work is paid for on the basis of results not the time taken to do it.
- The flexible workforce are all the part-time, temporary workers who provide the flexible workforce. Employed when needed and moving on to other organisations when required.

Each of these groups are likely to have a different level of commitment to the organisation and will certainly require different sorts of managing from the organisation. The largest growth of jobs are in the second two categories and increasingly so. Handy's fourth leaf is pencilled in as the Customers as they

Figure 6.1
Handy's shamrock organisation.

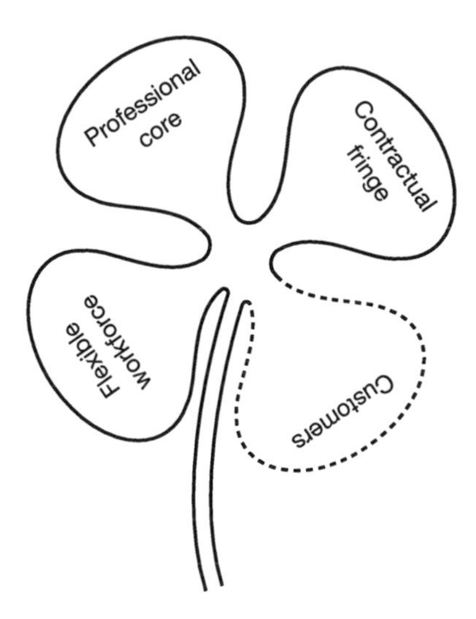

increasingly do some of the work that used to be done by the organisation such as self-service in shops, self-assembly of furniture or cleaning one's own shoes in hotels. This work is unpaid and unmanaged.

An example of a shamrock organisation could be a retail organisation who have a core staff of managers, professional buyers and a skeleton staff of shop workers. These are complemented by a contracted group of people for such tasks as advertising and transport. Seasonal variations in the requirement for shop workers is met by the flexibility of temporary staff with the customers helping in the fourth area by self-service.

Personnel effectiveness

Most of this book is about understanding the organisational context of work. However, if one is to be effective within this context one needs to be reasonably well organised oneself. This is the subject of the remainder of this chapter.

PAUSE FOR THOUGHT

Examples of the things the less well organised are frequently likely to say:

- *'Let's play it by ear.'*
- *'I'm still waiting for...'*
- *'Really, I don't remember that at all.'*

Although these may be useful tactics on occasion to get more information while developing a view on events.

As with the rest of this book I am not advocating any particular way of behaving but trying to give you various strategies for analysing your behaviour in an organisational context.

Managing time

One aspect of maintaining oneself in periods of high demand is to manage time more effectively. One way to start this is to keep a simple activity diary for a few days.

ACTIVITY **6.4**

Keep a diary for the next few days. List the activities as you go along; I put them on a separate line in a notebook but you may prefer to do something different.

When you have finished have a look at what you have got and ask yourself:

- How many of these activities am I doing to please other people?
- Is there anything I did not need to do here?
- What were the really essential things to do ?

A useful strategy for analysing how one spends one's time is to use Rosemary Stewart's (1982) categories of demands, constraints and choices of the job. She argues that different jobs have differing demands and that there are different constraints on the way that these can be met. Between these two are the choices available to the job holder in how the job could be done. So, for example, you might interpret these choices as being quite wide ranging, while if I were doing the job I might be much more inhibited and overwhelmed by the choices and constraints as I perceive them.

Demands come from:

- People within the organisation.
- Outside the organisation.
- From the system.

Constraints on developing things exactly as you would wish might be:

- Resources.
- Legal.
- Technical.
- Physical.
- Organisational.

It is also worth making a list of all the demands that come in to you over a couple of days to see just what decisions could be made about what to do. Most people experience too many demands in their jobs at the moment. This means making choices; some things clearly have to be done and some things can be left. The bulk, in the middle, are important things that need doing but not all of them can be done within the resources available. The normal advice is to prioritise these into 'must dos' and 'hope to dos' with, possibly, some consultation with one's boss or co-workers. However, it is not always clear how one should do this. Frankly, if it is impossible to discriminate between equally important things which need doing and you cannot do them all you might as well do the interesting ones and leave the others. You cannot do everything. Nowadays most of us are having to choose not to do things that appear worth doing, except, of course, for those who are not given the opportunity of being in work at all. It is learning to let go of some of these which can lead to greater job satisfaction.

ACTIVITY **6.5**

Make a list of all the things you ought to do in the next week. Now prioritise these into categories:

- Must do.
- Would like to do.
- Would be useful to do.

See how far you get down the list of things to do in the next week. Now ask yourself the following:

- Have I actually got more choice about what to do than I think?
- Have I carried on doing some things through habit even though they are no longer strictly necessary?

PAUSE FOR THOUGHT

I have met people who manage their diaries by only having meetings immediately before lunch or home time to ensure that people are not too verbose or lingering. They claim it gives them more thinking time.

Mind mapping

Another way of organising oneself is to organise one's ideas, information and understanding to find solutions to issues. One way of doing this is by mind mapping. This was introduced and developed by Buzan (1977). The idea is to encourage free thinking and creativity by allowing an individual's own connections to show through rather than being confined to the linear form of notes and written material. You start with the concept, issue or idea you want to examine in the centre of a page and then allow ideas to flow from that, rather like brainstorming. How you connect the words is entirely up to you and there are no rules. I drew Figure 6.2 to illustrate an organisation complaining that they had 'communication problems'. My task was to help them analyse the issue.

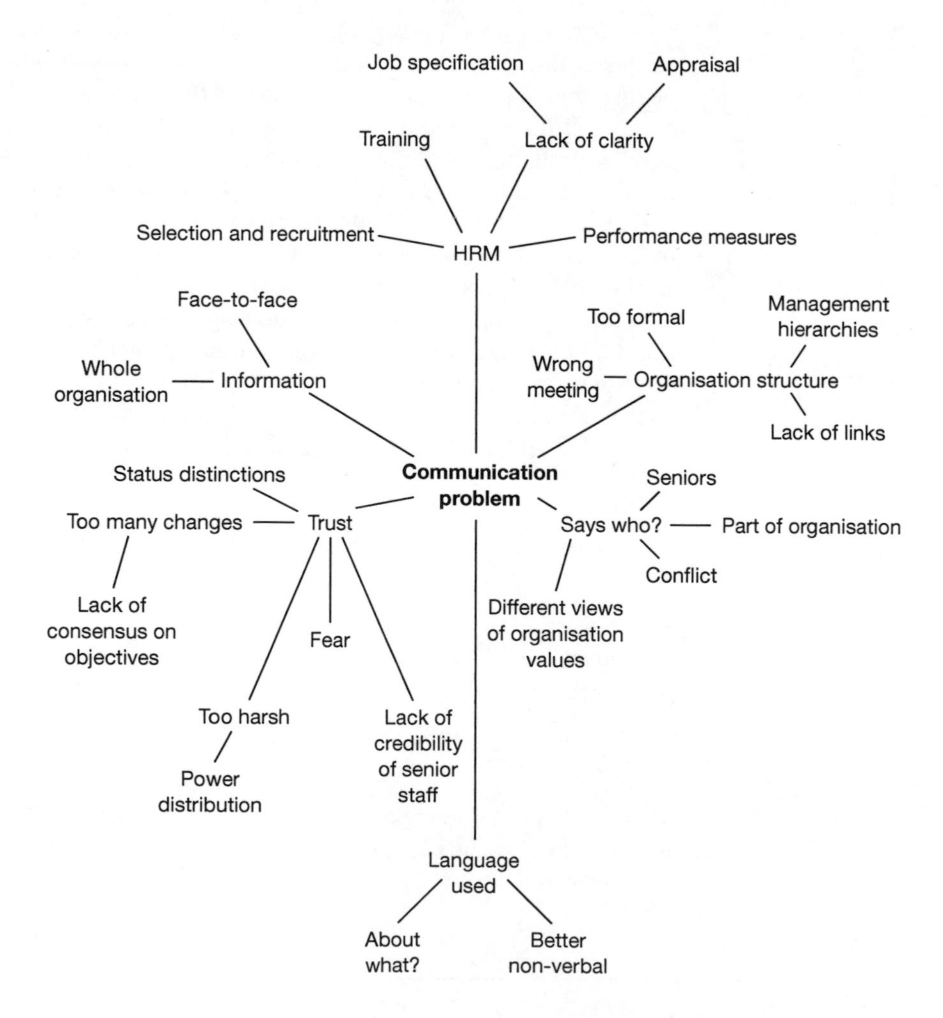

Figure 6.2
Mind map of an organisation with communication problems which I was asked to investigate.

ACTIVITY **6.6**

Draw a mind map of one of the following:

- A chapter in this book as a summary.
- An assignment you need to do.
- Some activity you need to organise, such as a party or event.

Coping with stress

The word 'stress' is very widely used these days and has come to mean a variety of things so some definitions are required. Stress can refer to a stimulus on someone, for example, 'the manager was putting a great deal of stress on the new person and they resented it'. Stress can mean their response, for example, 'the GP felt very stressed because of the number of patients who had been discharged early from hospital'. Stress can also refer to the transaction between the individual and their environment, for example, 'working in the offices which faced onto the main interchange for the city's road system meant they felt stressed'.

There can be good and bad stress, over- and under-stress. When people talk about being 'stressed' they are usually referring to being over-stressed with bad stress. The consequences of too much of this sort of stress are in the long term damaging to health and wellbeing. Research, see Mestel (1994), suggests that there is a link between the brain and the immune system which means that depression and chronic stress from work and insomnia are often bad for us as the activity of the immune cells goes up or down according to our different moods. If this is so, there is little wonder some illness is explained by the stress experienced by individuals (see Figure 6.3).

Figure 6.3 **Stress.**

Some examples of particular workgroups and the stress they experience are:

- Aid workers who often feel guilty about looking after themselves and have a tough-guy culture. Many aid organisations are introducing pre- and post-assignment counselling. This has led to the Red Cross lengthening their selection procedure from a one-hour interview to a one-day assessment at a centre where they evaluate capacity for teamwork and other requirements. Save the Children have improved their staff review process and make sure the annual appraisal includes something about 'looking after yourself'.

- Train drivers have to deal with sudden death with what they call 'one under' suicides. London Underground use traumatic incident reduction where the driver is asked to review the incident silently and then talk about it many times till the memory is no longer active.

So what are the identifiable stressors at work and what can be done about stress? The overwhelming conclusions of behavioural studies of stress are that it is experienced in all occupations, especially manual work, and particularly where there is routine, repetitiveness and lack of autonomy, see Cooper and Earnshaw (1996). This lack of control over what we do and how we do it appears to be the most stressful experience. Perhaps this is one reason so many people in organisations are claiming to be more stressed now as they feel more controlled by financial considerations. Individual members of professional staff feel as if they have less personal autonomy than previously, as managers have become more powerful.

Other areas to look for stressors at work include:

- In the environment – for example, a culture of never saying you are overworked.
- Internal – for example, being nervous all the time.
- Interpersonal relationships – for example, thinking the other is not trustworthy.
- Communication – for example, always insinuating and never getting round to saying anything clearly.
- Work load – for example, five shifts can be more stressful than four shifts even if the hours are the same as there is less time 'off work'.
- Noise and physical conditions – for example, noisy machinery and temperatures which are too hot or too cold are exhausting to work in and this is especially stressful if precise judgements are being made.

An example is Intensive Care Units in hospitals, which often have a high turnover of staff. This is associated with stressors such as grief, anxiety, guilt, exhaustion, over-commitment and over-stimulation.

There are various strategies for trying to cope with stress, besides the longer-term need to reduce the pressure; these are:

- Emotionally – crying, drinking, praying.
- Physically – diet, exercise, meditation, relaxation.
- Hobbies – distractions, holidays.
- Problem solving – confrontation, assertion, action planning.
- Personal and social support – family, friends, colleagues.

DID YOU KNOW?

In 1989 the Alliance and Leicester Building Society introduced term-time working for parents of school age children, see Spencer (1990).

Under the scheme, parents of children aged from five to fifteen can work during school terms only. Staff taking this option are given ten weeks unpaid leave every year to take during the school holiday, on top of which they are expected to take at least four weeks of their annual holiday entitlement during the school holidays. This minimum of fourteen weeks holiday amply covers the summer, Easter and Christmas breaks.

Another family-friendly initiative is the BBC's helpline for employees called 'family life solutions' which gives advice for staff who are responsible for children, elderly and disabled relatives. It is an extension of the Childcare helpline set up in 1995.

Each of these are for individuals to develop and there are well-established self-help groups in most localities, so I have not pursued 'how to' in more detail here.

ACTIVITY **6.7**

Questions to ask yourself if you are employed. (If not, ask someone who is employed about their experience.)

(a) What are the main causes of stress in your department?
(b) Does everyone have something to call their own in their job?
(c) Is there someone people can talk to in your department either formally or informally when they are feeling overwhelmed?
(d) Are staff encouraged to develop life outside of work?
(e) Do they have enough time to do so?

Conclusion

This chapter is rather different from the others. I have tried to give you a flavour of the issues that need analysing within the organisations by individuals in order to maximise their own performance. Over time different issues become more pertinent but understanding the basis of organisational behaviour allows one to recognise the issues and have some strategies for coping.

EXERCISE **6.1**

While you are studying, what are you doing to maintain yourself?

Check through the following list for helping to reduce pressure (reproduced from above).

- Emotionally – crying, drinking, praying.
- Physically – diet, exercise, meditation, relaxation.
- Hobbies – distractions, holidays.
- Problem solving – confrontation, assertion, action planning.
- Personal and social support – family, friends, colleagues.

Is there any area you feel is not well-covered? What are you going to do about it? If you find it difficult to think of ideas the students' welfare and counselling service often have good support services. They may be able to help.

Do it!

Self-check questions

1. Describe two trends in organisations.
2. What are the differences between strategic and operational jobs?
3. What is a portfolio job?
4. Describe the difference between core and periphery staff.
5. How can you organise time effectively?
6. What is a mind map?
7. Describe some strategies for coping with stress.

CASE STUDY **6.1**

Dino's Diner

This large Italian restaurant in the centre of the city is noisy and busy seven nights a week. The clatter of dishes, the sound of talking and occasional mayhem is part of the ambience. Charlie is the Maître d' who greets all guests and takes all orders. He wears flamboyant jackets, can be rude to guests and fusses around when things are quiet, pouring wine and filling olive dishes. He never clears plates or brings food to the table. Charlie is the highest paid member of staff! All the other waiters are young, untrained, good looking, part-timers.

1. Why would a management choose to have a Charlie?
2. Why would they have such a distinction between Charlie and the others?
3. What are the possible weaknesses of this approach?
4. What would be the feelings of the young waiters?

References

Buzan T. (1977) *How to Make the Most of your Mind*. Colt Books, London.

Cooper C. and Earnshaw J. (1996) *Stress and Employer Liability*. IPD, London.

Gates B. (1996) *The Road Ahead*. Penguin, Harmondsworth.

Handy C. (1989) *The Age of Unreason*. Business Books, London.

Hyman J. and Cunningham I. (1996) Empowerment in organisations: Changes in the manager's role. In *Managers as Developers*, Megginson D. and Gibb S. (Eds), Prentice Hall, Hemel Hempstead.

Mestel R. (1994) Let mind talk. *New Scientist*, 23 July, 26–31.

Morgan G. (1993) *Imaginization: The Art of Creative Management*. Sage Publications, Beverly Hills, CA.

Morgan K. (1993) *The Oxford History of Britain*, 2nd edn. Oxford University Press, Oxford.

Rick S. (1996) Managers as developers or developers as managers? In *Managers as Developers*, Megginson D. and Gibb S. (Eds), Prentice Hall, Hemel Hempstead.

Scholes K. (1994) *Strategic Management in Professional Service Organizations (PSOs) – The Finders, Minders and Grinders*. Sheffield Business School, Sheffield.

Spencer L. (1990) Parent power. *Personnel Today*, April, 32–3.

Stewart R. (1982) *Choices for Managers*. McGraw Hill, Maidenhead.

Udall S. and Hiltrop J.M. (1996) *The Accidental Manager: Surviving the Transition from Professional to Manager*. Prentice Hall, Hemel Hempstead.

Weightman J., Butler L. and Griffin J. (1989) *Management Competencies in Tameside and Glossop Health Authority*. Unpublished report.

Further reading

The more serious broadsheet newspapers have quite useful sections in them to keep you up to date with current management issues and fashions. For example, *The Financial Times* has a management page and *The Independent* has a city section.

Various self-help books on time management and stress are available in bookshops, local libraries, leisure centres and doctors surgeries. It's worth having a look at them.

Talking to friends is also useful to find out how they manage their work.

PART 2

Working in teams

CHAPTER 7

Group working

Objectives

When you have finished reading this chapter you should be able to:

- Distinguish between the process and content analysis of group behaviour and performance.
- Know what makes effective workgroups.
- Use a model for analysing group interaction.

Introduction

Working in an organisation inevitably means working in groups. A hospital could not take care of patients, a restaurant could not serve meals nor a plastics company make containers without individuals coming together in groups of different sizes and types. We have to do various things such as make decisions, delegate authority and set boundaries between us and the rest of the world. This distinguishes our activity at work from that of a mob according to Argyris and Schoen (1978). These demands require us to get together in groups. The groups may be of immediate colleagues in a section or department. They may be fulfilling a coordinating role, across a large organisation with area or management groups. They may also include people from different organisations coming together for a particular project such as a theatrical performance or a large construction project. There are also temporary and part-time groups such as meetings, working groups and task groups. It is hard to imagine any activity that does not involve some group work. The long-distance lorry driver, often used as an example of the lone worker, has to cooperate with others to get the vehicle loaded and unloaded with the correct paperwork and instructions.

Research on groups has taken various forms. Some was done years ago and has achieved classic status in the literature of both social science and management literature and is included here. Such studies look at things like the effect of groups on decision making, group stability and the different roles that people play. If we look at some of the classic studies we can see some pointers, warnings or confirmation of our own experience, which may help us to analyse organisational behaviour in groups.

DID YOU KNOW?

One popular metaphor about teams is to compare them with geese flying in a 'V' shape. Geese manage to migrate long distances by taking it in turn to lead the 'V', thus allowing the others to fly in their slipstream, each subsequent goose helps the one behind. By all helping and contributing the flock of geese travel further than any individual could have managed on its own.

Formal and informal groups

Groups at work can be both formal and informal. Formal groups are where the organisation structure groups together people to carry out a particular task or function. They may be brought together to carry out a sequence of operations, they may be put together because of geography or a shared profession. These groups are deliberately planned and organised by management and would often be written down in formal organisation charts with reporting relations made clear. Their main purpose is to ensure that the work of the individual members is coordinated. These groups can be quite permanent, even if individual membership changes, or may be short lived for a particular purpose. The formal group will have a formal distribution of power and authority, approved channels of communication, links between sections and also be constrained by some formal requirements about how the work is to be arranged. These are laid down in the formal job descriptions, charts and assessments. Part 3 of this book deals in more detail with the organisational setting of formal groups.

Within this formal structure there will also be more informal groups of people that are based on more personal relationships. These informal groups can often cut across formal groups and can be based on former working partnerships, common interests, sharing lifts to work, belonging to the same clubs and a whole variety of contacts. A very common informal group is the lunch group which may include people from different parts of the organisation and at different levels of seniority in the organisation. The topics of conversation may range over both work and private interests.

Buchanan and Huczynski (1997) suggest that groups, whether formal or informal, have the following structures about how they relate to each other:

- Status.
- Power.
- Roles.
- Leadership.
- Communication.

If you can analyse, describe and understand these aspects of the group you appreciate the nature of their behaviour.

PAUSE FOR THOUGHT *One blue chip company with prestigious open plan offices for its head office decided at a two day conference that the most important change they needed to make was to have a coffee room so that informal, creative contacts could be made. Top management agreed! The importance for groups to be able to meet informally to exchange information and ideas is now increasingly recognised in the design of new offices with their 'soft areas' of settees, plants, pictures and refreshments. This has come with the increased emphasis on individual effectiveness and empowerment rather than the controlled and prescribed traditions of many organisations. The last part of this book develops these themes in more detail.*

One particular sort of informal group is the 'network of contacts'. Networks are cooperative relationships between people who can help to accomplish things. The network is for sharing ideas, information and resources. These more informal networks are often an important part of getting things done as they allow for all sorts of connections, particularly across the organisation, that formal structures cannot meet. Kotter (1982) in his research on general managers came to the conclusion that individual managers had large networks of contacts which enabled them to carry out their agenda of things to be done.

PAUSE FOR THOUGHT

Marilyn Ferguson notes that networks are cultivated by:

> *conferences, phone calls, air travel, books, phantom organizations, papers, pamphleteering, photocopying, lectures, workshops, parties, grapevines, mutual friends, summit meetings, coalitions, tapes and newsletters.*
> *(Ferguson M. (1982),* Aquarian Conspiracy. *J.P. Tarcher, Los Angeles, CA.)*

We would probably need to add e-mail and faxes to this list now.

ACTIVITY **7.1**

On a piece of paper list all the individuals and groups who can influence how effective you are at what you do *but* with whom you do not have a formal working relationship. Give their names and their positions.

This will demonstrate your informal network.

Group theory

There is an important distinction made in the analysis of groups between *content* and *process*. Content is concerned with what groups do, the task they set themselves and why they are doing something. The process of the group is how they do things and how they interact with each other. Figure 7.1 describes various attributes of this process and content. The headings in Figure 7.1 are the headings for the next sections of this chapter so I will not go into further detail about them here.

In the following sections I outline some of the classic studies of group behaviour done by psychologists and sociologists. Some have studied real groups working and others have studied groups in the rather artificial setting of the laboratory. The first sorts of study have the merit of being real and therefore having credibility but there is always the question of how typical the experience is. The latter have the merit of being controlled and reasonably repeatable but not 'real'. So most people working in organisations like to take a bit of theory from both sorts of study to inform their own behavioural analysis in organisations.

Taking the headings in Figure 7.1 we will first look at the process side of groups with aspects of group dynamics, then group organisation. We will then look at the content aspects of group behaviour and performance, first looking at the purposes of the groups and finally the environment in which they operate. Like many aspects of organisational behaviour they all need to be considered together as all these aspects are important but the very nature of language (and books) is that things have to be looked at in a linear way despite the interactive nature of the material!

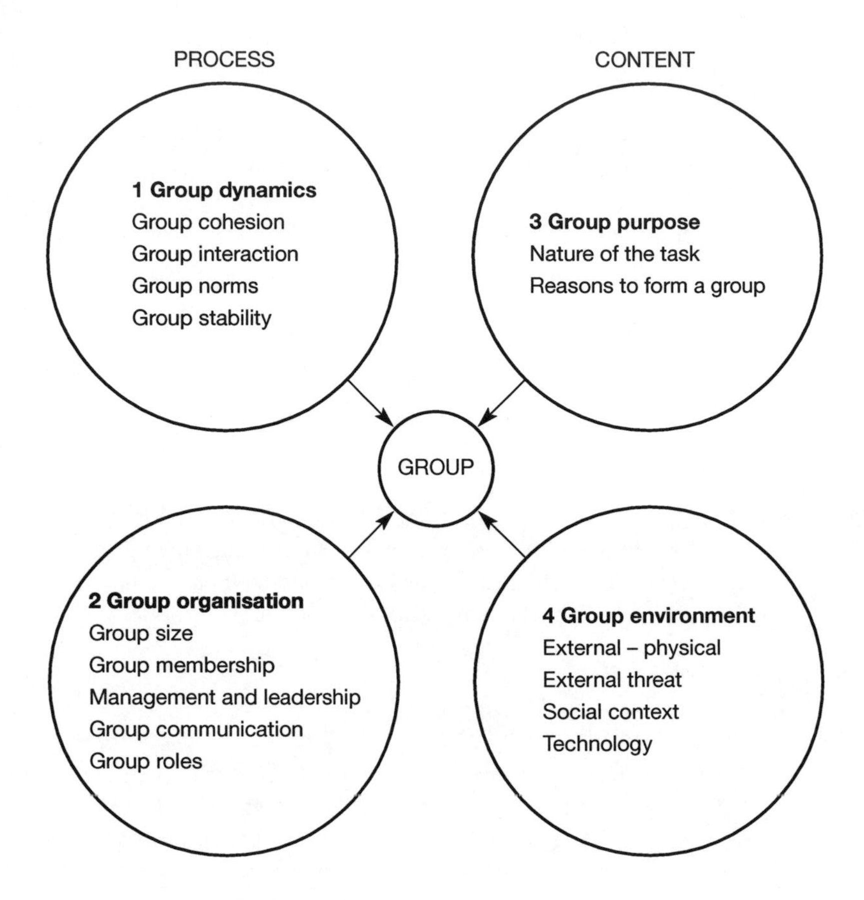

Figure 7.1
Factors influencing group behaviour and performance.

Group dynamics

This section is about how groups work together. It looks at such questions as:

- How are groups formed?
- Why do they stick together?
- What makes people want to stay with the group?
- What makes people not want to belong?

What you need to ask if you read these different models of group dynamics in the original is what sort of evidence is there for the conclusions drawn. This is good practice for academic study and particularly social science study where common sense is easy to claim. Normally I do not reproduce the evidence in this book as the detail would fill too much space but it is worth having a look at one or two studies from this chapter and comparing them with one or two from the next chapter to see the different types of evidence used. Social scientists ask for more evidence than managerial writers who make suggestions that might explain real situations, sometimes based on the findings of the more systematic social scientists. Both sorts of contribution are useful in analysing organisational behaviour.

Group cohesion

Tuckman (1965) suggests that there are various stages small groups go through before they are mature enough in their relations to be able to work together consistently. These stages are set out in Table 7.1. These stages are helpful in showing that group development takes time to become effective. This time will vary according to how long the group is going to work together. It may take several months for a long-term group because the degree of commitment required from each member is high and the risk of personal failure so great. Whereas in the short-term, part-time group the risk is lower and the tolerance higher. So when your workteam is going through an argumentative period you might consider whether this is a stage in developing group cohesion or whether it has some other cause. Another time to use this model is when you are setting up a new group and you expect some variation in the emotional climate of the group.

Table 7.1
Stages in the growth of group cohesion and performance. (Based on B.W. Tuckman (1965), Development sequences in small groups. *Psychological Bulletin*, 63, 384–99.)

Stages of development	*Process*	*Outcome*
1. Forming	There is anxiety, dependence on leader; testing to find out the nature of the situation and what behaviour is acceptable	Members find out what the task is, what the rules are and what methods are appropriate
2. Storming	Conflict between sub-groups, rebellion against leader; opinions are polarised; resistance to control by group	Emotional resistance to demands of task
3. Norming	Development of group cohesion; norms emerge; resistance is overcome and conflicts are patched up; mutual support and sense of group identity	Open exchange of views and feelings; co-operation develops
4. Performing	Interpersonal problems are resolved; interpersonal structure becomes the means of getting things done; roles are flexible and functional	Solutions to problems emerge; there are constructive attempts to complete tasks and energy is now available for effective work

Schutz (1966) and Schein (1969) have also looked at the stages of group development and emphasise that each phase has a core issue which the group must at least partly resolve before going onto the next phase. Both Schutz and Schein suggest that the concern of early meetings is the issue of inclusion – to what extent do individuals feel part of the group? It follows that individuals are most concerned about themselves at the beginning. There are likely to be rapid changes of topic as everyone raises issues that concern them and conflict is highly probable. Time needs to be taken to allow everyone the opportunity to establish an identity within the group. It is only then that the group is ready to work.

Group interaction

Bales (1950) found that effective groups needed people who helped get things done, that is, they were concerned with the 'what', the content or task facing the group. They also needed people who were concerned about the 'how', the process or social and emotional side of working in groups. Team members who were task-orientated were the most influential; those who were interested in the positive, social, emotional aspects were the most liked. Box 7.1 summarises his categories of behaviours. Behaviours from (a), (c) and (d) can all help to make a group work better whereas (b) type behaviours can be destructive. The important thing to remember is that groups, or teams, need both task- and process-orientated behaviours to be effective. Although one's own preference may be for particular sorts of behaviour it is as well to be tolerant of (a), (c) and (d) type contributions, whereas someone, including oneself, exhibiting (b) type behaviours might be encouraged to change the behaviours either by restating the aims of the group or learning strategies for effective team membership.

Group norms

These are the expectations or implicit rules that are developed within teams to define what is acceptable behaviour and what is not. Just think back to when you were new in a job, particularly if you were an experienced worker, to realise how important these group norms are. Newcomers are expected to comply with the group norms until they have gone through the socialising process of learning the expected behaviours. Eventually the norms become their own and are internalised. Or they are rejected and the newcomer remains outside the group. There are two main norms, task norms and maintenance norms.

- Task norms influence the way in which the group achieves its goals. What is considered a fair day's work for a fair day's pay varies considerably from one group to another.
- Maintenance norms develop within the team to help keep it together, for instance styles of speaking, little games that are played and cliquey behaviour that distinguishes your workgroup from that of your colleagues.

There are also group norms about defining the relations with others such as the boss or other departments.

Box 7.1
Bales's interaction process categories.

	(a) **Positive reactions**		(b) **Negative reactions**
SOCIAL EMOTIONAL	Shows SOLIDARITY, raises other's status, gives help, reward	← A →	SHOWS ANTAGONISM, deflates other's status, defends self
	Shows TENSION RELEASE, jokes, laughs, shows satisfaction	← B →	SHOWS TENSION, asks for help, withdraws out of field
	AGREES, shows passive acceptance, understands, concurs, complies	← C →	DISAGREES, shows passive rejection, formality, withholds help
	(c) **Questions**		(d) **Answers**
TASK AREA	ASKS FOR ORIENTATION, information, reception, confirmation	← D →	GIVES ORIENTATION, information, repeats, clarifies, confirms
	ASKS FOR OPINION, evaluation, analysis, expression of feeling	← E →	GIVES OPINION, evaluation, analysis, expresses feeling, wish
	ASKS FOR SUGGESTION, direction, possible ways of action	← F →	GIVES SUGGESTION, direction, implying autonomy for others

KEY:
A = problems of integration
B = problems of managing tension
C = problems of decision
D = problems of orientation
E = problems of evaluation
F = problems of control

PAUSE FOR THOUGHT

One work group I know in a technological industry does not consult the computing department when it has a computing problem. The computing people in their purpose built glass office are seen as too ivory tower. As someone in this company said to me 'Real people don't work in glass houses'.

ACTIVITY **7.2**

- What are the norms for your work group? For example, on this course?
- Who has helped to establish them?
- Did you inherit a set from other groups?
- What behaviour distinguishes you from other groups/courses/years?
- Do you, for example, have little rituals about lunch times or Fridays?
- Do you have nicknames?

Group stability

Rice (1958) studied working groups in an Indian textile mill. He concluded that the most productive group, and the most satisfactory to its members, was the pair or a group with between six and twelve members. Group stability was most easily maintained where every member of the group could understand the other's skills and when there were only a few differences of status and prestige among them. It was beneficial for a group if disaffected members could move elsewhere.

Rice's studies give us some strategies for building up long-term groups. For example, in departments where people need to work closely with each other and exchange ideas it seems that structures which do not emphasise differences of prestige or status are more likely to succeed. In secondary schools the most influential grouping for staff is the department, such as the science department or the humanities department; it is here that the main decisions about what happens to the pupils take place. Most secondary school departments have between six and eight people with few differences in status and the teachers are all concerned with the same subject area and so understand each other's skills. This all fits in well with Rice's conclusions.

ACTIVITY **7.3**

List as many team games as you can think of. Now list how many players there are in a team for each of these games.

Would these teams fit in with Rice's findings about the stability of groups? Why are there so few games that require 3–7 players?

Group organisation

This section is concerned with the 'nitty gritty' of organising groups. It looks at questions such as:

- What is the best size for the group?
- Who should be a member?
- What sort of management and leadership best suits groups?
- Can we communicate more efficiently?
- Do members need to play particular roles?

Some of these questions are also discussed in more detail elsewhere in this book, as is pointed out below.

Group size

The size of the group will effect the behaviour of members in the group. The larger the group the more formal arrangements are likely, and need, to be. Large groups, for example, will need clear communication and for the task to be clearly stated and understood for effective working. Smaller groups are able, and are likely, to be closer knit and can manage with more informal methods of communication and task definition. Various suggestions about size are given but usually it is between seven and twelve (see the Rice study mentioned above). The important attribute is expertise. Remember to ask whether you have all the necessary expertise in the group or whether there are too many people duplicating effort.

Group membership

The question of who should belong to a group is often decided in formal groups by the organisation structure. This will depend on decisions about tasks, coordination and reporting relationships. Temporary groups might be put together for tasks, projects and problem solving. It is also important to remember that the more homogeneous the members are in their style, assumptions and culture the easier they will find it to work together but there may be a lack of questioning and alternative views to reach robust conclusions. For example, some more formal business teams have representatives from other areas who are paid to present the view from different aspects of the business. Informal groups by contrast are much more likely to be based on shared assumptions.

Management and leadership

In the work setting groups are often managed and led. Clearly the nature of this will affect the nature of the group. A lot of the literature on leadership (see Chapter 8) is about the leadership of teams or groups. Similarly a lot of management literature is about how many people an individual manager should supervise, that is, what size groups should they be responsible for. Likert (1961) in a classic study of management and the interlinking of work groups suggests that no manager should supervise more than seven people.

Group communication

Leavitt (1951) examined which types of communication pattern were most appropriate for different tasks. He worked with experimental groups and asked small groups of people to communicate in different patterns of networks, as shown in Figure 7.2.

The patterns illustrated by Leavitt represent typical situations at work.

- The wheel is like a regional sales team with four sales people reporting to a regional manager.
- The chain is like a department with two executives, B and D, each reporting to manager C and having assistants, A and E.
- The circle is like a discussion group, particularly found in training groups.
- The Y is similar to an orthodox chain of command with one person, B, who is outside and who communicates only with C as is the case of a key supplier or customer.
- The completed network is the more normal discussion group found in real organisations.

Body language

There is usually a lot of communication in groups that is expressed non-verbally. Watch next time you sit in a group and see how much there is. Communications are usually of the supporting sort or the disagreeing sort. Body language is culturally specific and interpretation can be dangerous when

Figure 7.2
Types of communication networks in groups. (Based on Leavitt (1951).)

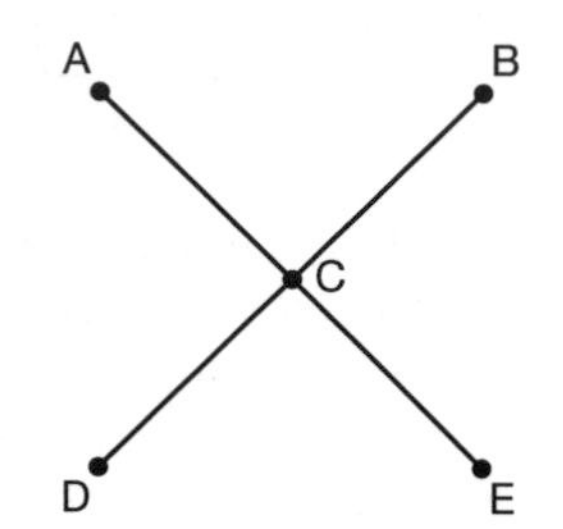

The wheel

All communication has to go through person C at the centre. This pattern provides quick answers to simple questions, but A, B, D and E tend to be dissatisfied with their roles.

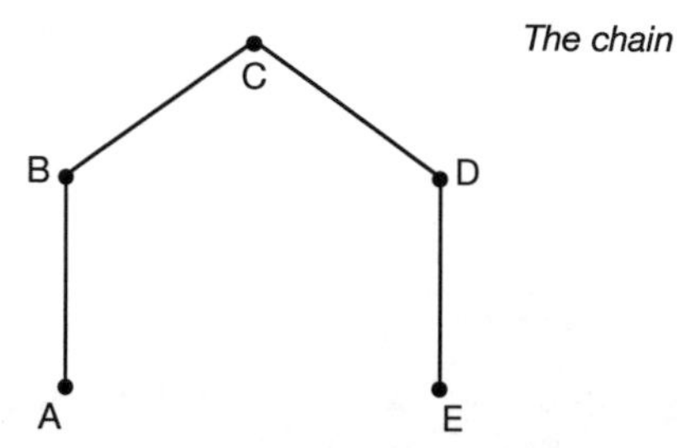

The chain

No one member is able to communicate with all the others. Members are reasonably satisfied with this system of communication, but it can be slow and lead to errors.

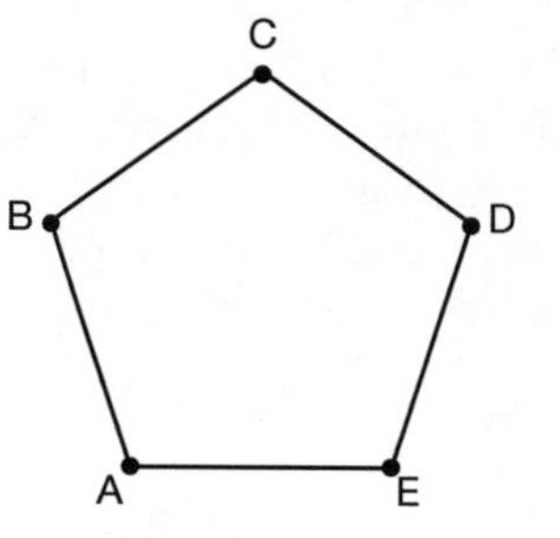

The circle

By closing the chain each member can communicate directly with two others. This provides the highest level of general satisfaction and can be effective for complex problems.

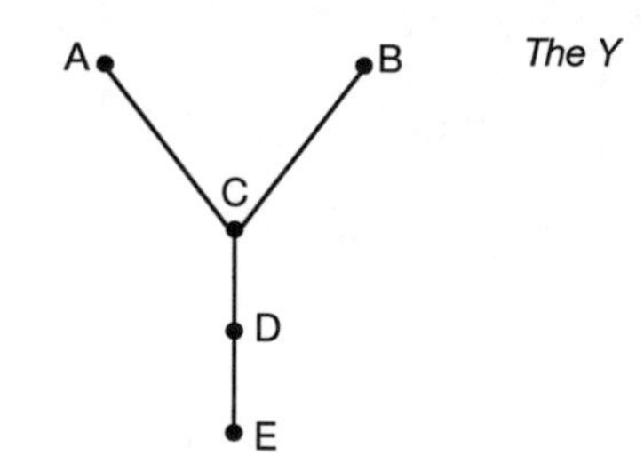

The Y

This combines features of the wheel and the chain in a centralised network.

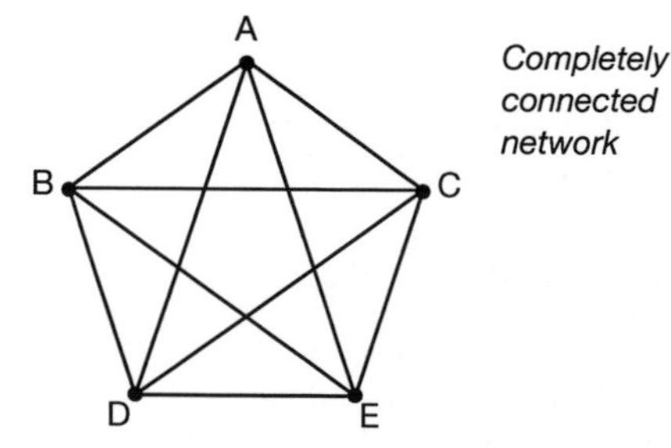

Completely connected network

Each person can now communicate freely with every other person and all are satisfied with their role. It can be effective when dealing with complex problems but is unsatisfactory for dealing with straightforward matters.

applied to groups from another tradition. It can, however, be a more useful guide to what people actually think in formal meetings than what they say! Examples are:

- Supporting gestures: Looking in the eye.
  Nodding head.
  Smiling.
  Turning body towards the person they agree with.
- Disagreeing: Shaking head.
  Raising eyebrows.
  Raised finger.
  Opposite of above.

Remember that disagreeing may be constructive or destructive.

Group roles

Belbin (1981) developed the work of Bales to look at the different roles that are necessary for management teams. He identified eight:

1. The *company worker* who works to keep the organisation's interests to the fore.
2. The *chair* who ensures that all views are heard and keeps things moving.
3. The *shaper* who influences by argument and by following particular topics.
4. The *ideas* person or plant who contributes novel suggestions.
5. The *resource investigator* who evaluates whether contributions are practical and finds out where and how to obtain resources.
6. The *monitor/evaluator* who assesses how valid the contributions are.
7. The *team worker* who maintains the group by joking and agreeing.
8. The *completer/finisher* who tries to get things done and suggests conclusions.

At different times each of these roles needs filling for teams to work effectively. Most of us fill more than one. Again the main use of this model is emphasising that different contributions are required to keep things moving in a group.

A more recent development of this is by Margerison and McCann (1990) who grouped Belbin's roles into:

- Explorer.
- Organiser.
- Controller.
- Advisor.
- Linker, coordinating the other contributions.

This is connected to a series of team development activities and shows the continuing usefulness of these models for practioners in organisations.

Group purpose

So far we have been looking at the process side of groups. That is the way people work together. It is also important to look at the content – what the group has to do. The two main questions are:

- What is the purpose of the group?
- Why form a group to do this?

Nature of the task

A group is unlikely to be effective if they do not know where they are heading. They must have a 'plan'. Their plans can be very long term, they are usually called strategic plans and refer to a period at least two years ahead and are often unreliable. Medium-term plans often cover periods of between three months and two years ahead and theoretically are derived from the long-term strategic plans with estimates of available resources, constraints and competitive considerations. The short-term plans of less than three months are most likely to be accurate as there is considerable inertia in most economic and natural phenomena.

I do not intend going into the details of planning techniques here but one important aspect is the very short-term planning known as target setting or goal planning that are statements of what you are trying to do. It is about prioritising. Answers to basic questions help managers, groups and individuals to deploy resources more effectively. The process includes the classic steps of:

- Where are we now?
- Where do we want to be?
- How do we get there?
- How are we doing?

A form for goal planning, or target setting, is shown in Box 7.2.

ACTIVITY **7.4**

Try using the form in Box 7.2 on something you have not quite managed to do recently. This could be something personal or at university. The more concrete you make your aims and objectives the easier it will be to judge whether you have achieved them or not.

For example, try making the following general aims more concrete:

1. Get agreement on budget.
2. Make more visits to customers.
3. Monitor budget more often.
4. Encourage staff to do better.

Reasons to form a group

People will form groups at work for a variety of reasons.

- Some tasks can only be done by a combination of people with different skills or their combined effort. For example, a theatrical performance needs actors, stage hands and make-up and wardrobe people at the very least.
- Some tasks are rather grim and so are better shared, when at least there is a social context. For example, telesales are usually located in one big room.
- Groups provide support for individual members. For example, they can share the stress of the work; groups of nurses in operating theatre work often strongly identify with their rota.

Box 7.2
Goal planning.

Goal planning

1. Decide what your goal is. Write it down with the criteria you will use to judge whether the goal has been met.
2. List the strengths you have already that will help you achieve the goal. Examples of the areas you might think about are given below.
3. List what you still need to reach your goal. Write these as concretely as possible so you can tell when you have met the need and it has become a strength. The same list as the strengths might help you to think about all the areas.
4. If a need is particularly difficult to achieve use the forms below to break the need into smaller, more easily achieved objectives.

Goal	
Strengths	Needs
1 Time 2 Place 3 Money 4 Materials 5 Cooperation of ... 6 Agreement of ... 7 Expertise 8 9 10	

Setting objectives

1. Objectives can be met to meet goals set down by oneself or others.
2. Make a list of the various possible ways of achieving the goal. Asking others for their ideas may increase your list of options but they are likely to be disappointed if their idea is not used.
3. Decide which is the most appropriate method by comparing the advantages and disadvantages of each.
4. The goal-planning form above can be used to establish the strengths and needs of reaching the goal in this way.
5. When dividing the needs into specific objectives it is advisable to state them so that an answer 'yes, that is done', can be given or not. Deadlines help the constantly-interrupted manager.

Need			
Objective	Method	Target date	Date done
1 2 3 4 5 6			

The group environment

Another influence on the behaviour and performance of the group is the environment in which it has to function. This can be the physical aspects of the environment and the social context. Questions here are about:

- What is the effect of discomfort on groups?
- What happens when they are threatened?
- What is the influence of the culture which surrounds the group?
- What effect does technology have?

Physical environment

It was always understood that the closer physically to each other a group was the more effective this was. However, the introduction of open plan offices where people are often sitting metres away from each other has not always been matched with efficiency as many people start creating barriers with plants, bookshelves and any other means for establishing privacy that they can find. However, where teams of people are very scattered it can lead to people feeling isolated. For example, British Gas Service people were moved to home-based working in 1996 and they lost their morning meeting at the 'depot'. Now they meet once a month for a general briefing and get together to maintain the cooperative working necessary if they need to call for help from a colleague when a problem is too big for a single service engineer.

Threats to the group

When there is some external threat to a group it can often become much more cohesive. For example, when a change to working practice is proposed some groups can become very close. This can also happen when there is a clash between two groups: some schools which have amalgamated have found that the two previous schools' staff have become much stronger groups than they ever were when the schools were separate.

Social context of the group

The general culture of the organisation and its own external environment will affect the behaviour and performance of a group (see Chapter 11 on organisation culture). The degree of formality/informality in the organisation as a whole will affect the behaviour in the group. Issues such as participation or control, the amount of rules, and whether the organisation is orientated towards results or creativity, will affect the group's style. A workgroup or team is most likely to reflect this general culture, or style. However, there will be differences across the organisation as different groups do set some of their own norms and traditions, as we saw earlier in the discussion of process aspects of groups. But on the whole a group working in, say, a hospital trust will have a different social context from a group working in a merchant bank even if they are actually charged with a similar task such as drawing up selection criteria for a new appointment.

Technology

The effect of technology on how work can be organised is easily seen. If you have a large piece of machinery then clearly everyone has to come to it whereas if the work involves using a PC then this can be done literally anywhere thanks to portable PCs and modems. Just compare the different group experience of working on an offshore oil rig in the North Sea with being part of the cosmetic sales team for an international perfumery house. The nature of the technology and task clearly affect the nature of the group. Some of the smaller differences in technology are often introduced precisely to enable people to work more efficiently as a team. For example, on a biscuit baking line there used to be a hold-up at the label attachment section which meant other groups were getting frustrated that their work was held up and they were not meeting their targets. All it needed was a small improvement to the adhesive and all the workgroups were better synchronised.

Effective groups or teams

Guirdham (1990, p. 374) offers the following characteristics of a fully effective team:

- Team objectives are clearly understood by all members.
- All members are committed to the objectives.
- Mutual trust is high.
- Support for one another is high.
- Communications are open and reliable, not guarded and cautious.
- Team members listen to one another, understanding and being understood.
- The team is self-controlling.
- Conflicts are accepted and worked through.
- Members' abilities, knowledge and experience are fully used by the team.

Other writers such as McGregor (1960) have very similar characteristics of effective groups.

Most of these characteristics concentrate on the *process* side of groups working. That is, the way people work together. It is also important to look at the *content* – what the group has to do. This is emphasised by Guirdham putting this aspect first. Effective teams have both a good task orientation and a cohesion amongst the group. The words 'process' and 'content' are important terms for analysing groups and are worth keeping in mind if you find yourself in an ineffective team, group or meeting. Is the problem a content one, that is, an unclear or impossible objective, or is it a process problem, that is, the group is not working well together for this sort of task? The reason many team building exercises consist of outdoor activities is that the objective is clear and it is clear what the result is. This makes the analysis of the process, the purpose of the exercise, clearer, rather than involving endless debates about the exact nature of the goal and whether it was achieved.

The disadvantages of groups

Throughout this chapter there has been an emphasis on the effectiveness of groups and how best to enhance this. There are, however, some difficulties with emphasising group or team work.

Individuals

Not everything is best done by a group despite the current emphasis on teams. Some things need to be done by individuals and it is counterproductive to involve a team. Even some decisions are best made singly, although you then do not have the commitment of others in putting that decision into practice. But involving groups in decision making can be an expensive process if it means flying people in from all over the world, paying the hotel costs, losing their normal productivity and then asking them to take a minor decision or confirm one that has already been made.

Conflict

Although competition in the marketplace is at the very heart of capitalism, competition in the workplace can be a waste. Kolb *et al* (1991) point out that competitiveness in the organisation usually results in energy being expended at the expense of the overall aims and objectives of the organisation. But some competitiveness is encouraged by employers when they feel that competing teams will egg each other on to greater performance levels. For example, many sales teams compete for monthly prizes. Like studying organisational behaviour, it all comes down to a balance between extremes.

Groupthink

Janis (1972) studied the decision making of the United States foreign policy groups. He found that a cohesive group of individuals, sharing a common fate, exerts a strong pressure towards conformity. He found that President Kennedy's 'Bay of Pigs' fiasco in the early 1960s, where the USA and Russia came close to war over the placing of missiles in Cuba, and the disaster in Vietnam in the 1960s and 1970s, where the USA were fighting the local communists of North Vietnam, could not be accounted for by individual incompetence. He coined the phrase 'groupthink' to cover the exaggeration of irrational tendencies that seem to occur in groups. He argues that the group setting can magnify weaknesses of judgement.

This groupthink concept is perhaps most useful as a warning that groups are not always a good thing. For example, when change is being proposed there is a tendency to dismiss those individuals who are reluctant to support the innovation as dull, unimaginative, obstinate or behind the times. This may be so but it is sometimes the case that the change is not so good after all and the proposing group were suffering from some sort of groupthink.

Conclusion

In the last decade the world has gone mad about team work. Managers call on people to do things on behalf of the team often using sporting metaphors to gird everyone along. People often belong to lots of teams. Typical examples are: the grading committee, the systems implementation group, the working party, the European group. Work is increasingly organised around processes and projects with any one person belonging to many teams. So how can these teams be made to work effectively? Perhaps by using some of the things you have learnt in this chapter in order to look after both the process and content. As you can see from the list of references at the end of this chapter there is a lot of material here on both the academic social science side of analysing how groups work and on the practical management side of trying to make teams function.

DID YOU KNOW?
Thorn Lighting were running, in 1997, five-day workshops with the unemployed on team building because they found that people were only learning individual skills. They argue that not everyone can be a high flyer so they need to encourage team work.

EXERCISE **7.1**

Use one of the following questions as a starting point to bring in the material from this chapter. Ideally, ask someone in work. If this is not possible, look at your own position as a student doing this course, or your work, paid or not, or in some other area of your life such as a sports team or student activity. If you have time, try another.

1. Using Tuckman's sequence where do you think your team fits in?
2. Next time you are in a meeting use Bales's or Belbin's list to check the behaviours of your colleagues.
3. Do a role analysis of your own job. This involves asking all the people who come into contact with you what they expect of someone doing that job. It is not an assessment of how you do it but what they would expect. It can be quite revealing to realise just what a range of views there are and how they might conflict, or be simpler than you thought, or even just what you thought!

EXERCISE **7.2**

To get an understanding of informal groups one common investigative tool is sociometry. This is where people rate their fellows privately and anonymously in terms of some context or characteristic. For example, who would you prefer to work with? Or, who would it be good to go out with for the night? Usually people are asked to make a first and a second choice. When this has been done the results are collated. For example:

Person	*1st choice*	*2nd choice*
A		
B	II	
C	IIIII	II
D	I	IIII
E	II	IIII

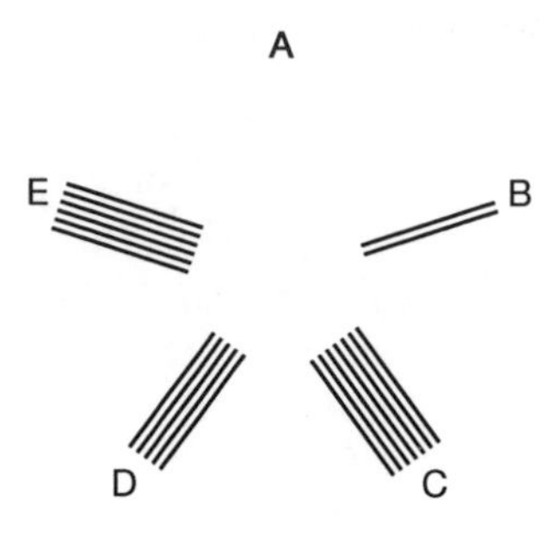

Figure 7.3
Example of sociometry.

Or the results can be given as shown in Figure 7.3. Clearly C, D and E are the preferred people for this task. There are more elaborate versions of this methodology available and it is a technique frequently used by sociologists.

Have a go yourself with a group of colleagues or friends but try to keep the topic light-hearted such as:

- With whom would you most prefer to go to a fancy dress party?
- With whom would you prefer to spend Sunday morning?

You are not trying to give someone a crisis because no one chooses them, you are just looking at a investigative device!

Self-check questions

1. Why are informal networks important at work?
2. What are Tuckman's stages for group cohesion?
3. What were Bales's findings?
4. What is meant by the word 'norm'?
5. What is the best communication pattern for complex communications?
6. Identify Belbin's team roles.
7. What factors influence the behaviour and performance of groups?
8. What is 'groupthink'?

CASE STUDY **7.1**

We have probably all seen the Red Arrows flying display team from the Royal Air Force performing their dramatic flying and close formation manoeuvres, if only on the television. Have you ever wondered how they manage to do it? Clearly there is very precise flying involving tight control of the airplane by highly-trained pilots and support crews. There is also a behavioural aspect to it. They have to coordinate closely with each other.

The Red Arrows team rely on each other to do their job correctly otherwise everyone is in danger. They feel that the biggest barrier to communication, delegation, empowerment, quality and team work, which are all seen as critical in their success, is lack of trust. They develop this trust by concentrating on the following:

- Open criticism.
- Public praise.

- Organisation goals.
- Individual goals.

(This is based on material from H. Owen in *People Management*, 21 March 1996, p. 34.)

How does this approach fit in with the models of teams and groups discussed in this chapter? Which models, if any, work best to explain these assumptions?

References

Argyris C. and Schon D. (1978) *Organizational Learning*. Addison-Wesley, Reading, MA.

Bales R.F. (1950) *Interaction Process Analysis*. Addison-Wesley, Reading, MA.

Belbin R.M. (1981) *Management Teams: Why they Succeed or Fail*. Heinemann, London.

Buchanan D. and Huczynski J. (1997) *Organisational Behaviour*, 3rd edn. Prentice Hall, Hemel Hempstead.

Guirdham M. (1990) *Interpersonal Skills at Work*. Prentice Hall, Hemel Hempstead.

Janis I.L. (1972) *Victims of Groupthink*. Houghton Mifflin, Boston, MA.

Kolb D.A., Rubin I.M. and Osland J. (1991) *Organizational Behaviour*, 5th edn. Prentice Hall, Englewood Cliffs, NJ.

Kotter J.P. (1982) *The General Managers*. Free Press, New York, NY.

Leavitt H.J. (1951) Some aspects of certain communication patterns on group performance. *Journal of Abnormal and Social Psychology*, 45, 38–50.

Likert R. (1961) *New Patterns of Management*. McGraw Hill, New York, NY.

McGregor D. (1960) *The Human Side of Enterprise*. McGraw Hill, New York, NY.

Margerison C. and McCann D. (1990) *Team Management: Practical New Approaches*. Mercury Books, London.

Rice A.K. (1958) *Productivity and Social Organisation*. Tavistock, London.

Schein E.H. (1969) *Process Consultation: its Role in Organization Development*. Addison-Wesley, Reading, MA.

Schutz W.C. (1966) *The Interpersonal World*. Science and Behaviour Books, New York, NY.

Tuckman B.W. (1965) Development sequences in small groups. *Physcological Bulletin*, 63, 384–99.

Further reading

Handy C. (1997) *Understanding Organisations*, 3rd edn. Penguin, Harmondsworth. This is a delightful book that has been very influential in Britain for the past two or three decades. He has a very easy readable style with lots of examples.

Mullins L.J. (1996) *Management and Organisational Behaviour*, 4th edn. Pitman, London. Part 3 of this impressive textbook deals with groups. This is the textbook that is frequently used on courses dealing with organisational behaviour in more detail than this book.

There are lots of training videos in this area. Two you might like to look at are: *High Performance Teams* (1996) Industrial Society, which includes some of the material on the Red Arrows mentioned in the case study.

Team Spirit? How to be an effective team member, Video Arts, Dunbarton House, 68 Oxford St, London W1N 0LH.

CHAPTER 8

Developing leadership and autonomy

Objectives

By the time you have finished this chapter you should be able to:

- Give some definition of what leadership is.
- Describe several different models of leadership style.
- Discuss contingency models of leadership.
- Distinguish between managing and leading.
- Know what makes a credible leader.
- Understand the importance of valuing the led for leadership.
- Use the term empowerment appropriately.

Introduction

This chapter is about some of the aspects of organisational behaviour that help to make some teams work better than others. As we saw in the last chapter there are two aspects that need to be considered for any team. First, is there something for them to do? If so, is it clear what that is, who is going to do it and how? Is there a consensus about what the task is and is it agreed by not only those within the team but those outside who may overlap or need to coordinate with the team? The second issue that needs to considered is how the people within the team work together. Are they complementary and do they help each other to get the best out of the team? Are there some processes which are hindering the team? Are there some sorts of task that the team is better at than others?

To answer these questions about particular groups or teams we often end up asking questions about how the team is managed or led and about how much autonomy the group has. How united do they feel about what they are doing? What sort of pressures are placed on them to conform? It is these sorts of question that we will be looking at in this chapter. The currently preferred term in management circles is to talk of leadership which it is claimed is different from management in that it is about enabling others to perform rather than making them perform. The language of leadership often uses vocabulary from theology as well as the more traditional language of the social sciences. The sometimes spiritual and mystical associations with leadership creep in even in the most 'objective' texts – it is worth looking out for as it is a very different voice to that normally heard in the analysis of organisational behaviour.

Developing leadership and autonomy

Leadership is the Holy Grail of management writing and talking. Everyone would like to claim it as a personal attribute but it is very difficult to achieve consensus on quite what it entails. All the early studies that looked for the personality traits that make up a leader failed to find any conclusive evidence of special traits, except that leaders on the whole were taller than the led!

Although we find it difficult to agree quite what leadership is, it is useful to have some sort of definition. It is usually thought to include the ability to get people to do different things, things which they normally would not have done, and to do these different things with some degree of commitment and enthusiasm. Surprisingly it is quite easy to get people to obey orders at work without the manager using any particular skill or personal charm. However, if we want more from the performance of duties than a bare minimum then something else is required.

DID YOU KNOW?

Davies (1972) in a review of the research found the four general traits related to leadership success were:

- *Intelligence; leaders usually have a slightly higher general intelligence than their followers.*
- *Social maturity; having self-assurance and self-respect leaders are mature and able to handle a wide variety of social situations.*
- *Achievement drive; leaders have a strong drive to get things done.*
- *Human relations attitudes; knowing that they rely on other people to get things done leaders are interested in their followers.*

This model of leadership concentrated on the person leading rather than on the job to be done.

Nowadays you will hear phrases about leadership competencies like:

- Maintain the trust and support of colleagues and team members.
- Set up collaborative and consultative working arrangements.
- Provide the environment for people to excel.
- Nurture individual development.
- Recognise success.
- Encourage enthusiasm through teamwork.

None of us would disagree with these as worthy ambitions for leaders, they are what are called 'motherhood terms' in that you can't really be against either motherhood or the above phrases! But it is quite difficult to see exactly how a team leader should go about the task of leadership. The two essential ingredients seem to be clarifying the tasks to be performed and establishing suitable enthusiasm and expertise in the people to undertake these tasks effectively. However, there are, as ever, several different approaches to analysing leadership and we will look at these in the following sections.

ACTIVITY **8.1**

Answer the following questions about people you have worked with or come across in other activities such as clubs or groups you have belonged to.

- Who have you worked for who seemed to be a good leader?
- Who have you worked for who was not a good leader?
- What characteristics distinguished them from each other?
- Could you use any of these characteristics to lead others more successfully?

The roles of the leader

After the early studies had failed to come up with any useful personality traits (qualities) that were associated with leaders, another more pragmatic approach was to look at what functions a leader fulfils for the group. Various studies have looked at the work done by managers and leaders, see, for example, Mintzberg (1973) and Stewart (1967). This sort of research led to a description of the various roles that leaders could or should fill in organisations.

A useful summary by Krech *et al* (1962) suggests the following possible roles for the leaders (Figure 8.1).

- Coordinator.
- Planner.
- Policy maker.
- Expert.
- External group representative.
- Controller of internal relations.
- Controller of rewards and punishments.
- Arbitrator and mediator.
- Symbol of the group.
- Role model.
- Ideologist.
- Parent figure.
- Scapegoat.

Styles of leadership

An early influential model of leadership in Britain was Adair's (1982). Adair used his model to develop leadership at the Royal Military Academy, Sandhurst, but the methods have been adopted in a wide variety of organisations. He argued that people working in groups have three types of need, two of which are shared with all group members, the third being related to each individual.

Figure 8.1 **Leadership pill.**

1. The task to be accomplished together.
2. Maintaining social cohesion of the group.
3. Individual needs of team members.

These three types of need are interdependent. If the group fails at the task there is diminished satisfaction for the individual and the group tends to fall apart. If the group lacks unity this will affect performance. If the individuals are discontented then they will not give their best performance. Figure 8.2 shows these three sets of needs, that it is the leadership's function to provide, as three overlapping circles. This emphasises the essential unity of leadership, and shows that a single action by a leader may have an influence in all three areas.

Figure 8.2
Adair's three circle model of leadership.

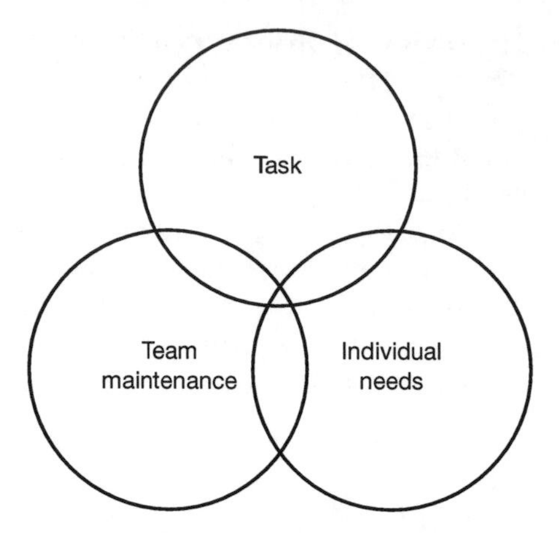

Another well-tried device for identifying individual leadership style is Blake and Mouton's (1969) managerial grid. This is used as an exercise in finding one's current leadership style with the hope that it can be modified at least slightly to become more appropriate to the situation in which one is working. The managerial grid identifies concern for production and concern for people as the two axes of the grid (see Figure 8.3).

Figure 8.3
The managerial grid. (Based on Blake and Mouton (1969).)

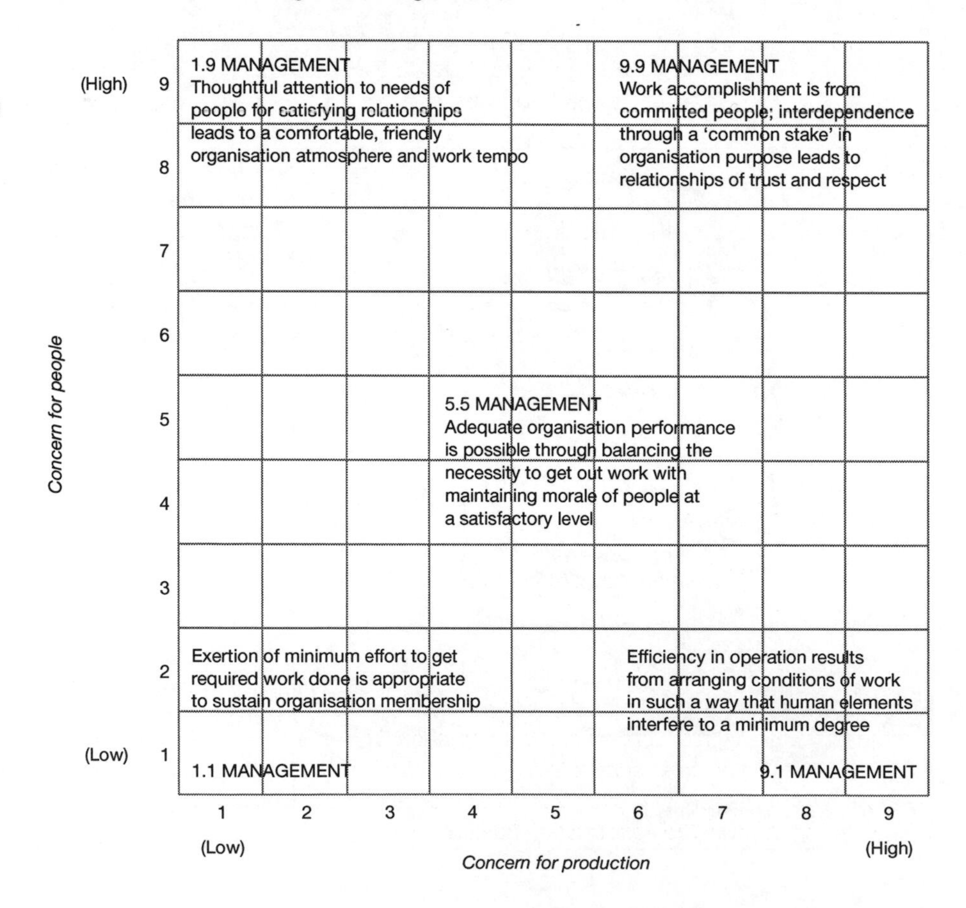

These result in a grid of different types of leader. For example, at the extremes:

- At the lower left-hand corner is a 1.1 management style which is the style of managers with a low concern for both people and production, who try to stay out of trouble and simply do what they are told.
- In the upper left-hand corner is the 1.9 style of high concern for people but low concern for production. This is the utterly delightful leader, full of charm and consideration who never quite gets round to making anything happen.
- The bottom right-hand corner is the 9.1 person with high concern for production and little concern for people. They are full of ideas on what to get done and what needs doing but are very frustrated when no one pays any attention or cooperates with such a leader.
- The top right-hand style of 9.9 of high concern with both people and production is the obvious goal.

This emphasis on style, rather than personal characteristics, is probably the secret of the success that the grid method has enjoyed since it provides useful criticism of the type that most people can accept. This grid could also be used as a way of analysing the general culture or behaviour in organisations and whether the concern for people and tasks is in balance or not and whether some changes are required.

Another useful model is that of Tannenbaum and Schmidt (1973) who suggest a continuum of behaviour by leaders and those who work for them. The continuum is demonstrated as follows:

- At one end the leader makes all the decisions and announces them as a fait accompli.
- The leader sells the decision.
- The leader presents ideas and invites questions.
- The leader presents tentative decisions subject to change.
- The leader presents problems and gets suggestions and makes the decision.
- The leader defines the limits and asks the group to make the decision.
- At the other end the leader permits the group to function within limits defined by others.

DID YOU KNOW?

Heathrow Express Construction Projects faced indefinite delays in completing the railway line following the collapse of a number of tunnels. They changed the way of working by emphasising that all the different organisations and contractors and the British Airports Authority who had commissioned the work were a single team. They ran development courses for staff on the front line with an emphasis on the 'soft' skills for supervisors, engineers, tunnellers and support staff. These were seen as crucial to the change away from blame and confrontation. The project was soon back on schedule and in 1997 they won an award from the Institute of Personnel and Development for changing the way the construction industry worked.

Moving along this continuum illustrates the amount of control that the leader has over the led. This has led to the use of four words to define these different sorts of leader.

- Tells.
- Sells.
- Consults.
- Joins.

This brief summary is often used informally in organisations to describe a boss's behaviour.

ACTIVITY **8.2**

Get into pairs and ask your partner to do each of the following things in each of the four modes of:

- Telling.
- Selling.
- Consulting.
- Joining.

Ask them to:

- Go and get something for you from the other side of the room, library or coffee room.
- Come and do something with you such as a trip to the library, coffee room etc.
- Discuss how you should celebrate the end of term.
- Discuss what should go into the next assignment.

You could do half with you asking and half with you responding.

Now examine your responses and think which felt the most appropriate way of leading in each question. Did they vary? Was one approach consistently the better way or was there a difference depending on the task?

Contingency models of leadership

This approach emphasises the importance of the situation that the leader and the group find themselves in. Fiedler (1967) was the first to use the term 'contingency' in the context of leadership. He argues that any leadership style may be effective depending on the situation, so that the leader has to be adaptive. He also appreciates that it is very difficult for individuals to change their style of leadership as these styles are relatively inflexible: the autocrat will remain autocratic and the free-wheeling, laissez-faire advocate will remain free-wheeling. As no single style is appropriate in all situations effectiveness can either be achieved by changing the leader to fit the situation or by altering the situation to fit the leader.

Three factors will determine the leader's effectiveness:

- Leader–member relations. How well is the leader accepted by the other members?
- Task structure. Are the jobs of the group routine and precise or vague and undefined?
- Position power. What formal authority does the leader's position confer?

Fiedler then devised a novel device for measuring leadership style. It was a scale that indicated the degree to which a person described favourably or unfavourably their least preferred co-worker (LPC). Those who used relatively favourable terms tend towards permissiveness, with a human relations-orientated and considerate style; he called them high LPC. Those who used an unfavourable style of criticism tend to be managing, task controlling and less concerned with the human relations aspects of the job; he called them low LPC.

It is then possible to combine all these elements to show how the style of leadership that is effective varies with the situation in which it is exercised. Table 8.1 shows the results from Fielder's study of 800 leaders.

High LPC leaders are likely to be most effective in situations where relations with subordinates are good but task structure is low and position power weak. They do reasonably well when they have poor relationships with the other members but there is high task structure and strong position power. Both of these are moderately favourable combinations of circumstances. Low LPC leaders are more effective at the ends of the spectrum, when they either have a favourable combination or an unfavourable combination of factors in the situation.

Table 8.1
Leadership performance in different conditions. (Based on Fiedler (1967).)

Condition	*Leader–member relations*	*Task structure*	*Position power*	
1	Good	High	Strong	Low LPC leader more effective
2	Good	High	Weak	Low LPC leader more effective
3	Good	Low	Strong	Low LPC leader more effective
4	Good	Low	Weak	High LPC leader more effective
5	Poor	High	Strong	High LPC leader more effective
6	Poor	High	Weak	Similar effectiveness
7	Poor	Low	Strong	Low LPC leader more effective
8	Poor	Low	Weak	Low LPC leader more effective

The value of Fiedler's work is that it concentrates on effectiveness as its yardstick and demonstrates the fallacy of believing that there is a single best way to lead in all situations. It is interesting that the majority of situations he describes appear to call for a generally less attractive type of person as leader, but we should remember that he was examining a range of situations for the purpose of explanation and that situations which are at the extremes of his continuum may not be very common in organisational life. Not everyone agrees with Fiedler's view that leaders cannot change their style.

The drive for leadership in organisations

In the 1980s there was increasing emphasis on leaders rather than managers. Several people addressed the distinction.

Watson (1983) used a well-known organisational framework known as the 7 Ss of strategy, structure, systems, style, staff, skills and shared goals. Watson suggests that managers tend to rely on

- strategy
- structure
- systems

whereas leaders use the softer Ss of

- style
- staff
- skills
- shared goals.

Kotter (1982) made perhaps the more detailed distinction. He saw management as predominantly activity-based whereas leadership means dealing with people rather than things.

Management involved the following:

- Planning and budgeting. This involves target setting. Establishing procedures for reaching targets. Allocating the resources necessary to meet plans.
- Organising and staffing. This is setting the organisation structure. It means recruiting the right people and giving them incentives.
- Controlling and problem solving. This involves monitoring the results compared with the plan and identifying problems and working out solutions.

Everything is concerned with logic, structure, analysis and control and if well done it produces predictable results on time.

Leadership on the other hand is:

- Creating a sense of direction. This is usually as a result of dissatisfaction with the status quo. It is challenged. Out of this challenge a vision for something different is born.
- Communicating the vision. The vision must be the realised or unconscious needs of other people and the leader must work to give it credibility.
- Energising, inspiring and motivating. These words encapsulate much of what a leader must be seen to do. People must be kept moving, enthusiasm must be bred and maintained in them and when the going is tough they must be supported and helped.

If done well, and with passion and commitment, then it will produce impetus for change. If no change is necessary, frankly, management might be better! Where change is necessary management will be found lacking and the need for leadership will be paramount.

In management, and Human Resource Management circles in particular, there is presently a great deal of emphasis on developing leadership in those with responsibilities. They speak of moving from management to leadership. The factor prompting this move is an ideal of moving from compliance to commitment based on the humanistic approach of many working in this field (see Chapter 1 for discussion of this topic). There is also a feeling that as organisations become less hierarchical and more team- and project-based, individuals will belong to several teams and will be required to offer their contribution rather than have it demanded of them.

Mobilising this commitment through effective leadership has become one of the buzz words of management at the turn of the millennium. There is a particular emphasis on the visionary constituents of leadership and the ability to inspire others through a suitable statement of the purpose and mission of the group. Words about how people can be taken out of themselves and achieve more than they imagined are often bandied about. It remains to be seen whether this will work and whether criteria for effective leadership behaviour can be distinguished. It is also worth remembering that leaders can only lead as far as followers allow unless some coercion is involved.

A popular distinction between leaders is that made by Burns (1978) and Kuhnert and Lewis (1987) among others, who distinguish between *transactional* and *transformational* leaders.

- Transactional leaders use styles of communication and techniques to clarify task requirements and ensure that there are appropriate rewards when the task is completed.
- Transformational leaders are those who articulate a mission and create and maintain a positive image in followers and superiors.

The latter sort of leader has become the more accepted definition of what leadership is about. It is this transformational leadership that we are concerned about for the remainder of this chapter.

What makes a credible leader?

Managers are people with authority, stemming from the position they hold: they are *in* authority, with all the formal power that the position confers. Successful managers have something more: they are *an* authority, possessing skill, knowledge and expertise that others consult willingly. Credibility is the word used in organisations, particularly among professionals, to describe this prerequisite ability that you need in order to get things done. In the increasingly informal working of organisations this credibility is something you have to earn and maintain for yourself. The job title and organisational position will help but will not be sufficient. Those with high credibility are worthy of belief, trustworthy, convincing and respected. They are listened to and can get things done willingly and quickly, whereas colleagues who lack credibility meet resistance and have to rely more heavily on the glacial speed of formal mechanisms.

What is credibility? It is the ability to get things done based on expertise and personal qualities rather than position and power. This means relying on one's own abilities and informal ways of getting things done. It means being able to get things done more quickly and with less fuss. Those who do not have credibility have to rely on the formal procedures and positions of power. The reluctance of others to comply where there is no credibility leads to long delays and tedious battles in implementing change. In our increasingly informal organisations the importance of credibility cannot be underestimated.

The basis of credibility is usually an appropriate expertise and some contribution of personal qualities such as hard work and enthusiasm. It is a very rare individual who can rely on personal attributes alone to be credible. Leadership is more often made up of hard work, understanding of the position and position power. The components of a leader's credibility might be:

- Keeping in touch with the main task. It is only by keeping in touch with the main task of the organisation as a whole and the section in which the leader is located that new ideas can be based in reality. If they lose touch with their operational expertise they risk losing credibility with their colleagues. Staff can become sceptical about how much they understand current operational problems and the manager will retreat further into management and administration. This in turn creates unnecessary and superfluous systems of control that infuriate the staff.
- Legitimacy. Staff on the receiving end of managers exercising authority respond readily only when they perceive the authority as legitimate. The formal organisation charts, job titles and pay structures provide *in* authority legitimacy. Western society and its organisations have developed a taste for informal means to supplement these. Keeping in touch with the main task and maintaining technical competence is the main feature but *an* authority is also legitimised by such personal characteristics as willingness to do things, working hard and demonstrating enthusiasm. Belonging to the organisation and being seen to be committed to it can be crucial in being able to influence things. Experience enables some people to develop a 'nose' for appropriate times and actions. They have invaluable legitimacy. The fact that these cannot be learned does not reduce their importance.
- A clear role. We have found that many managerial jobs do not have any clear role. People with these jobs are not in charge of anything and consequently the individuals, who are often hard working, experienced and keen, will find work to do. Not all of this is helpful as it often interferes with other people's work, particularly where the work created is predominately administrative and increases the amount of administration done by those required to respond.

For further details of these components of credibility see a series of studies by Weightman (1986), and Torrington and Weightman (1982), (1987) and (1989).

The characteristics which undermine credibility are appearing to do useless things, adding to the burden of others unnecessarily and bandwagoning for personal gain. But different cultures and organisations will reflect different things so any particular organisation may well have other behaviours that add to or subtract from credibility. The important thing is to know what is the basis of your credibility and work on maintaining it.

The consequences of not having credibility are that those working with you will be frustrated and less compliant, peers will take you less seriously, bosses may only include you as a back up to themselves and customers, clients and others outside the organisation may come to devalue the whole organisation.

As important as acquiring credibility is the process of maintaining credibility. It is no use relying on an expertise and practical experience built up five or ten years ago. No young member of staff will be impressed with 'well, we used to do it like this and it was fine' or ' fifteen years ago we had the same problem and I managed to fix it'. Far better to offer the advice as current and try to encourage a mutual problem-solving approach.

ACTIVITY **8.3**

Questions to ask yourself particularly once you start work. You might like to ask someone who is a manager these questions.

- Who has real credibility round here?
- What is the basis of this credibility?
- What is the basis of my credibility?
- Is this based on old expertise?
- What am I doing to maintain my credibility?
- Is this mostly based on technical expertise or personal qualities?
- What do you do to maintain your credibility with your staff?
- What do you do to maintain your credibility with your colleagues elsewhere in the organisation and outside?
- What are we doing to ensure that others can build and develop their own credibility?
- Are we doing anything to undermine their credibility?
- Can we do something about it?

Valuing: consideration, feedback, delegation and participation

If staff are to work so they willingly contribute their efforts and commitment there has to be something in it for them. Clearly the salary and interest of the work are important elements, but where extraordinary commitment is given there is usually something more. This may be because the work itself is seen to matter, because of the unusually effective leadership of the manager or because the individual member of staff feels valued.

Most organisations are suffering from innovation overload. This is often happening just when staff morale is lowered because of redundancies and a general levelling of staff differentials. Staff respond to this in different ways, some by withholding commitment, see Scase and Goffee (1989), for example, on how middle managers removed their commitment. Some withdraw from extra work. Some increase their militancy. Some simply bow their heads and resolve to work harder – like Boxer the horse in *Animal Farm*.

So what can a line manager or leader do about it? It is not usually possible to reduce the innovation overload. But, maybe, there is something that can be done about morale. There are several ways that people can help improve the morale of their team by valuing each other. Valuing is a complex social interaction which has something to do with valuing the member of staff as a person as well as the job which they do. Four types of valuing are consideration, feedback, delegation and consultation.

- Consideration. People tend to feel a lack of consideration from their colleagues when the organisational culture is one of keeping to oneself rather than talking to colleagues. Even at the simplest level such things as eye contact in corridors, saying 'good morning', smiling and the everyday courtesies of the working day can make a difference. Evidence from research we (Torrington and Weightman) have done in a variety of organisations suggests that most people would welcome more of these small gestures at work. Lack of consideration may be one of Hertzberg's dissatisfiers (see Chapter 3).

- Feedback. All too often the enormous contribution and exhausting effort that people put into their jobs seems to lack any perceptible output. People need feedback from their colleagues. This can be the formal performance appraisal dealt with in Chapter 9. It can also be informally taking an interest in what others are doing. It is not hierarchy bound; a junior saying 'That's great! How do you do it?' can be very pleasing.
- Delegation. Members of staff are valued when responsibility is delegated to them, but this involves delegating real responsibility not just giving people jobs to do. Individuals must be trusted to make decisions about what, whether and how to do things not just given the job of completing tasks. Otherwise they are likely to work to rule and feel like machines. Responsibility cannot be delegated and then taken away without devaluing confidence and future effectiveness.
- Consultation and participation. Due to the innovation overload it is difficult to create the conditions in which people will respond to change with enthusiasm. However, if they are to respond with commitment rather than stoical compliance then some sort of participation in at least the 'how' even if not the 'what' will help. Although it takes longer to get a decision if you involve more people, they are at least then committed to trying to make it work if they have been involved in the decision process. Whereas if you do not include people in the decision process it will take much longer to persuade them afterwards and they will often use all their creative powers to prove it cannot be done.

ACTIVITY **8.4**

Describe your approach when you ask a friend to:

- Wash your favourite jumper.
- Look after your pets/plants.
- Buy you a book.
- Perform some other favour.

Do you:

- Let them decide whether to do it or not?
- Let them decide what to do or not?
- Let them decide how to do it or not?

Empowerment

If there is one concept from the Human Resources field that has become popular with senior managers it is 'empowerment', see, for example, Foy (1994). This simple idea means that employees at all levels are responsible for their actions and should be given the authority to make decisions about their own work. This is not just to make people more satisfied with their work but is done to enable organisations to respond quickly. The advantages claimed for an empowered workforce are better services, flexibility, speed, cross-department links, improved morale and compensation for limited career paths.

Empowerment is about ownership of the problem and the solution. True empowerment means employees having the discretion to take decisions about what they feel it is appropriate to do at the time. This empowerment, presumably, also includes the right to be consulted about the nature of the empowerment proposed and indeed the power to say 'no' to empowerment.

Typical elements of a system to ensure the success of an empowered workforce, from a management perspective, include:

- Performance evaluations drawn from a variety of sources.
- Variable rewards, including some group element.
- Tolerance of errors.
- Enhanced communication.
- Generalist managers and staff.
- Giving yourself time to develop the confidence in each other.
- Sufficient resources to deliver some of the solutions that are generated.

Empowerment can really only happen where there are sufficient resources to take on any training that is necessary for individuals. Too often empowerment procedures are initiated as a substitute for sufficient resources to get on with the job. It also requires roles to be clearly defined and for the previous managers to give up some of their power.

It is worth thinking about what is in it for each empowered person. It could include such things as:

- A team bonus.
- Increased recognition.
- Security of employment.
- The satisfaction of developing new talents.

Very often claims to have empowered the staff fall well short of these ideals. The difficulties with empowerment from the organisation's point of view are a greater potential for chaos, a lack of clarity, breakdown of hierarchical control and demoralisation of those staff who do not want more responsibility. But without there being something in it for the staff they will feel very put upon, the whole initiative will sink in a flurry of accusations about the latest fashion and fad and it will not work. Empowerment should not feel like dumping! As Hyman and Cunningham (1996) found in their research on empowerment in several UK organisations:

> empowerment in many cases is little different from earlier prescriptions for job enlargement, or at best job enrichment, where employees can exercise discretion and influence over the execution of their immediate tasks, but the overall parameters within which they operate are in many cases not so flexible.

Conclusion

Leadership is currently a popular term in management circles. There have been many studies of leadership behaviour but it is still a confused area. Some of this confusion is because of the aspects of power, authority and control implicit in the relationship of leader and led. Chapter 12 about power, authority and influence develops this further.

EXERCISE **8.1**

Over the next week see if you can collect ten examples of behaviour that you consider demonstrate leadership. These may be among your friends deciding what to do, in lectures from your fellow students or lecturers, it may be in an emergency, it may be complete strangers you observe or see on the television.

If you are in a seminar group compare your examples with others.

- Do you all agree that each other's examples demonstrate leadership?
- Are there different degrees of leadership examples?

Now try to group the examples using the Blake and Mouton grid or Adair's circles.

- Do they fit?
- What difficulties do you have?

Self-check questions

1. Can we define leadership?
2. List some roles for leaders.
3. Describe Adair's model of leadership.
4. What is Blake and Mouton's grid?
5. Describe the continuum of leader control/led participation in four simple words.
6. What is the contingency model of leadership?
7. What is the difference between transactional and transformational leaders?
8. What is credibility?
9. What are the main components of valuing?
10. What is empowerment? How do organisations try to implement it?

CASE STUDY **8.1**

Walkabout

Sid was the care and business manager in the theatre and high dependency directorate of a large NHS hospital trust. He was responsible for ensuring that the operating theatres and the intensive care, high dependency and day wards worked efficiently. These were spread over two sites, three miles apart. Every morning he visited each of the theatres before operating began and then visited the wards. Sid had worked at the hospital as a nurse for twenty years, his wife and daughter both worked in the hospital as well. This daily 'walkabout' involved talking to many of the surgeons and anaesthetists about equipment, rotas, developments and budgets. It also involved talking to nursing staff about problems they were having with getting sufficient experienced staff to cover for a series of maternity leaves and sickness. Sid also spent time, on the day I shadowed him, with the technicians in the intensive care ward over the introduction of a new piece of equipment. As Sid went round he joked with people, heard people's personal stories and made notes of things he needed to look into further. By 10.30 am he had covered a lot of ground both physically and mentally. His notebook was full of jottings made on his tour.

So what were the strengths of this walkabout?

References

Adair J. (1982) *Action Centred Leadership*. Gower, Aldershot.
Blake R.R. and Mouton J.S. (1969) *Building a Dynamic Organization through Grid Organization Development*. Gull, Houston, TX.
Burns J.M. (1978) *Leadership*. Harper and Row, New York, NY.
Davies K. (1972) *Human Behaviour at Work*, 4th edn. McGraw Hill, New York, NY.
Fiedler F.E. (1967) *A Theory of Leadership Effectiveness*. McGraw Hill, New York, NY.
Foy N. (1994) *Empowering People at Work*. Gower, Aldershot.
Hyman J. and Cunningham I. (1996) Empowerment in organisations: changes in the manager's role. In *Managers as Developers*, Megginson D. and Gibb S. (Eds), Prentice Hall, Hemel Hempstead.
Kotter J. (1982) *The General Managers*. Free Press, New York, NY.
Krech D., Crutchfield R.S. and Ballachey E.L. (1962) *Individual in Society*. McGraw Hill, New York, NY.
Kuhnert K.W. and Lewis P. (1987) Transactional and transformational leadership: a constructive/developmental analysis. *Academy of Management Review*, October, 648–57.
Mintzberg H. (1973) *The Nature of Managerial Work*. Harper and Row, London.
Scase R. and Goffee R. (1989) *Reluctant Managers: Their Work and Lifestyles*. Unwin Hyman, London.
Stewart R. (1967) *Managers and Their Jobs*. Macmillan, London.
Tannenbaum R. and Schmidt W.H. (1973) How to choose a leadership pattern. *Harvard Business Review*, May–June 162–75, 178–80.
Torrington D. and Weightman J. (1982) Technical atrophy in middle management. *Journal of General Management*, Vol. 7, No. 4, 5–17.
Torrington D. and Weightman J. (1987) The analysis of management work. *Training and Management Development Methods*, Vol. 1, 27–33.
Torrington D. and Weightman J. (1989) *The Reality of School Management*. Blackwell, Oxford.
Watson C.M. (1983) Leadership, management and the seven keys. *Business Horizons*, March–April, 8–13.
Weightman J. (1986) *Middle management dinosaur or dynamo*. PhD thesis, UMIST.

Further reading

John Harvey Jones was chair of ICI and has written several very readable books about management which are really about leading people. For example, *Altogether Now* (1994), Heinemann, London.

The Admirable Crichton by J.M. Barrie is a play about an Edwardian family who are shipwrecked and are led by their butler. It has several insights into leadership. (See Case study 12.1.)

Shakspeare's *Henry V* is about leading men into battle and is worth reading, or seeing, to get a perspective on the human needs of leadership.

CHAPTER 9

Performance management

Objectives

When you have read this chapter you should be able to:

- Give some definitions of performance.
- Debate some ethical considerations of performance management.
- Describe the normal stages of performance management.
- Discuss issues associated with measuring performance.

Introduction

Managing performance has become a buzz phrase of management. What is meant by performance management or managing performance varies enormously. For some it means manipulating pay and other reward systems so that people will work harder. For others it means telling staff what they should do. Other people think it means increasing people's understanding of the whole process so that they know what they are doing. We will look at a variety of different models or methods in this chapter and some of the variety of claims that are made about managing performance.

The one certain thing is that nothing quite distinguishes our underlying assumptions about the working relationship as our approach to managing performance and what is seen as acceptable and what is not. Some would argue for the autonomy of individuals to offer their work in whatever way they feel is appropriate. Some would argue that there is a need for outside authorities to ensure standards that individuals apply in their work although individuals should be able to offer this work as and when they wish, like, for example, professional groups such as lawyers and doctors. Others, usually managers, want things much more tightly controlled by the employers or managers. Questions about quality and rewards for work and how it should be done are all associated with performance management. Who should take the decisions about these is inevitably wrapped up in the politics of the debate.

This chapter looks at some of the issues associated with performance management as well as describing some of the normal procedures for managing performance.

Ethics of managing performance

What right does anyone have to manage another person's performance? Can those who are senior in the hierarchy be blamed for the poor performance of an individual at work? When there is a serious accident questions such as these become focused. For example, was it the captain of the ship who failed to close the bow doors who was responsible for its sinking or was it his bosses who were constantly putting pressure on the captain to quicken the turnaround time to make more journeys per day? This question of the social responsibility and ethics of organisations is increasingly a subject for discussion, see, for example, Connock and Johns (1995).

We have earlier distinguished between hard and soft approaches to organisational behaviour. So it is with performance management. Those with a hard approach will see it as a continuing right and responsibility of those senior in the organisation to set out formal requirements for performance and to monitor the results. Those with a softer approach will prefer to see the developing individual with the flair to cope with autonomy and consequently offering their best performance to the organisation.

These two approaches are at the extremes and most organisations use a mixture of both. Increasingly these are brought together in the contract of employment. This has explicit terms which detail that the employer can control the work of the employee and what the employee will get in return. It also has implicit aspects, sometimes called the psychological contract, which include such things as the maintenance of mutual trust and confidence by the employer and that the employee will obey lawful and reasonable orders. This explicit and implicit contract of employment is at the core of performance management. See Foot and Hook (1996) for further discussion of this topic.

Some of these issues have been brought together under the concept of job satisfaction. Although originally studied from the point of view of motivation studies, job satisfaction seems to be something more complex and is now associated with job design and the quality of working life. Whatever is involved, job satisfaction does seem to be an attitude of mind and is undoubtedly an internal state associated with a feeling of achievement. The relationship between job satisfaction and performance is controversial. Earlier researchers felt that satisfaction led to improved performance but it could be that performance leads to satisfaction. However, Luthans (1992, p. 123), suggests that:

> Although most people assume a positive relationship, the preponderance of research evidence indicates that there is no strong linkage between satisfaction and productivity.

We will return to aspects of job satisfaction and its implications for job design in Chapter 13.

The important concept to help make sense of performance management from an organisational behaviour perspective is that of some sort of contract between the employer and employee. The nature of the contract will vary enormously and individuals vary in what they consider acceptable. Analysing these contracts will tell you a lot about the particular organisational behaviour.

Defining what is performance

Who defines what performance is required and whether it has been achieved will be determined by the nature of the organisation, its environment and the politics and power associated with the players involved. This context is dealt with in Chapters 11 and 12. Whoever runs the organisation ultimately is responsible for its performance. They may be accountable to shareholders, customers, clients, staff, the country and other stakeholders. The performance can be organisational, group or individual.

The interaction between members of the organisation about performance will be both formal and informal. We will often say to colleagues 'that's great' or 'what's that you're doing?' We will observe their behaviour, look at their production, listen to them on the telephone or see them with a client. These observations give us informal information about performance. We are constantly on the look out for clues as to what others are doing and learning about their performance and picking up on what is acceptable and what is unacceptable performance in this particular context. We are also learning new ways to do things that improve our own performance. For example, my ability to use word processing was greatly improved by sitting next to an experienced secretary while we finished a report – she was wizard at using all the devices and short-cuts! Performance management is about formal, systematic ways of doing this.

One approach to directing the performance of people in organisations is Management by Objectives (MBO). This phrase is used to describe a system of management that tries to relate the organisational goals to the behaviour and performance of individuals in the organisation. It involves:

- Setting targets and objectives.
- Getting individuals to agree these objectives and the criteria for measuring performance.
- Continually appraising and reviewing the outcomes.

This concept was introduced by Drucker (1954/1989) and was initially related to the behaviour of senior managers. Since then it has been widely adopted and is now applied to all levels in the organisation through performance appraisal systems. The cycle of management by objectives is a cycle of interrelated activities, see Figure 9.1.

The advantages claimed for such a system are that it:

- Concentrates on the perceived important areas.
- Identifies problem areas before they become critical.
- Identifies training needs.
- Improves communications.
- Makes managers actually manage their staff.

Some difficulties, identified by Kane and Freeman (1986), are:

- That individuals do just enough to get the reward.
- The emphasis is on the short term.
- A lack of discretion for managers.

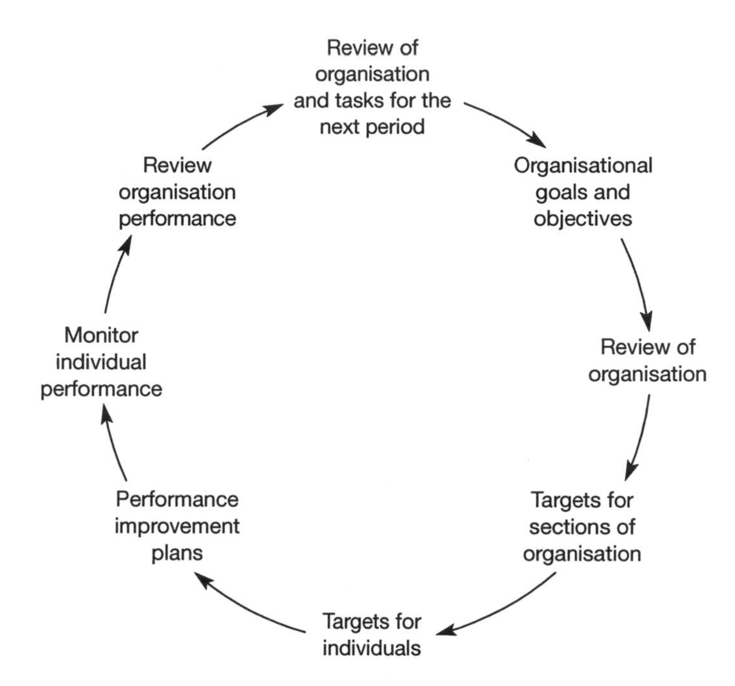

Figure 9.1
The MBO cycle.

- A lost flexibility as individuals 'work to objectives'.
- The annual bottleneck of interviews after the organisation's goals have been set.

An overriding issue for some is that it can be a top-down procedure if there is no feedback to the original target setting from those asked to implement the targets.

Stimulating improved performance

The increased interest in systematic management in the past ten years has led to the development of performance management. A variety of influences have contributed to this: increased competition from other countries and realisation of their better productivity, the findings of Peters and Waterman mentioned in Chapter 1 and pressure from government bodies such as the Training section of the Employment and Education Department.

Performance management is usually taken to mean an increased emphasis on specifying what is wanted and rewarding those individuals who are able to deliver it satisfactorily. The normal stages of performance management, as described by the literature and those advocating performance management, are:

- Written and agreed job descriptions, reviewed regularly.
- Objectives for the workgroup which have been cascaded down from the organisation's strategic objectives.

- Individual objectives derived from the above, which are jointly arrived at by appraiser and appraisee. These objectives are results- rather than task-orientated, are tightly defined and include measures to be assessed. The objectives are designed to stretch the individual and offer potential development as well as meeting business needs.
- Development plan devised by the manager and the individual detailing development goals and activities designed to enable the individual to meet their objectives. These could be competency-based. The emphasis here is on managerial support and coaching.
- Assessment of objectives with ongoing formal reviews on a regular basis designed to motivate the appraisee and concentrate on developmental issues.
- There is usually also an annual assessment which affects pay received, depending on the performance in achieving the objectives.

For many organisations this has led to three separate interviews with staff, the appraisal interview which looks at the past performance, the performance interview which looks at what is expected for the next period and the development interview which deals with training and development needs and future career prospects. Clearly for some these might actually be done successively on the same day but maintaining the distinction between the three is felt to be useful in keeping the concept of performance management clear. One of the major advantages of performance management is that managers are forced to give emphasis to formal and planned employee development. Another advantage is that it also enforces a clear role description and set of objectives agreed by managers and individuals. On the down side there is potential conflict between the aim of improving performance which requires openness and a developmental approach and the link with pay. This conflict is sometimes resolved by separating the performance development and performance pay reviews and holding them at different times of the year.

ACTIVITY **9.1**

- How many of the performance management techniques have you experienced?
- Would it have been appropriate to have used more?
- How would this coexist with the desire for some people to be seen as autonomous professionals?

Before we get on to the specifics of performance management let us look briefly at some of the ways people in organisations arrive at the strategies and targets that are supposed to start the whole process. There are a large number of books on strategy and planning from all possible points of view, an interesting and influential British one is Kay (1993). Perhaps the most commonly used technique is the simple form of a SWOT analysis (Figure 9.2). This is a useful device for analysing the situation and then making some decisions.

- Strengths. What are the positive attributes of the organisation, department or group in this situation? This might include people, tradition, technology

Figure 9.2 **SWOT.**

and know-how, customer loyalty, resources, location, reputation.

- Weaknesses. What are the negative attributes of the organisation, department or group in this situation? This might include any of the above! What needs doing to overcome these weaknesses?
- Opportunities. These are usually changes in the environment of the organisation such as changes in the market, legislation, transport, economy, other competitors' positions, technology. There needs to be a sensitivity to picking up on these for a successful organisation.
- Threats. These can be any of the above! Particularly if changes are ignored or not noticed.

The device can be used in all sorts of circumstance for both large and small projects. Box 7.2 on goal planning is related to this SWOT analysis.

ACTIVITY **9.2**

Do a SWOT analysis of your preparedness for your next assignment.

It might be useful in helping you sort out where the bottlenecks are in your completing it on time and help you to prioritise your work. Can you use it?

Performance related pay

The way in which people are rewarded is central to the regulation of the employment relationship. Pay arrangements are also central to any changes, including cultural initiatives, as they are the most tangible expression of the working relationship between employer and employee. Managerial perceptions of appropriate payment systems have been subject to considerable change and fluctuation over time. The basic principles of paying either for time and/or performance are at the heart of any system. Payment for time is relatively straightforward with hourly or weekly rates determined. Paying for performance is altogether more complicated. The nature of the performance and whether it is achieved by an individual or the group can all be considered. Over time many organisations end up with some hybrid system that includes both these factors as well as all sorts of custom and practice. For example, we, Weightman, Blandamer and Torrington (1991), found that people in the North Western Regional Health Authority were paid on 2008 different levels of pay, 78 per cent of these pay points had ten people or fewer being paid that amount. We also found wide ranges for such things as weekly hours, annual holidays, pay for 'on call' and so on.

PAUSE FOR THOUGHT

Kanter (1989, p. 223) said:

> *Can anyone be against the idea that people's pay should reflect their performance? Isn't that how the system is supposed to work?*

Compare this view with that held in many British organisations as late as the 1980s, that men should be paid more than women doing the same job as they had families to support.

It is outside the scope of this book to discuss the advantages and disadvantages of different pay systems, for further information on them see Kessler (1995). However, it is worth noting that the current fashion of 'pay for performance' approaches to managing performance can really only work in an environment in which the staff are given enough discretion in their jobs to be able to affect their actual performance in a significant way. Otherwise they will become cynical about the whole initiative. It is also the case that performance related pay schemes add about 10 per cent to the salary bill. This is because the performance element of the pay needs to be substantial, say 30 per cent to be sufficiently motivating and to make a significant difference, otherwise it feels derisory and not worth working for. This is not always affordable or appropriate.

Despite all this talk of performance management the reality is that a line manager's responsibilities for pay are often merely the administrative ones of ensuring the paperwork associated with hours, overtime and rotas worked is up-to-date and returned in time for the pay records to be updated before the pay date. Pay administration is a classic Herzberg hygiene factor, if it is OK no one bothers but if there is an administrative error then people can be very upset.

DID YOU KNOW?

In 1996 Price Waterhouse offered their staff a cafeteria of benefits that they called Flex. Eighty per cent of the reward figure had to be taken in cash, plus a minimum of 20 days holiday, plus a choice from 19 benefits such as holidays, pensions, health insurance, accident insurance, childcare vouchers, retail vouchers, company cars, health club membership at a discount. This had a tax and National Insurance contribution benefit for the company as well as the obvious benefit for the individual.

Mercury Telecommunications also have a large scheme like this.

A line manager is responsible for engendering commitment from the staff. Rewarding them in other ways than through pay is within their powers. People work for a variety of reasons as we saw in Chapter 3. To gain commitment, rewards can include such things as valuing the contribution, allowing autonomy, supporting people through personal crises and generally treating people as they would like to be treated. The personal credibility and leadership of a manager will probably enhance the value of these rewards in the eyes of the staff.

ACTIVITY 9.3

Answer the following about any work you have experienced:

- What does the pay you receive tell you about the organisation you work in?
- Do the terms and conditions of the people who work in your section vary?
- What about the non-qualified staff?
- What about the difference between the conditions of the core and periphery staff?
- In what ways were you rewarded other than financially?

Hendry, Bradley and Perkins (1997) summed up some of the areas that need considering when looking at performance management generally from a managerial perspective.

➤ Reasons	why are we reappraising rewards?
➤ Objectives	goals critical performance contract with employees performance system to do what? Attract/motivate/retain/control?
➤ External	what stage of the business cycle are we in? national culture
➤ Internal	assumptions groups
➤ Systems	to support
➤ Design	how to define rewards? incentives what measures are appropriate? can we measure performance? can people see this? is it manageable? how does this get communicated to everyone?
➤ Outcome	effect on behaviour success criteria
➤ Monitoring	what review process?

We might also add costs – how much will it cost and is it worth it.

Measuring performance

Measuring anything about people inevitably means judging them in some way. Despite efforts to try to reduce the subjectiveness of this judgement, such as the use of a competency approach described in the next chapter, there is always a point at which someone is judging another. Where this judgement is to last a long time and may affect the individual's chances of employment or education very careful consideration of the assessment process is necessary. This may explain why you can find almost mystical discussion of the assessment process in education journals. Box 9.1 gives a list of basic questions to ask about measuring someone's performance. The answers to these questions will be contingent on the particular setting of the assessment.

As well as these questions there is also the question of who should do the measuring and how the measuring should be done. People involved in measuring performance might include:

- Self-assessment – where the individual decides whether they are having difficulty or not with some required behaviour and this can then be the basis of discussion.
- Peer assessment – not usually done formally unless looking at how effective the team is. But a great deal of informal measurement is done.

Box 9.1

Questions to ask yourself about assessment.

Why are we assessing this person?
- to recruit them?
- to develop them?
- to promote them?
- to redeploy them?
- for them to gain national qualifications?

How important is it that the assessment is very accurate?

Is the assessment compulsory?

How much time and effort are we prepared to put into the process?

How frequently do we want the assessment done?

Who should do the judging?
- the person themselves?
- their colleagues?
- someone within a position of authority?
- someone with expertise?
- a variety of people?

What sort of evidence is needed to assess the competency?
- can the individual collect written materials to prove they have done something?
- must the competency be observed?
- are simulated exercises appropriate for assessing these competencies?
- can the competency be demonstrated during normal work?

Who has sight of the conclusions of the assessment?
- is it confidential?
- just the individual, their line manager and personnel records?
- can the information be used for purposes other than the original?
- should the assessment result be used outside the unit?

What will happen as a result of the assessment?
Who is responsible for ensuring this follow up takes place?

Figure 9.3 **Targets**

- Boss assessment – certainly the most common technique in the workplace. This may include observation, exercises and collecting evidence. Usually it does not involve such systematic measures and is much more informal.
- Others who come into contact with the job holder – for a true 360 degree picture of the job holder some assessment by their customer, client or other contacts would be logical but rarely happens in works organisations.
- Outsiders – sometimes used to give a certain objectivity. For example, in assessment centres. These can be expensive and there is the question of confidentiality.

Techniques for measuring performance could include:

- Observation – this can be both formal and informal. It has the advantage of actually seeing the behaviour to be judged and has high credibility. However, it is very time consuming and not everything worth doing is observable.
- Assessment or development centres – these are where individuals come together for a day or two and carry out various activities while being observed by assessors, see Woodruffe (1994). They are useful for focusing on the individual and getting outsiders involved in the assessment. However, they are expensive to run and are simulations of activities not the real thing.
- Portfolios – this is where individuals collect documents and evidence of work they have been involved in and done. The advantages are that the individual is responsible, they celebrate achievement rather than failure and it concentrates on continuous development. However, they can become very unwieldy to read through and there is the issue of comparability.
- Record systems – such as work sheets. This enables comparisons with others but may emphasise quantity at the expense of quality.

The problems encountered in running any scheme of assessment are formidable. Here are a few of these problems, mostly based on the experience of appraisal schemes in organisations.

- Paperwork – any system of assessment always involves paperwork and documentation as the essential feature is reporting and schemes invariably include attempts to make the judgements and the reporting consistent between different assessors. This unavoidably involves forms and detailed instructions.

- Formality – the forms introduce an inhibiting feature into the everyday working relationships between the participants who dislike the idea of formal evaluation. However, the desire for informality has to be balanced with the usefulness of a considered view.
- Outcomes ignored – often a development or promotion is agreed at the appraisal review and then the manager responsible does not deliver the promised development or promotion. There may be good reasons for this but if it happens too often it can undermine the whole process.
- Performance measured by proxy – this is where the performance cannot be measured easily so some other behaviour, such as time keeping or pleasant manner, is measured instead. This is the 'halo' effect.
- Easily measured bits – people do the easily measured bits and get the bonus whereas the difficult, soft parts of the job get ignored. This can become a powerful message in the organisation as everyone becomes more and more hard headed and wonders why they are all feeling so stressed.
- The just-above-average syndrome – there is a reluctance to say people are not good enough so many assessment schemes introduce a forced marking down of some area so that not everything for everyone is marked just-above-average. Where this happens the high-flyers continue to be developed and promoted but nothing is done to develop and deal with poor performance.
- Incomplete coverage – no system ever covers everyone. For example, those just arrived and those just leaving will not be covered. Where there are others being excluded, because they are 'past it' or 'on the fast track', can also undermine the system.
- Ill-informed assessors – sometimes the assessor is asked to make the assessment because of their job title and rank rather than their knowledge of the job and job holder's performance. This can be made worse if they do not know the context in which the individual is trying to operate.

Performance review

Performance appraisal is a well-established way of providing milestones, feedback, guidance and monitoring to staff. A further development, as described above, is tying this appraisal into a larger and more complete system of performance management. These performance management systems, which are increasingly used (see, for example, Fletcher 1997), highlight appraisal as a central activity in the good management of staff. The difference from traditional appraisal 'chats' is that the assessment process in performance management tends to be more rigorous and objective, is more clearly linked into precise job definitions and is based on organisational objective setting, individual development plans and has links with the pay system. For many systems an element of self-appraisal is also included, which has the advantage that the individual, who really knows what they have been doing, can suggest ways of improving their own work. Self-appraisal is also useful in engendering commitment to any agreed changes.

DID YOU KNOW?

Clergy in the Church of England are not considered employees as they 'work for God' so when they wanted to introduce appraisal they opted for peer appraisal.

W.H. Smith use upward and 360 degree appraisal to identify managers' training and development needs.

The essential elements of any performance appraisal are *judgement* and *reporting*. The performance is not simply being measured as in the completion of a work rota, it is being judged. This obviously involves discretion, worry about bias and the possibility of being quite wrong. This judgement not only has to be made but also passed on to other people in such a way that the other understands what is intended and takes action upon it. Those devising performance appraisal schemes devote most of their energies to finding ways of making the judgements as systematic as possible and the reporting as consistent as possible between different appraisers.

Much of what has been written about the appraisal process concentrates on the personal interaction. In addition, George (1986, p. 32) suggests that an effective appraisal scheme is dependent on the style and content of appraisal not conflicting with the culture of the organisation. He suggests that the degree of openness that is required in the appraisal process is:

> unlikely to materialise without an atmosphere of mutual trust and respect – something which is conspicuously lacking in many employing organisations.

The appraisal, therefore, needs to reflect the wider values of the organisation in order for it to be properly integrated into the organisation and to survive in an effective form. The appraisal system can, in fact, be used to display and support the culture and style of the organisation.

The reasons why managers might want to appraise their staff include:

- Human resource considerations – to ensure the abilities and energies of individuals are being used effectively. They would hope to find out more about the staff and make better use of each individual's talents and expertise.
- Training – it is useful to identify training needs both for new tasks and to remedy poor performance among their staff.
- Promotion – talking to individuals about their aspirations as well as finding out about their performance can assist decision making about which staff are ready for promotion.
- Planning – to identify skill shortages and succession needs. If there is a widespread lack of particular skills then some serious planning will need to take place.
- Authority – the appraisal system sustains the hierarchy of authority by confirming the dependence of staff on those who manage them. It is one of the rituals which underlines who is boss.

The reasons why staff might wish to be appraised by their managers include:

- Performance – here is an opportunity to discuss what could be done and how one might go about doing it.
- Motivation – talking about the job and the work it involves may remind us why we do the job and why we wanted it in the first place.
- Career – a boss can be helpful as they understand the promotion route and may well have travelled the same route themselves.

PAUSE FOR THOUGHT *Improving the training, appraisal, targets and rewards of part-time and temporary employees might benefit the organisation as well as the individuals.*

Many things can impair the judgement, reporting and effectiveness of the performance appraisal. For example:

- Prejudice.
- Insufficient knowledge of the individual.
- The 'halo' effect of general likeability or recent events.
- The difficulty of distinguishing the performance from the context in which the person works.
- Different perceptions of what are appropriate standards.
- Marking everyone 'just-above-average'.
- Ignoring the outcome of the appraisal process. For example, if there are no improved resources, training or changes everyone will be frustrated.

Despite these problems of judgement, reporting and follow-up the potential advantages of performance appraisal are generally felt to be so great that the effort is worth expending to make it work.

Most people find a problem-solving approach the most effective form of appraisal interview when both appraiser and appraisee have the skill and ability to handle the situation. This approach is similar to the counselling interview where neither party knows the answer before the interview begins. It develops as the interaction takes place. Training in this type of interviewing is widely available. This does not mean there is no preparation before the interview. Indeed quite the contrary. Both parties need to have a good think about the past year's performance, the next year's expectations and where the changes are expected. It is the comparison of each of their views of these that can be the real stuff of a trusting, problem-solving appraisal interview. Experience suggests that the quality of the interview improves as the confidence and trust of the participants develops. So do not expect too much the first time!

Performance appraisal in various guises is now very common. Different forms are constantly introduced to try to resolve some of the difficulties listed above. Despite the problems, most people feel that a regular, formal encounter between themselves and their boss is an appropriate, if sometimes disappointing, procedure.

DID YOU KNOW?

Stages in a counselling interview:

1. *Factual interchange – focus on the facts of the situation first. Ask factual questions and provide factual information. This provides a basis for later analysis.*
2. *Opinion interchange – open the matter for discussion by asking the client's opinions and feelings but not offering any criticism or making any decisions. Gradually the matter is better understood by counsellor and client.*
3. *Joint problem solving – ask the client to analyse the situation described. The role of the counsellor is to assist in the analysis and focusing, not to produce answers.*
4. *Decision making – the counsellor helps to generate alternative lines of action for the client to consider and they both share in deciding what to do. Only the client can behave differently.*

Poor performance

A particular aspect of managing performance is managing the poor performer. We can all perform badly at times. Usually there is some tolerance of this but where it persists something has to be done about it for the sake of the customers/clients, other colleagues and the individual concerned. Avoiding the issue of managing poor performance does not mean it goes away. Problems with people at work can be short term or long term. For example, most of us are not very good when we have a cold. But there are others who never seem to perform well. It is these individuals who have a long-term performance problem that I want to discuss.

Before anything can be done to improve poor performance it is important to establish that there really is a *gap between the required and the actual performance*. Required performance can be communicated to individuals in several ways. For example, through:

- Contracts of employment with an outline of duties.
- Formal rule books.
- Job descriptions.
- Training manuals.
- Lists of standards.
- Procedures.
- Briefing meetings.
- Training sessions.
- Meetings.
- Individual conversations.
- Professional training and monitoring.

There may be reasons for an individual having difficulties with any of these. For example, the written requirements may be poorly thought out, inappropriate or out of date. Any of them may be poorly communicated.

When we need information about the actual performance this can be collected in several ways. For example, through:

- Personal files.
- Time sheets.
- Sickness and absence records.
- Record cards.
- Customer complaints.
- Inaccurate work.
- Mistakes.
- Colleagues.
- Comparison with other people's work.
- Unfinished work.

After looking at what is expected and what has actually been done the question is whether there is sufficient gap between the two to require attention.

If a gap is established the next task is to find the *reason for the gap*. Only by finding the reason, or reasons, for the gap can we begin to do something about it. There are three main types of reason for poor performance. First, are personal reasons that arise from the person's domestic and individual circumstances outside the organisation's control. The main issue is how long and to what extent do we allow the personal problems to interfere with work. Second, are reasons to do with poor management and organisation. Third, there are individual reasons that arise from the person not fitting in with the organisation. (See Box 9.2.)

Having established the gap in performance and found the reasons for it we are in a better position to do the important management work which is to *do something about it.* Usually having established some of the reasons these will give us starting points for dealing with them. There are some other starting points given in Box 9.3. Whatever the starting point, there is a need to discuss the problem performance with the individual concerned and a coun-

Box 9.2
Reasons for poor performance.

Personal characteristics

- Intellectual ability inappropriate due to poor selection or changes.
- Lack of emotional stability due to poor selection or changes.
- Poor physical ability which may change with age or job changes.
- Health problems.
- Domestic circumstances such as child care, parents or partner.
- Family break-up.

Organisational characteristics

- Assignment and job impossible to do or understand.
- Lack of suitable planning in touch with reality.
- Job changes do not make sense to the individual.
- Pay felt to be too low or poorly administered.
- Poor investment in equipment.
- Inadequate training.
- Inappropriate levels of discipline, too excessive or too lenient.
- Poor management – an individual poor manager or a poor management system.
- Physical conditions distract from the performance if they are irritating.
- Location and transport problems when relocated.

Individual characteristics

- Group dynamics where someone does not fit in and is made not to fit in.
- Personality clash usually means one of the other reasons though we all feel this clash occasionally.
- Sense of fair play abused when different views on the right way to do or say things occurs.
- Conflict of religious or moral values.
- Inappropriate levels of confidence – both over- and under-confident.
- Poor motivation although usually this really is a symptom of some of the other reasons given.
- Poor understanding of the job despite everyone's best effort.

Box 9.3
Ways of dealing with poor performance. (Source: Torrington and Weightman (1991).)

The following are not given in order of execution but as starting points to assist thinking when a problem arises.

- *Goal setting*. Jointly agree specific, reasonable goals, and a date to review the performance.
- *Training*. Make sure you give appropriate training, preferably on the job, so there is no problem in making the connection between the training and the working situation.
- *Dissatisfactions*. Fill the gap where appropriate; remedy particular problems such as pay or conditions.
- *Discipline*. Measures range from the informal discussion through to increasingly formal procedures and punishment ultimately including dismissal.
- *Reorganising*. This can be helpful where the problem has arisen through difficulties with the work materials, reporting relationships; physical arrangements being no longer adequately organised.
- *Management*. Improve the clarity of communicating the task, the monitoring systems or the expertise of a particular manager.
- *Outside agencies*. Particularly appropriate where there are personal and family reasons.
- *The job*. Transfer to a more appropriate job or department; redesign the job.
- *Peer pressure*. Where an individual performance is very different from the average, those working alongside will feel it inappropriate and may put pressure on the individual to change.

selling interview technique based on problem solving would be appropriate (see Pause for thought, p. 152).

DID YOU KNOW?
The red hot stove rule was originally advanced by the American Douglas McGregor, who likened effective discipline to the touching of a red hot stove:

- *The burn is immediate; so there is no question of cause and effect.*
- *There was warning; the stove was red hot, and you knew what would happen if you touched it.*
- *It is consistent; everyone touching the stove is burned.*
- *It is impersonal; you get burned, not because of who you are, but because of what you have done.*

Conclusion

This chapter about performance management has inevitably had a more managerial feel to it than some of the others. (After all it has management in the title!) The whole question of the right to manage someone else's performance, when and how can be questioned. The contract of employment and how this is interpreted is at the heart of this relationship. Understanding performance management and some of the associated issues is important for analysing organisational behaviour.

A related area to performance management is that of what task or job is actually given to individuals. This is dealt with in Chapter 13.

EXERCISE **9.1**

The mini appraisal interview

Give each person a copy of the following document and group into pairs, calling yourselves A and B (or possibly threes, A, B and C). Alternative topics to 'Last week' could be: liaising with other courses, coordinating with other activities, fitting assignments in. Ideally the topic should suit the person.

Document

The subject for this interview is Last week. You may look at all the work of last week or some part of it.

1. A interviews B for information about their week (15 minutes).
2. B interviews A for information about their week (15 minutes).
3. A and B prepare for feedback and discussion (15 minutes).
4. B conducts appraisal interview with A about the week (30 minutes).
5. A conducts appraisal interview with B about the week (30 minutes).
6. A and B discuss with each other what they liked and disliked about the process.

Points to remember:

- The first interview is about information gathering – you might use some of the ideas explored in Pause for thought on page 152.
- The second interview is for feedback. This should include looking for good practice. Only criticise those things that can be changed.

A final discussion among all the group could focus on the various issues that have developed such as:

- How useful was it to talk about your work?
- How useful was the feedback?
- What would make the feedback have greater usefulness?
- Was the credibility of the 'appraiser' important?

Self-check questions

1. What is meant by the psychological contract between an employer and an employee?
2. Is job satisfaction an indication of job performance?
3. What is MBO?
4. What are the normal stages of performance management?
5. Isn't all pay for performance?
6. Who might be involved in measuring performance?
7. Why might managers want to appraise their staff?

CASE STUDY **9.1**

The people manager as performance manager

Phillipa is the clinical nurse specialist for critical care in a large teaching hospital. She has been in the post for a year having come from another hospital outside the area. She found a hard-working group of 81 nurses and technicians in place when she came who had in many cases worked in these wards for as long as 20 years. Most of the nurses are on high grades to reflect their professional skills. There is a constant flow of new techniques and technology coming on stream in this department. Phillipa wants to discuss with her staff the changes they are having to deal with and prioritise the development of each of them. The unit is rather isolated geographically from the rest of the hospital and by their own admission is élitist. Phillipa wants to find some way of getting all the staff to work together despite the problems of shifts, nights, part-timers and professional commitments. She also wants to tackle some of the interpersonal difficulties which arise when there are shortages of staff through illness.

What would you do in her position?

References

Connock S. and Johns T. (1995) *Ethical Leadership.* IPD, London.

Drucker P.F. (1989) *The Practice of Management.* Heinemann Professional, London. (This includes reference to his earlier 1954 work.)

Fletcher C. (1997) *Appraisal: Routes to Improved Performance,* 2nd edn. IPD, London.

Foot M. and Hook C. (1996) *Introducing Human Resource Management* Addison Wesley Longman, Harlow.

George J. (1986) Appraisal in the public sector: dispensing with the big stick. *Personnel Management,* May, 32–5.

Hendry C., Bradley P. and Perkins S. (1997) Missed a motivator? *People Management,* 15 May, 20–5.

Kane J.S. and Freeman K.A. (1986) MBO and performance appraisal: a mixture that's not a solution. *Personnel,* vol. 63, no. 12, December 26–36.

Kanter R.M. (1989) *When Giants Learn to Dance.* Unwin, London.

Kay J. (1993) *Foundations of Corporate Success: How Business Strategies Add Value.* Oxford University Press, Oxford.

Kessler I. (1995) *Reward Systems in Human Resource Management: A Critical Text.* J. Storey (Ed.) Routledge, London.

Luthans F. (1992) *Organisational Behaviour,* 6th edn. McGraw Hill, New York, NY.

McGregor D. (1960) *The Human Side of Enterprise.* McGraw Hill, New York, NY.

Torrington D. and Weightman J. (1991) *Action Management.* IPD, London.

Weightman J., Blandamer W. and Torrington D. (1991) *Pay Structures and Negotiating Arrangements.* Report for The North Western Regional Health Authority.

Woodrufe C. (1994) *Assessment Centres,* 2nd edn. IPD, London.

Further reading

Current practice is often discussed in the management pages of the *Financial Times* and other broadsheet newspapers. Look at current personnel journals such as *People Management* from IPD for specific examples of current practice. Also, any Human Resource Management textbook will have material on this, for example, the sister volume to this title by Foot and Hook (1996) mentioned above.

There are several videos in this area you might like to try:

- *The whole picture – 360 degree appraisal.* Four case studies such as ICL and Thomas Cook, from the Industrial Society (1997).
- *Coaching for improved performance at work.* Case studies such as NatWest and easyJet from the Industrial Society (1997).

These can be hired by the day.

CHAPTER 10

Development

Objectives

When you have finished reading this chapter you should be able to:

- Discuss the pressure on British organisations to increase training of their staff.
- Discuss some of the different assumptions that can be made about training, education and development.
- Describe the use of a competency approach.
- Describe different ways of training.
- Suggest different levels of evaluating development.
- Understand what lifelong learning and personal development is.

Introduction

Training and developing staff is seen as an important part of work organisations. However, finding the time and the money to pay for resources can be tricky. So why bother? There seems a wide consensus in Britain that training is a good thing. It is certainly felt to be at the heart of dealing with change. The government exhorts us to train through initiatives such as National Vocational Qualifications (NVQs) and Investors in People (IIP). Employers organisations see training as the way to upgrade the skills of the workforce to take on new technologies and challenges from overseas. Trade unions see training and development as the way forward for members to keep jobs. All agree that encouraging people to undertake training and development is one of the main tasks for British organisations. This may be the induction and training of a junior, the developing of an experienced member of staff or the switching on of a jaded member of staff to adapt to the changes sweeping through the organisation.

The argument goes that the best way of dealing with the demand for constant change that is currently experienced in most organisations is to become an active learner. This has led to an increasing emphasis at work on training. Where there are professional trainers involved there is likely to be an emphasis on systematic training. This system has an in-built logic to it, it is advocated by the Department of Employment and is called the systematic training cycle. In this approach identifying what needs training is carefully analysed before training is planned; carrying out the training and then evaluating the whole process completes the cycle. This approach clearly fits the use of competencies as they can be used for identifying the training needs and evaluating any improved performance. This cycle requires time and careful monitoring so presumes, in practice, a training specialist or department to carry it out.

Not all organisations have such training departments and there can be a wide range of development opportunities available in different organisations. Like most other organisational behaviours, developing is contingent on the specific circumstances of the individual person and the organisation they find themselves working in.

The national scene

Increasing competitive pressures, particularly from overseas international companies, are forcing firms to adopt market strategies with an increased emphasis on product quality and customer-focused products. The increased internal competition and the threat of takeovers has had a similar effect. Resulting production techniques with their increased worker discretion, management structures which are flatter and increased decentralisation all highlight the importance of skills and competencies in the workplace. They also raise questions about how adequate current arrangements are to generate these skills and competencies. The technology changes of recent years have also required rapid retraining of individuals. The changes in employment patterns have meant that government felt the need to do something about the employability of those caught up in this restructuring. Add to this pressure from the EU to make qualifications equivalent so that workers can cross borders to work more easily and you have quite a lot of pressure for a formal, central, government-controlled, system of qualifications. The UK traditionally had quite an informal system.

DID YOU KNOW?

In Spain when electrical work is done in a house the electrician issues a certificate that they have done the work and that it is safe. Only those with suitable qualifications can get and issue these certificates. In the UK there are electricians working with varying levels of qualifications including those with no formal qualifications; and no certificate of safe installation is expected or given. Although they can be prosecuted if they ignore the regulations concerning electricity in the bathroom.

Three enduring government training initiatives are:

- NETTs – National and Educational Training Targets which are set nationally for young people and adults. It is assumed that employers will play a large part in this through IIP.
- IIP – Investors in People is a government scheme to acknowledge organisations that comply with various systematic training approaches such as identifying training needs, recording these and giving opportunities for development.
- NVQs – National Vocational Qualifications are a framework designed by each industry to focus on the skills and knowledge used in particular jobs. Within the framework there will be jobs at differing levels of responsibility and complexity. Level 1 is foundation and level 5 is senior management. These are not universally approved of as some see them as the lowest common factor in training standards and there has certainly been a lot of debate about the nature of the standards that make up the qualifications, not least in the arguments over the management standards.

Organisations' approaches to development

Organisations differ in the assumptions they make about education, training and the development of the people working in the organisation. Several writers, such as Handy (1989) and Reid and Barrington (1997), discuss the nature of education and training at work. Some organisations and their managers define education very narrowly to include only formal qualifications whereas others take education to mean the widest possible development of individuals through values and opinions. There can be differences in the assumptions about both the purposes and the methods of development.

One distinction that is frequently used is between training and education. Reid *et al* (1992) suggest that education and training can normally be distinguished by the following;

- Objectives – training can be expressed in behavioural terms whereas education tends to be put in more general abstract terms.
- Time – training plans tend to be shorter than education's plans.
- Methods and content – training usually involves mechanistic techniques of stimulus, response and practice whereas education involves more organic learning methods.
- Context – if it is to do with work it has traditionally been called training whereas study away from the workplace was education, even where the very same learning was taking place.

Increasingly the word development is used to describe both education and training at work.

So what influences the assumptions that organisations make about training and development at work? Some of the influences are:

- The underlying political view of the government, the employer and the individual.
- People's expectations about access to development opportunities.
- What obligation the learner has to the provider of the development opportunity.
- The power of the gatekeepers, such as trade unions and professional bodies, to entry and status within a given trade or profession.
- The relative stability of occupations.
- The scale of unemployment.
- Who is considered responsible for funding the development.
- Whether the development is highly specific or a transferable attribute.
- The speed and level of new technology.
- The expense of providing the development opportunity.
- Whether certain groups of people are to be specifically targeted.

Each of these influences can vary, so any one person in a particular organisation can have quite different development opportunities from another person in a different organisation. For example, if you work in a well-established large organisation that operates in a stable environment there will be long-established skills that you will be expected to acquire in a 'conventional' way. If, on the other hand, you are at the leading edge of development in a newly established organisation you are likely to be expected to see to your own development as and when it becomes necessary.

PAUSE FOR THOUGHT

The quandary is that learning and development is necessary for change so by its very nature it will sometimes question and undermine the very philosophy that set up the training in the first place.

How the differing factors listed above are put together leads to various different philosophies of development. Reid *et al* (1992) distinguish the following differing philosophic views of training:

- Élitism – has its roots in long-established patterns of provision over long periods of time. Training is reserved for high status work and was the dominant view throughout the UK till the 1960s.
- Voluntarism – the onus is on individuals to seek out, and pay for their own development in their own time. This often results in organisations not knowing who can do what and staff leaving when they have become qualified through 'night school'.
- Centralism and authoritarianism – this is where training is imposed by a personnel or training department after identifying training needs using the authority of top management. The so-called systematic approach that is very commonly described in textbooks falls into this category.
- Conformism and non-conformism – the development of national vocational qualifications (NVQs) to which individuals conform is an example of such a philosophy where the government felt there was a need to set some central targets.
- Humanism – this view gives the learner centre stage with what they want to learn and how. Many management consultants run such sessions where there is no agenda for a two-day conference and people are encouraged to set their own agenda.
- Continuous development – is currently in favour with training people, personnel practitioners and writers in this area. It assumes that learning should be endless for all as the world is changing so fast.

We might also add the traditional approach of sending the 'spare body' who is sitting around on a course, irrespective of need.

DID YOU KNOW?

BICC Cables when closing their Wakefield plant offered all the employees the chance to get their skills accredited on NVQ to help them get new jobs. This included the variety of experience gained over the years using different technical and personal skills. Many were surprised how well qualified they were when their skills were analysed and accredited.

Competencies

One particular approach to development that is widely used, and increasingly so, is the competency approach. Essentially, competencies underlie the behaviours thought necessary to achieve a desired outcome. A competency is something you can demonstrate, for example, driving a car or slicing bread, where it is clear when the behaviour has been successful. These in turn can be broken down into smaller steps, when the overall competency is too difficult to achieve in one go. Not all necessary work behaviours are easy to describe and analyse. Many of the most useful involve subtle application and experience to achieve. Where general statements of competency are wanted and these reflect higher-order attributes, competency lists include knowledge, understanding and personal attributes to temper the strictly behavioural descriptions of simpler competencies.

This competency-based learning has been well established for learning technical skills over a long period. Just think of all those practical periods for scientists and engineers! However, this approach has increasingly been taken on by top management to look at core competencies as part of strategic thinking, personnel departments to improve recruitment and training and by individuals as a base for establishing and demonstrating their expertise.

Core competencies are defined by Prahalad and Hamel (1990) in a very influential paper as the combination of individual technologies and production skills that underlie a company's myriad product lines. For example Sony's core competence is miniaturisation, which allows them to make everything from Walkmans to video cameras to notebook computers. These core competencies explain the ease with which successful companies are able to enter new, and seemingly unrelated businesses. The process of identifying core competencies is a strategic issue and outside the domain of this book. However, in many organisations some of the core competencies of the organisation are individually controlled. For example, hospital departments rely on the reputation of particular consultants to attract patients. Similarly hairdressing salons rely on particular stylists and restaurants on chefs for their reputation. This dependence is often reflected in contracts which forbid individuals who leave practising their trade within several miles of their previous employment. Some manufacturing organisations are also finally beginning to realise their dependence on technically competent individuals and are introducing reward systems of pay and status commensurate with management scales for technical people. Competencies are discussed further on page 77 and in Weightman (1994).

ACTIVITY **10.1**

Here are two lists of competencies required for particular groups. The first, Box 10.1, was for heads of department in secondary schools. The second, Box 10.2, was for personnel managers in health establishments. Both were developed during periods of rapid change for the organisations following political decisions about local management taking over from national directives so increasing the management responsibility of professionals.

Have a look at each of these and ask how easy would it be to assess people against these lists. Is there anything surprising about these lists?

Deciding what skills to train and develop

The technical skills associated with training systematically are increasingly described in terms of identifying the competencies required; measuring the competencies of the post holders; identifying training needs and then develop-

Box 10.1

Core competencies for Heads of Departments in secondary schools in one LEA.

1 Vision

- (a) Ability to seek goals and desire appropriate objectives.
- (b) Able to perform beyond the immediate needs of the situation.
- (c) Able to predict the need for appropriate tasks.
- (d) Producing original, expressive or imaginative responses to tasks.
- (e) Able to demonstrate an awareness of value dimensions and preparedness to challenge assumptions.

2 Planning skills

- (a) Able to forward plan to meet a target.
- (b) Able to judge a range of alternative strategies before implementing a plan.
- (c) Able to be aware of appropriate timescale.
- (d) Ability to prioritise.
- (e) Ability to analyse into discrete elements.
- (f) Ability to sequence appropriate strategies.
- (g) Ability to take account of the need for contingency plans.
- (h) Ability to develop detailed and logically sequenced plans to accomplish goals.

3 Critical thinking

- (a) Ability to think analytically and systematically.
- (b) Ability to apply concepts and principles to a problem.
- (c) Ability to differentiate between intuitive and analytical thinking.
- (d) Lateral thinking.

4 Leadership skill

- (a) Ability to direct the actions of others towards an agreed goal.
- (b) Structuring interaction to the purposes in hand.
- (c) Arranging the effective deployment of resources.
- (d) Willingness to accept responsibility:
  - (i) for the actions of others
  - (ii) for the achievements of goals.
- (e) Ability to act decisively in appropriate situations.

5 Persistence

- (a) Preparedness to make use of a range of strategies to achieve a problem solution.
- (b) Ability to demonstrate a commitment to task completion.
- (c) Ability to recognise when circumstances require a flexible response.

6 Influence skills

- (a) Ability to have an impact on others by action or example.
- (b) Ability to get others involved in the processes of management.
- (c) Persuading staff to balance individual needs and institutional requirements.
- (d) Persuading others to consider a wide range of options.
- (e) Able to negotiate effectively.
- (f) Ability to use a wide range of strategies to obtain agreement.

7 Interpersonal relationships

- (a) Ability to establish and maintain positive relationships.
- (b) Ability to perceive the needs, concerns and personal circumstances of others.
- (c) Able to recognise and resolve conflict.
- (d) Able to use effective listening skills.
- (e) Able to notice, interpret and respond to non-verbal behaviour.
- (f) Able to make effective use of a range of oral and written communication skills.
- (g) Ability to give appropriate feedback in a sensitive manner.

8 Self-confidence

- (a) Able to feel assured about personal ability and judgement.
- (b) Ability to demonstrate assertive behaviour without generating hostility.
- (c) Ability to seek and accept feedback about personal performance and management style.
- (d) Able to offer a challenge to others in order to enhance their self-confidence.

9 Development

- (a) Able to actively find ways of enhancing self-knowledge.
- (b) Able to demonstrate an understanding of learning style (in self and others).
- (c) Able to actively seek opportunities to enhance growth in self and others.
- (d) Ability to assess development needs.
- (e) Ability to design, implement and evaluate development programmes.
- (f) Able to implement a positive climate conducive to growth and development.

10 Empathy

- (a) Ability to demonstrate awareness of the needs of the group.
- (b) Ability to demonstrate awareness of the needs of an individual.
- (c) Ability to listen and communicate in a constructive manner.
- (d) Able to indicate sensitivity to the implications of decisions (for others).

11 Stress tolerance

- (a) Able to demonstrate appropriate behaviour in stressful circumstances.
- (b) Able to demonstrate resilience in pressure situations.
- (c) Able to remain effective in a range of working situations.
- (d) Able to retain a balance between priorities.
- (e) Able to take into account level of stress in others.

Box 10.2
Job composite model of competencies. (Source: Torrington, Waite and Weightman (1992).)

Name .... Date ....

Current post ....

Using the job composite model of personnel competencies, complete the following checklist by assessing your present expertise in each of the following competencies as either A, B, C, D or E, indicating:

A Little or no expertise.
B Some expertise, but a need for further development or updating now.
C Expert.
D Considerable expertise, but some further development or updating necessary soon.
E Not relevant to the present post.

Professional competencies

1 *The Personnel Manager (PM) as selector*
.... Vacancy identification
.... Job analysis
.... Recruitment advertising
.... Selection process
.... Psychometric testing
.... Selection decision making
.... Letters of offer
.... Contracts of employment
.... Employee records
.... Induction/socialisation

2 *The PM as paymaster*
.... Job evaluation
.... Pay determination
.... Employee benefits
.... Performance related pay
.... Salary administration
.... Salary structures
.... Pensions and sick pay
.... Taxation and National Insurance

3 *The PM as negotiator*
.... Consultation
.... Employee involvement
.... Negotiating bodies
.... Trade union recognition
.... Agreements and procedures
.... Grievance and discipline
.... Redundancy and dismissal
.... Industrial tribunals

4 *The PM as performance monitor*
.... Appraisal/assessment
.... Attendance management
.... Management of poor performance

5 *The PM as welfare officer*
.... Health and safety
.... Counselling services
.... Occupational health
.... Health and safety legislation

6 *The PM as human resource planner*
.... Supply and demand forecasting
.... Modelling and extrapolation
.... Manpower utilisation
.... Planning
.... Statistical method
.... Computer analysis

7 *The PM as trainer*
.... Identification of training needs
.... Design of training
.... Delivery of training
.... Evaluation of training

8 *The PM as communicator*
.... Bulletins
.... Community relations
.... Team briefing
.... In-house magazines

Generic competencies

9 *Managing oneself*
.... Personal organisation
.... Time management
.... Interpersonal communication
.... Assertiveness
.... Problem solving and decision making
.... Report writing
.... Reading
.... Presentations
.... Managing stress

10 *Working in the organisation*
.... Networking
.... Working in groups
.... Power and authority
.... Influencing
.... Negotiating

11 *Getting things done*
.... Setting objectives
.... Goal planning and target setting
.... Managing external consultants
.... Using statistics
.... Information technology literacy
.... Keyboard skills
.... Minute-taking
.... Record keeping
.... Setting up systems and procedures

12 *Working with people*
.... Interviewing
.... Listening
.... Counselling
.... Conducting and participating in meetings
.... Team building

ing those competencies which are less well developed. This is the most systematic way to decide what needs developing. Comparing the planned needs of the department with the assessed competencies of the people in the department and attending to the difference between these is an ideal few organisations achieve. Reality, fortunately, is never quite as mechanical as that!

Training needs are commonly identified in the following ways:

- At appraisal sessions when the manager and the individual discuss what training would be appropriate over the next year to help improve and develop the individual's contribution and career prospects.
- As a result of changes that the department is taking on and which may involve a training and development programme for the whole department.
- At the instigation of the individual who wants to improve and develop their abilities either for current work or for career purposes.
- As part of the systematic progress of induction and initial training of new members of staff.
- As part of a recovery programme after the identification of poor performance of an individual or group.

These training needs can be skills, knowledge or understanding. Increasingly they are expressed in competency terms.

Lists of competencies appropriate for a particular job, profession or qualification can be drawn up by analysing and describing the behaviours and associated activities necessary to do specific aspects of the job. To this list is added the other behaviours that are likely to be required in the foreseeable future. Then appropriate assessment procedures can be devised for individuals to be assessed for selection, qualification, training and development purposes. Training specialists have led the way in the use of these competency lists. Implicit in the whole competency approach is that the line manager is really involved in ensuring that those people they manage are given appropriate opportunities to develop their competencies.

With a list of the competencies required in the job and a measure of the competencies of the post holder made, a comparison between the two can be made and the areas for development or training needs identified. Then a programme of development can be agreed for the following period.

DID YOU KNOW?

Beeton Rumford Catering, part of P&O, have 105 full-time workers and 500 temporary staff. They decided in 1995 to eradicate the casual ethos of the temporary workers by training and developing them in the same areas as the full-timers and developing a six-tier career structure for temporary staff. They also had a pool of 200 of these temps who would not be laid off at 24 hours notice. The hope is that by making this commitment the temporary staff would show more commitment in return.

ACTIVITY **10.2**

Think back to a work experience you have had, or currently are having, and answer the following questions:

- How were training needs identified?
- Did they leave it up to individuals to volunteer for training or was there another method as well?

- What opportunities for development on the job did they encourage?
- Had they started using a competency approach?
- Should they?

Deciding how to train and develop

Having decided what needs training and developing the next question is how to go about it. Like most decisions in organisations those about training and development have to be made on the basis of resources and opportunities available. There is no point in planning a perfect but impracticable programme. This pragmatism also needs to be applied to what makes sense. There is absolutely no point in sending someone off on a long course if there is no prospect of them implementing the newly learnt skills when they come back. Equally, there is no point in trying to learn a new technique at work where the equipment to put it into operation does not exist. There is also a cultural aspect to this decision making. In more centralised organisations staff are told what they need to learn and are given training experiences to deliver this, whereas more self-managing organisations will expect the staff to identify their own learning priorities and find the resources available to achieve them.

A lot of different methods for training and development do exist and I have included a brief description, in alphabetical order, of some of the more common ways of training and developing people's competencies and some of the associated advantages and disadvantages.

Acting up

Acting up is doing a more senior job temporarily to cover for absence or vacancy, for example, maternity leave. It gives an individual the opportunity to broaden their experience and skill within a position of greater responsibility. The difficulty can be that returning to the original post after the acting up period is difficult and this re-entry needs sympathetic managing by the returning senior post holder.

An example is the catering manager acting up for the hotel services director while he or she is off work having a major operation.

Action learning

This involves the linking of a real, structured task and action within the learning process using action learning sets. Action learning sets are groups of people who discuss the problems associated with the task using an identified facilitator. It can be difficult to keep the group on the task as individuals develop, but it is a technique found particularly useful by senior staff who enjoy being part of a group as they can feel very isolated.

An example was a group of six personnel directors from two regional health authorities who came together to develop a personnel auditing form. The six originally met on a course and continued meeting infrequently with a facilitator over two years to complete the task.

Audio-visual presentations

These include slides, films and video. The technique is similar to a lecture in what it can achieve but video has an advantage over the lecture as it can be stopped and started as required and be taken home to study at leisure.

An example are the numerous videos promoting new techniques and apparatus made by companies to market their products. Similarly many journals now present their material on tape so they can be listened to in the car on the way to work.

Case study

This is where a history of some event is given and the trainees are invited to analyse the causes of a problem or to find a solution. This provides an opportunity for a cool look at problems and for the exchange of ideas about possible solutions. However, trainees may not realise that the real world is not quite the same as the training session.

An example is the use made of case studies for business development and taking on financial control. This might include such things as the position of British supermarkets faced with low cost competition from abroad in the early 1990s and how they coped.

Coaching

This is improving the performance of someone who is already competent rather than establishing competency in the first place. It is usually done on a one-to-one basis, is set in the everyday working situation and is a continuing activity. It is gently nudging people to improve their performance, to develop their skills and to increase their self-confidence so that they can take more responsibility for their own work and develop their career prospects. Most coaching is done by the more senior person but the subordinate position of the person coached is by no means a prerequisite. What is essential is that the coach should have the qualities of expertise, judgement and experience that make it possible for the person coached to follow the guidance.

An example can be found in almost any contact between professionals. Just think of some of the best interactions between solicitors and barristers and their juniors.

Delegation

Delegation is not just giving out jobs to do – it is giving people the scope, responsibility and authority to do it in their own way. It allows individuals to test their own ideas, develop understanding and confidence. This is often called empowerment. The more specific the instructions and terms of reference, the less learning will be managed as a result of the activity. With the assignment delegated, the individual starts to work on their own. The decision about when to seek guidance and discussion on progress from the manager is also in their own hands.

An example would be the director of estates handing over a portfolio of buildings to a junior who is given the autonomy, and budget, to decide how to maintain these buildings.

Discussion

This is where knowledge, ideas and opinions on a subject are exchanged between trainees and trainer. This is particularly suitable where the application is a matter of opinion, for changing attitudes and finding out how knowledge is going to be applied. The technique requires skill on the part of the trainer as it can be difficult to keep discussion focused or useful.

One example was the staff of a specialist department who at the end of a day's training about performance appraisal discussed with the trainer and the senior staff how to go forward with an action plan.

Distance learning

This method involves the individual utilising a range of printed, audio-visual and other teaching materials outside the traditional course environment. It is self-learning and requires high levels of personal discipline and can be difficult to sustain in isolation.

The Open University is probably the best known example.

Empowerment

See Delegation above and Chapter 8.

Exercise

This is where the trainees do a particular task, in a particular way, to get a particular result. This is suitable when trainees need practice in following a specific procedure or formula to reach a required objective. The exercise must be realistic.

Most of us have had to do exercises to master the latest technology such as PCs, faxes, answerphones and video.

Group dynamics

Using this method, trainees are put in situations where their behaviour is examined. The task given usually requires them to cooperate before they can achieve the goal. Observers collect information about how the trainees go about this and then give feedback to the group and the individuals after the task is completed. Trainees learn about the effect they have on others. This may be threatening and anxieties need to be resolved before the end of the session. This sort of developing is very dependent on the quality of the trainer and can be dangerous if entered into too casually. Usually the task is relatively remote from work.

The most common types of example are outdoor activity centres with their courses on leadership for managers.

Job rotation

In job rotation individuals do different jobs within the section or organisation over a period of time. By setting up flexible working patterns within the organisation, individuals can be facilitated to broaden their experience and skills. The disadvantage can be the loss of highly specialised staff and their commitment to ensuring that things are right.

One example is the operators on a chemical plant who rotate on all parts of the plant from managing the raw materials, making the product, sampling for quality control and checking the final packaging and labelling.

Learning contracts

These are usually agreed between an individual, their boss and whoever is providing the learning experience. They specify what learning opportunities are expected, when these will occur and what outcomes are expected. The aim is to ensure everyone agrees and the individual is then expected to monitor their own performance against this contract. Contracts can also be used in conjunction with informal learning and to generate learning opportunities at work.

Second year care students from a Further Education college had contracts agreed between the student, tutors and the residential homes they were going to for work experience placements.

Learning opportunities

Many opportunities come up in the normal working environment which can be used to develop oneself or others. Look around and see what already exists before using time-consuming outside opportunities. The difficulty is that these can be missed or by concentrating on the learning, the task is not carried out as efficiently.

Walking the floor is classically a way managers learn about what are current concerns in their patch, they can also pick up on new ways of working and the relationships that exist in the department. By using these to ensure that individuals learn how to be more effective useful development takes place.

Lectures

A lecture is a talk given without much participation by the trainees. The method is suitable for large audiences where the information to be got over can be worked out precisely in advance. There is little opportunity for feedback, so some in the audience may not get the point. It requires careful preparation and should never be longer than 40 minutes.

A lecture on development and training to first year students at a university is an obvious example.

On the job

With this method, trainees work in the real environment with support from a skilled person. This gives the trainee real practice and it does not involve expensive new equipment. However, not all skilled people are skilled trainers. The essential ingredients are briefing, feedback and support that help the individual to achieve the objectives in a structured way.

A new business manager was in the office for two weeks before the old business manager moved to a new job. This overlap meant a smoother handover of procedures and commitments, and provided an example of on the job training.

Programmed instruction

This can also be called Computer Assisted Learning (CAL). Trainees work at their own pace using a book or computer program which has a series of tasks and tests geared to teaching something systematically. It is suitable for learning logical skills and knowledge. However, it does not allow for discussion with others which may be important where the application is debatable.

Examples are libraries with programs on how to use their services, and there are several on how to work out budgets, taxes and business planning.

Project

This is similar to an exercise but a project allows greater freedom to display initiative and creativity. They can allow feedback to be given on a range of personal qualities as well as technical abilities. They need the full commitment and cooperation of the trainee and specific terms of reference.

The Royal College of Nursing's Institute for Advanced Nurse Education management students have projects as part of several modules. These are expected to be work-based and practical and usually are an opportunity for doing a more detailed study of something that needs to be done anyway, such as a business plan for a new development within the unit.

Role play

In this training method people are asked to act the role they, or someone else, would play at work. It is particularly used for training for face-to-face situations and is suitable for near real-life situations where criticism would be useful. The difficulties are that people can be embarrassed and the usefulness of the exercise is very dependent on the nature of the feedback given.

An example are the staff on an appraisal workshop who practised interviewing each other using different techniques. They then role played by conducting a mini-appraisal interview about each other's work in the previous week.

Secondment

This involves organising a placement in an alternative department or organisation for the achievement of a specific purpose. It is often used for management and professional development. The individual may, of course, choose not to come back!

An example is a researcher from the laboratories who covers for a maternity leave in the manufacturing plant for six months.

Simulation

This training method involves the use of mock-ups of real life situations and equipment. It gives people experience before they encounter the real thing. It can be used for initial training, updating, keeping in practice or introducing new techniques. The expense of creating a realistic mock-up is really only justified where practising on the real thing is totally impossible or a mistake would be catastrophic. The increasing sophistication of computer graphics have enabled all sorts of simulations and 'virtual reality' to be created for workplace training and development to take place.

Obvious examples are the computer simulators used for pilot training, cadavers for medical students and mock battles for the military. However, the increased use of 'virtual reality' may make this an increasingly accessible training methodology.

Sitting by Nellie

This is where the new person sits by an experienced person to see what they do and slowly learns all the little tricks of the trade as well as the main task. It is much derided as being unsystematic and dependent on the observer knowing what they are looking for. It does, however, pass on the little bits of experience that never get formalised.

Current examples can be found in abundance in the way most of us learn the little short-cuts on our computers.

Skill instruction

Here the trainee is told how to do it, shown how to do it and then does it under supervision. This is suitable for putting across skills, as long as the task is broken into suitable parts. What is considered suitable parts will vary with the task and the person receiving the training. Breaking things down into small steps is not suitable for all skills as some are better learned as a whole.

Any of the mechanical skills would be a good example here, such as learning how to put on a car exhaust, how to service machines or stripping down the airconditioning in a building.

Talk

A talk allows participation by the trainees, by asking them questions or inviting questions from them. It is useful for getting over new ways of looking at things which involve abstraction. It is appropriate for up to 20 people. It can only be used where people are willing or able to participate. Where people do not want to participate it becomes a lecture.

Examples are when ideas about management or the future are being explored. Management consultants usually report their findings to the board by giving a presentation and then individuals ask questions and test out their understanding of the findings.

ACTIVITY **10.3**

- Which of the above would be best suited to short-term (less than six months) training and development?
- Which would be better suited to longer-term goals?
- Which of the methods are appropriate for introducing new working practices where everyone needs to do it?
- Which methods require a degree of self-confidence and motivation?
- Which methods would you find it easy to resource and which require major expenditure?

Evaluating development

If organisations and people are to spend time, effort and money on training and development it is important to evaluate whether it really has been useful. 'Validation' is the word used to describe the process of seeing whether the training and development has achieved its objectives and 'evaluation' is the process of ascertaining whether the training has affected the performance of the job. It may be that the outward-bound leadership course has met all the objectives (validation), but we cannot see any change in performance at work (evaluation). Evaluation is much more difficult because of the problems of deciding, defining and measuring performance or competency. Hamblin (1974) suggests five levels at which evaluation may take place:

- Reaction – trainees give their personal view and impressions of the experience.
- Learning – the amount of learning is measured.
- Job behaviour – work behaviour is looked at six to nine months later to see if it has changed.
- Organisation – productivity, time taken to do things, absenteeism, turnover and labour costs are examined to see if there is a difference after the training.
- Ultimate level – the effect on profitability and growth over a period of years.

Normally, assessing the reaction of participants is the only evaluation done, with feedback given to the providers of the training or development. The cost of doing the others usually puts people off trying, particularly as it can become very time consuming. However, where a major investment in development is being made some of the longer-term evaluations do take place.

PAUSE FOR THOUGHT *Ask the following about any training you have been involved with, such as learning to drive a car, your current course or sports coaching.*

- *Which sort of evaluation was used?*
- *Would it be cost effective to do some more?*

Encouraging lifelong learning or lifetime personal development

Much of this chapter has been about the organisational approach to development but what about the individual in all this? As we discussed in Chapter 4

Figure 10.1 **Lifelong development.**

individuals are being encouraged by various government bodies, professions, employers and trade unions to see learning as a lifelong commitment. As we saw in Chapter 6 there is also increasing emphasis on individuals managing themselves rather than relying on their bosses to provide appropriate opportunities for learning and development. So what can the individual do?

First, there are the opportunities available in the normal working environment for learning and developing one's skills and knowledge. Taking on the challenge of the new task, making the presentation, answering the question when you are not absolutely sure will all give you experience, increase confidence and a certain amount of increased competence. Hanging back all the time from exposure to new ideas, experiences and technology means being one of the last to learn the new. Examples would be chairing the meeting when the chair is away, using the new software on the PC, helping the customer who phones up with a complaint rather then passing them on to someone else.

Second, there are the outside opportunities to keep up to date. Reading the relevant material in the papers, journals, e-mail and Internet will keep you up to date with advances in your field and current issues of concern. This reading should become an automatic part of any professional's working week, particularly those with a demand for CPD, see page 64. Similarly, there are outside networking opportunities for learning about the new such as conferences, symposia, shows and fairs. Many professional bodies and interest groups run these. Examples would be the local Institute of Personnel and Development monthly meetings or the yearly Royal Show for agricultural people.

Third, there is keeping in touch with how careers in your chosen profession are developing. For many this is done by signing on with one or two headhunters or recruitment agencies. For others it is done by looking in the relevant journals and newspapers to see what is currently on offer and what experience is being valued. Keeping your curriculum vitae (CV) up to date and suitably presented for when an opportunity comes up so that you are in a position to take it would seem sensible.

Fourth, choose to work for employers who will not only value your current contribution but assist your development through training and development plans such as IIP, see page 64. This is often referred to as a learning organisation and is further discussed in Chapter 14.

PAUSE FOR THOUGHT

Kanter (1989, p. 321) states:

> *If security comes from being employed, then it must come from being employable. In a post-entrepreneurial era in which corporations need flexibility to change and restructuring is a fact of life, the promise of very long-term employment security would be the wrong one to expect employers to make. But employability security – the knowledge that today's work will enhance the person's value in terms of future opportunities – that is a promise that can be made and kept. Employability security comes from the chance to accumulate human capital – skills and reputation – that can be invested in new opportunities as they arise.*

The individuals in organisations are increasingly asked to take on their own development and to seek opportunities for doing so. Individuals are also being encouraged to keep their own records of what they have actually done, records of achievement. These can be portfolios of events experienced, documents of work done and references of satisfied customers or they can be demonstrations of competencies. These records are useful for compiling CVs and for claiming competence at a later date.

Conclusion

The issue of development will always concern those analysing organisational behaviour. The balance between the interests of the individual and the organisation is perhaps the most critical. This 'contract' will vary depending on the relative interests, power and environment in which they find themselves. We will return to this topic in Chapter 14.

EXERCISE 10.1

Try justifying a skiing holiday, or some other activity holiday, in terms of the opportunities it gives for team building and developing the skills in a group of managers.

EXERCISE 10.2

Look at the list of training methods in this chapter. Judge which would best suit a Kolb learning cycle (see Chapter 4). Which would be useful for each of the CRAMP types of learning (see Chapter 4)?

Self-check questions

1. What are NVQs?
2. List six different views of training.
3. What are competencies?
4. How can training needs be identified?

5 What are the following:
   action learning
   learning contracts
   distance learning
   job rotation
   role play?
6 What is
   CPD
   IIP?

CASE STUDY 10.1 Particular individuals at work in a secondary school

1 Helen

Last year after completing her probationary year on a low timetable, Helen volunteered for all sorts of extra tasks including organising a day for the whole school on environmental issues. She was an active member of the school band and the school play and was always ready to see pupils at lunchtime and after school. She had volunteered for some of the more difficult year ten and eleven classes. We met her in her seventh term of teaching. She was having problems with the year ten group and a deputy head had taken the group over. She was now off work sick about 40 per cent of the time. She also complained of being tired and was seriously thinking of leaving the profession.

2 Gary

Gary is in his late twenties, teaching maths and computing. His enthusiasm for computing has led him to develop all sorts of systems for whole school use. He has a knack for seeing where computing can relieve teachers of day-to-day administrative tasks. The local authority and headteacher have introduced a new computing system into the school office and he was not involved at all. Gary cannot understand why with his experience and expertise he was not consulted. He has started putting satirical writing on the staff noticeboard and is becoming embittered.

3 Doreen

Doreen is head of house and teaches an 80 per cent timetable. Her lessons are constantly interrupted by the phone in her classroom or people coming in with messages about pupils in her house. She feels she is doing neither job properly and that somehow she is to blame for not being better organised. She looks very harassed and worn.

1 Why might a keen, lively, energetic teacher like Helen become tired and disillusioned so quickly?
2 Is there anything the school could have done to help?
3 How would you help Helen?
4 What would you do in Helen's position?

5 Do you agree with Gary's perception that he should have been consulted about the office system?
6 If not what could you do to persuade him?
7 What would you do to keep Gary involved in the school?
8 Why do you think Doreen found herself in such a situation?
9 Could it be anything to do with her personality?
10 Are there some sorts of people more likely to find themselves in this position than others?
11 How can Doreen's work be sorted out?

References

Bowden V. (1997) The career states system model: a new approach to analysing careers. *British Journal of Guidance and Counselling,* Vol. 25, No. 4, 473–90.
Hamblin A. (1974) *Evaluation and Control of Training.* McGraw Hill, London.
Handy C. (1989) *The Age of Unreason.* Business Books, London.
Kanter R.M. (1989) *When Giants Learn to Dance.* Simon and Schuster, London.
Prahalad C.K. and Hamel G. (1990) The core competence of the corporation. *Harvard Business Review,* March–April, 79–91.
Reid M.A., Barrington H. and Kenney J. (1992) *Training Intervention: Managing Employee Development,* 3rd edn. IPD, London.
Reid M.A. and Barrington H. (1997) *Training Interventions,* 5th edn. IPD, London.
Torrington D., Waite D. and Weightman J. (1992) A continuous development approach to training health service personnel specialists. *The Journal of European Industrial Training,* Vol. 16, No. 3, 3–12.
Weightman J. (1994) *Competencies in Action.* IPD, London.

Further reading

The Institute of Personnel and Development (IPD) have a large selection of books about training at work. I would suggest having a look at:

Reid and Barrington (1997) above – This has been the standard text in this area for a long time; good sensible stuff.

Harrison R. *Employee Development.* This is a detailed, well-thought-out text aimed at students specialising in this area. It covers both theory and practice with lots of examples.

Hackett P. (1997) *Introduction to Training.* This is probably the most accessible of the three but obviously has less detail.

Bee F. and Bee R. (1994) *Training Needs Analysis and Evaluation.* IPD, London.

I would also have a look at Handy C. (1997) *Understanding Organisations,* 3rd edn. Penguin, Harmondsworth. He has been very involved in influencing organisations to changing their attitudes to training and development particularly in respect to management development. He was at one time at the London Business School.

PART 3

Analysing the whole organisation

CHAPTER **11**

The organisational setting

Objectives

When you have read this chapter you should be able to:

- ➤ Describe several different ways of looking at organisational structure.
- ➤ Distinguish between power, role, task and people organisations.
- ➤ Understand the concept of organisational culture.
- ➤ Describe the context of organisations.
- ➤ Understand your own preferred style of organisation.

Introduction

Throughout this book I have referred to the organisation as if it existed as an entity, clearly this is not the case. An organisation is made up of the component parts of the individuals and groups that cooperate with each other and comply with implicit and/or explicit rules to try to achieve some common goal. Organisations vary enormously in their goals. They may be set up as profit making or non-profit making organisations. They may be in the public sector, privately owned or multinational. They may have very specific, focused aims or be general trading companies. The range of organisations is vast; is it any surprise that their setting and structures and cultures are equally varied? This chapter is about ways of analysing organisations as a whole and the different theories that can be applied to them.

PAUSE FOR THOUGHT

Most of us talk abut our work organisation as if it existed in its own right. You will here people say things like 'M & S have some wonderful foods' or 'The Prudential is very quiet at the moment' or 'Ford is coming up with something new, I wonder what it is'. One of my friends refers to his employer, Shell, as 'The mighty, yellow mollusc' such is the felt, strong identity of the organisation. This process of talking about organisations as if they were a person is technically called 'reification'. It certainly suggests that organisations are felt to exist and are not just a figment of the imagination.

Classic theories of organisational structure

The traditional way of analysing organisations is to look at the structures in the organisation. This means looking at who reports to whom and where decisions are made. This is usually described in the organisation chart, sometimes called an organigram. Organisation charts show how people relate to each other formally within the organisation and where decisions are expected to be made. How an organisation is structured can vary depending on such things as size, function and geographical distribution. So you will find one organisation with a structure of departments called sales, purchasing, personnel and manufacturing that is based on function. Another organisation will have departments based on Northern England, Southern England, Scotland, Wales, Western Europe and the rest of the world. There are all sorts of factors that can influence how an organisation is structured.

Theories of how organisations are, could or should be structured tend to concentrate on one of the following: task, technology, structure, people, management or context. Below is a quick review of how some of the classical studies of organisational behaviour can be fitted into these slightly different views of organisational structures. As many of the studies are discussed elsewhere in this book I have not given a detailed description of them here. The idea is really to remind you that the structure of organisations is influenced by a variety of factors and can be understood in many different ways.

Task efficiency

This is where the goals or objectives of the organisation are to the fore. The nature of the inputs, outputs and the transformation between them is the focus of theories here. Later theories of organisation developed from the early writing of Fayol and Urwick in this area. They were concerned with the process of organisation and sets of principles for increasing efficiency. For example, Fayol (1949) defined the five functions of management as planning, organising, co-ordinating, commanding and controlling. Another writer to focus on the structure of an organisation from this task perspective is Weber with his analysis of bureaucracy.

Technology

Under this heading we are looking at the way in which the task is carried out. The material, system, procedures and equipment used can affect the behaviours of people and so the structures of the organisation will be different. The early scientific management theories of Taylor (see Chapter 1) were developed by the systems theories which try to bring together previous understanding of the technical and social variables that affect behaviour within the organisation and how it affects the ability of people to get things done. Later systems theories were developed by the Tavistock researchers, for example Trist *et al* (1963) who looked at changes in the coal mines, Walker and Guest (1952) who looked at the effects of assembly production methods on people's behaviour and Blauner (1963) who looked at alienation (discussed in Chapter 3) in relation to different technologies.

Structure

The classic ingredients of structure are job descriptions, patterns of authority, formal relations between members and channels of communication across the organisation. The division of work and the coordination of tasks are major concerns for theories in this area. The early classical theories were concerned with the principles of management and organisation, see above, and have much to say here. This has led to a vast bibliography of management literature and theory. Classic names are Fayol and Urwick. Later twentieth century writers with well-listened to advice in this area are Drucker (1977) and Handy (1985) (see below).

People

The basis for organisation structures have also been studied from the perspective of the nature of the people doing the work and how their attitudes, needs and relations can be affected by the groups and leaders they work with. This work started with the early human relations approach (see Chapter 1) and continues with concerns about leadership, see, for example, Adair (1982), and the continuing emphasis on human resource management. (See Chapter 8 of this book for further discussion.)

Management

Organisational structure has also been looked at from a management perspective. Here the emphasis is on coordinating the activities of the organisation by developing strategies, policies and procedures that direct the activities of the organisation and its interactions with the external environment. Classic references here are Porter (1980) and Mintzberg (1973).

Context

A development of these models has been the influence of contingency theory which suggests that there is not one best way of doing things but rather a question of 'if you have these conditions then this is probably the more likely outcome'. Classic references are Burns and Stalker (1966) and Lawrence and Lorsch (1967). The rest of this chapter in many ways has this perspective as I tend to the rather pragmatic view that finding an analysis that fits is often about using bits from differing perspectives.

One summary of all this that I particularly like is by Handy. To see how organisational structures are influenced by a variety of factors and how the different analytical tools can be helpful Handy (1985) gives us four 'ideal' types of organisation, that are based on the idea of Harrison. He shows us how there are quite different organisations with different structures, cultures, procedures and ways of getting things done. The four types of organisation he gives are the power organisation, the role organisation, the task organisation and the person organisation.

1)The power organisation, which is often found in small, entrepreneurial organisations, depends on a central, all-powerful head. The structure is best seen as a web, see Figure 11.1(a). Influence and power spread out from the centre on a line of personal contact. There are few rules and systems, but often precedent is followed. Such cultures have the ability to move quickly and react well to threat or danger. Size is a problem, as the web cannot support too many activities, something that a small company has to bear in mind as it expands. The quality of the central figure or figures is critical, and succession is often a problematic issue. A web without a spider has no strength.

The role organisation is found in large bureaucracies. It depends on rational and logical arrangements. It has a structure like a Greek temple, see Figure 11.1(b). The pillars are the functional specialisms, with a coordinating top management represented by the pediment. The emphasis is on the role of particular jobs, not on the individual who fills the role. It is most successful in a stable environment, a monopoly, long product life, or where the market is stable. Successful examples have been the civil service, the oil industry and retail banking. It becomes insecure when things change.

The task organisation is a job- or project-oriented organisation. The emphasis is on getting things done. It is best represented by a net, see Figure 11.1(c). Influence is based on expertise, and most people working in this type of organisation expect to have some sort of expertise. It is very much based on teams of people working together. An example would be a television company, where individuals from different professions work together on a particular production and then disperse. This style works well for quick adaptation to change but has difficulty developing economies of scale or great depth of expertise. Control can be difficult, particularly when resources are tight.

The person organisation is far less common than the others. The individual is the central point. The structure and systems are there to serve the individual. Examples are professional partnerships, families or barristers' chambers. A cluster best represents it, see Figure 11.1(d). Systems and procedures can be introduced only by common consent. Few organisations of this sort exist but many people hold it as an ideal. They can be difficult to organise and manage as the individuals can always move elsewhere.

Handy continues his analysis by explaining that most large organisations will have different sorts of organisation operating in different parts of the structure. For example, head office may well have a powers culture for top managers with a person culture for the specialists. The manufacturing plants may well be operating with a role culture while the research unit is a task culture. Only by understanding these differences can one begin to understand the behaviour in the organisation.

Organisational culture

A special way of analysing organisations, and so being able to work more effectively in them, is the understanding of organisational culture. There has been a move away from emphasis on formal procedures and structures as the most important organising device in organisations and there is increasing emphasis on the organisation's culture, that is, its characteristic spirit and beliefs. This is sometimes called the organisation climate (Figure 11.2). Culture is seen in how people treat each other, the nature of their relationships and their normal atti-

Figure 11.1
Examples of Handy's forms of organisation.

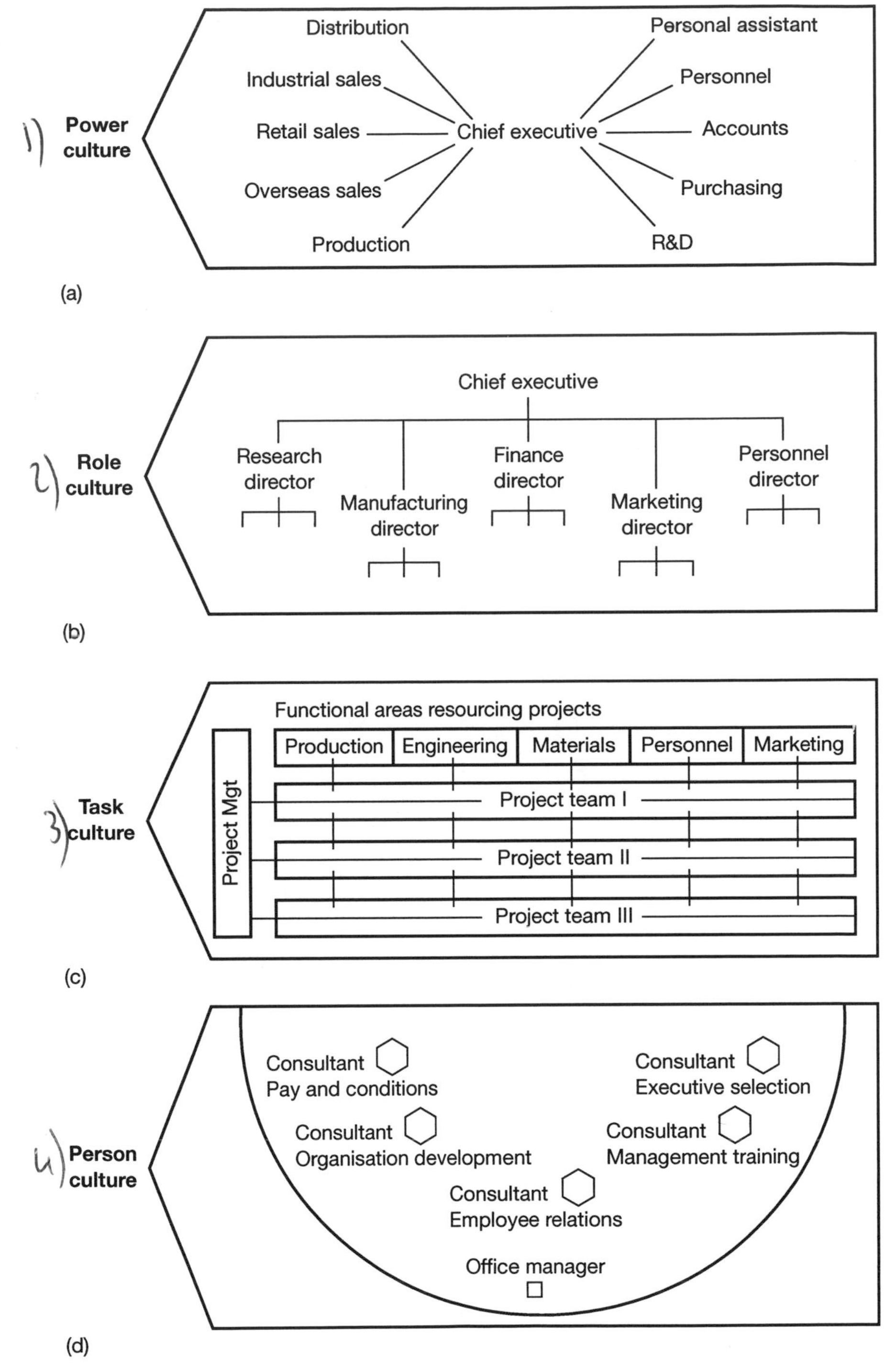

Figure 11.2 **Organisational climate.**

DID YOU KNOW?

Different national cultures affect work-related competencies. For example Yuet-Ha (1996) suggests the following is true for East Asian countries.

- *Relatively easy to implement:*
  Team work and cooperation
  Interpersonal sensitivity, listening and impacting on others.
- *Relatively difficult to implement:*
  Open communication
  Participation
  Decisiveness
  Empowerment
  Delegation
  Sharing information.

This is probably because East Asian cultures are deferential and so tend not to have such open communication as we do in the West. Participation is on defined terms, for example, you do not challenge the boss otherwise there is a loss of 'face'. Trade unions are often illegal or under government control. The different approach to individual identity means this is subordinated to family and social needs. It is important to remember that this book's terms will often refer to Western organisations and their assumptions and definitions would be understood differently elsewhere.

tude to change. In other words the values and norms of the organisation are manifestations of the organisation culture. It is these features of organisational life that are likely to have more effect on people's behaviour than formal reporting relationships or procedures.

Organisational culture is seen as the characteristic spirit and beliefs of an organisation. This is demonstrated, for example, in the conventions about how people behave and treat each other and the types of working relationship that develop. It is developed in all sorts of ways and is mostly taken for granted. You really only notice it when you go and work for another organisation and realise that they do things differently and treat each other in strangely different ways. Culture is difficult because it is intangible – you cannot draw it like an organisation chart. It is none the less felt to be real and powerful. If you are unwittingly working against it you will feel as if you have hit a brick wall.

There are innumerable studies of organisational culture, it was very much the buzz word in the 1980s. These in turn have been used to help in the managing of change which we return to in Chapter 14. One of the most penetrating analyses of organisational culture is by Schein (1985). He suggests that there are three levels of culture: artifacts, values and assumptions.

- Artifacts are the most visible level of culture and include the physical layout, the language used and the behaviour of people.
- Values are people's convictions about reality and will affect how they deal with a new task.
- Assumptions are unconsciously-held learned responses that guide people's thinking and feeling about things and consequently influence their behaviour.

Schein argues that these assumptions are the essence of culture and that the others are manifestations of the culture.

Schein goes on to distinguish two sorts of mechanism for organisational change, primary and secondary. By implication these factors are probably the most influential on organisational culture as well. The primary mechanisms of culture change are:

- What leaders pay most attention to.
- How leaders react to crises and critical incidents.
- Role modelling, teaching and coaching leaders.
- Criteria for allocating rewards and determining status.
- Criteria for selection, promotion and termination.

The first three emphasise the importance of leading by example. All are about showing people what matters. The last two are to do with emphasising people as individuals. Those who fit in or help the organisation are selected and rewarded, those who do not are not.

The secondary mechanisms for the articulation and reinforcement of culture are:

- The organisational structure.
- Systems and procedures.
- Space, buildings and facades.
- Stories and legends about important events and people.
- Formal statements of philosophy and policy.

These secondary mechanisms are the formal aspect of management and organisation. Interestingly they have been the traditional areas of study and training for managers, partly because they are easier to write about than the difficult subjects of leadership and people. In Schein's view they still have a role to play but as support to the more important aspects of showing people what is important and recognising those who demonstrate the desired behaviour. Note that the formal statements come second. It is the informal aspects of the organisation which are seen to be the more powerful in influencing people's behaviour.

Alternative views of organisation culture question whether it can or should be managed. Smirchich (1983) summarises the fundamental debate about organisation culture. In many ways there is a fundamental difference in the literature of organisational behaviour between those with a positivistic approach and those with a phenomenological approach (see Box 11.1).

DID YOU KNOW?

Bisto Foods had a tradition of risk averse management that concentrated on producing existing products with lots of rules about what, how and when things could be done. A cultural change was undertaken to make the staff more adaptable and to increase product innovation. It was decided to try to get everyone interested in food by offering everyone a two-day course in prestigious hotel kitchens. A serious haute cuisine chef was brought on to the staff and multifunctional teams of manufacturing and product development people were set up. So far the results have been encouraging – have a look in your nearest supermarket for the current state of progress.

Box 11.1
Debate about organisation culture. (Based on Smirchich (1983).)

Positivistic	***Phenomenological***
Single culture	Several parallel cultures
Reality outside of self	Mental state only
Maintains status quo	Conflict leads to change
Senior people direct the culture	Negotiated and shared by all members
Senior people manipulate the culture	All members seek to influence the culture
Examples are:	
Management writers	Organisation theory writers
Pascale and Athos (1981)	Morgan (1986)
Peters and Waterman (1982)	Smirchich (1983)

ACTIVITY **11.2**

If you have worked in two or more organisations think how they differ over the big things such as job allocation, rewards and management. Think also about how they differ in the small things such as style of dress, how they greet each other and the lunch arrangements.

If you have only ever worked in one organisation go and visit another. You will be amazed how different they can be even when they are in the same business. For example, just think back to the differences between the universities you visited before coming to your present place of study. What would they have been like to teach in?

Another useful analysis of organisational culture is by Hofstede (1991). He suggests that we can distinguish between different cultures by considering differences in the following four areas: power distance, uncertainty, individualism and values.

- The *power distance* is the distance between the least powerful and the most powerful and the degree of acceptance of this. For example, some organisations have very formal relations between senior and junior members of staff and only the most senior are consulted about changes. Other organisations use first names and would consult everyone affected by the changes.
- The degree to which *uncertainty is accepted* varies and affects whether risks are acceptable. For example, departments differ in how much they cross-check results. This then affects how they handle errors.
- Differing cultures differ in the *degree of individualism* that is normal or whether a cooperative collective is encouraged. We can probably all point to examples of units where everyone acts as an individual and seem very loosely coupled as a unit. We can also think of other units which are very close and have a strong unit identity. Often the style is determined by the nature of the work. For example, research departments relying on dedicated individual insights may accept higher individualism than the flight deck of an aeroplane where the collective group need to be closely coordinated.
- A fourth aspect of culture is the degree to which it is dominated by the *traditional male values* of rationality, logic, competition and independence rather than the traditional female values of intuition and caring. Again there may be differing examples within one organisation but the overriding culture of senior management may tend towards one or the other.

Strategy and planning models of the organisational context

Figure 11.3 **Strategic decision.**

A completely different set of models about the context of organisations are those relating to strategy and planning. Because of its association with decision making and objectives, strategy is generally viewed as a top management activity. The grim comparison with nuclear weapons makes the point. Tactical weapons may kill thousands but strategic weapons can kill hundreds of thousands. Strategic decisions in organisations are the ones that really matter (Figure 11.3). They do not, however, involve only top managers. Because of an emphasis on analysis and precision when developing strategies there is a tendency to concentrate on economic data and overlook the way in which people and their values can influence the implementation, or failure to implement, a chosen strategy. Nowadays a strategic model must take account of the various interested parties or stakeholders in the outcome.

Strategic planning is the process of deciding priorities, setting targets and agreeing the main purposes of the organisation. It may include short-, medium- and long-term goals. It is likely to include some changes which have been imposed from outside but has been tuned to local conditions. This ability to monitor various environments, seek out and synthesise multiple sources and types of information and develop and implement a plan of action that anticipates trends before they are obvious is one of the most useful competencies for senior staff.

DID YOU KNOW?

When Shell wanted to dispose of the Brent Spar oil platform at the end of its practical life in the late 1990s they planned to sink it in the Atlantic ocean. They consulted the various statutory and professional bodies about their plan. They did everything legally and thoughtfully. But they completely failed to consult with the various environmental groups nor did they try to take the public along with them. Although the technical evidence was supportive of their position they had completely failed to grasp the beliefs and emotions of the German population about preserving the wildness of the ocean bed. Consequently Shell had to back-off and reorganise the decision making surrounding Brent Spar's disposal. The understanding of the organisational context by senior management has changed completely in the light of this case.

Another example is Stagecoach's handling of a pay round in South West Trains. In November 1996 the train drivers were offered increased pay and reduced hours in return for more driver-only trains. This led to 71 drivers being made redundant. In March 1997 there were not enough drivers, trains were cancelled and South West Trains had a public relations nightmare that led to running free trains. This failure in the planning and implementation of the changes to account for the time it took new drivers to learn to drive and learn the routes was a great embarrassment and financially costly.

ACTIVITY **11.3**

Think of an organisation that you know. Now list all the different people and organisations that can affect what happens to that organisation. To get you started here are some general categories to think about:

- customers/consumers/clients
- local community
- shareholders/constituents/members
- employees/past employees/pensioners
- sources of finance
- suppliers
- politicians and legislation
- lobbying groups
- competitors
- pressure groups within the organisation

This gives you some idea of the context of the organisation. If your list is accurate you could get an even better idea of this context by specifying in detail how each can influence the organisation and where future difficulties could lie.

No organisation can ignore the environment in which it operates. Porter (1980, 1985) developed his classic model to describe the four forces of competition which make up the environment of an organisation:

- The threat of new entrants.
- The threat of substitute products.
- The bargaining power of buyers.
- The bargaining power of suppliers.

Strategic management is mostly about trying to defend the organisation from these forces or trying to actively influence them. The balance between them will vary over time, place and circumstance. For example, legislation on pollution may well prohibit new entrants to the business so reducing the threat of increasing competition, while reduction in the number of buyers, for example house buyers in a recession, reduces the price an organisation can charge.

Thompson and Strickland (1990) describe the five tasks of strategic management as a continuous process which starts with defining the business, continues with getting specific performance objectives and deciding how to achieve the objectives, and ends with implementing the performance and evaluating the performance. The whole process is then recycled. A typical sequence for the planning process is to start with simple questions such as:

- Where do we want to be? – Establishing the mission.
- Where are we now? – Internal and external analysis.
- How do we get there? – Setting objectives, developing actionable plans, integrating the plans.
- How are we doing? – Providing adequate controls, evaluation measures, and review.

This is not a book about management and particularly not about senior management and planning, but the usefulness of thinking about the organisation's context and how this affects the behaviours of those working for the organisation cannot be underestimated. Some aspects of the context you can influence, others you cannot; some will be opportunities, others will be constraints. The clever players are those who can analyse the context and use the information.

Communicating with the outside world

Another way of looking at the organisational context is to think about the various people and groups which people within an organisation have to contact in order to get on with their work. Many jobs require people to communicate with a large number of different individuals and organisations outside their own organisation. Figure 11.4 gives examples of two such jobs in the health service.

Figure 11.4 **Examples of communication webs.**

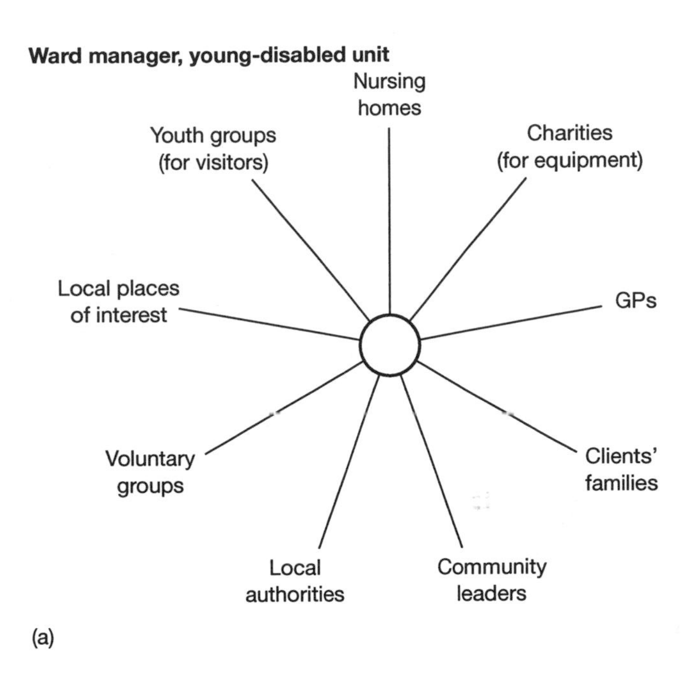

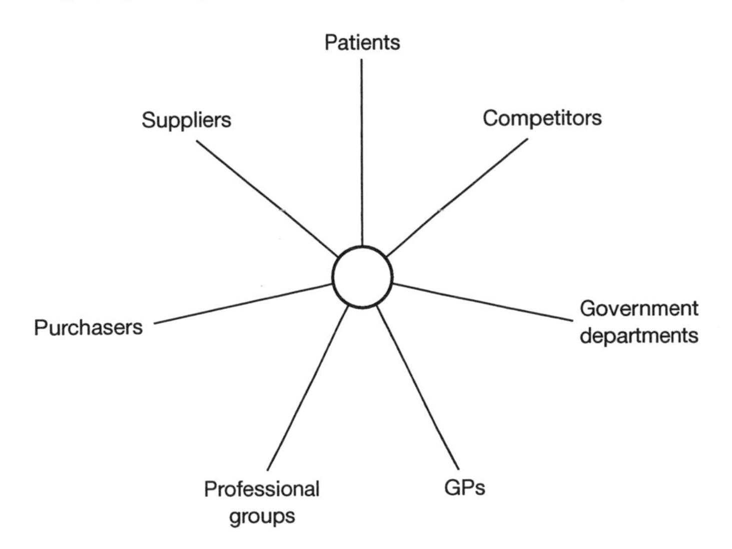

Usually this communication is informal on the phone, face-to-face or through routine formal meetings and letters. However, one sometimes has a more elaborate communication to make and it is worth taking some time to think about it. The importance organisations attach to this communication can be seen in the increasing use of professional public relations people and agencies to handle this area (see Chapter 5). There are several questions to do with the nature of this communication that need answering, especially in an increasingly well-informed world that has higher and higher expectations that accurate, accessible, information is available.

The first question you need to consider is *what do we want to communicate to whom?* By clarifying this *what* and *whom,* the how to do so should be relatively straightforward. What we may need to communicate could concern policies, our vision of the future, practicalities, understanding, information and feelings.

The second question to answer is *do we want to ensure that our audience is willing?* By being clear about the message you want others to hear and by making yourself willing to hear their point of view the degree of misunderstanding could be reduced. The ideal is for an honest, frank, accurate communication to take place between you at all times. The reality of life, however, is that often the message is not clear because of conflicting demands, uncertainty, misunderstandings and lack of time. It is also the case that promising more than can be delivered is more damaging to a reputation than saying no in the first place, see, for example, Bourke (1994). Similarly, if the communication is merely dealing with image and not getting down to dealing with underlying problems, the problems become worse and the reputation of the organisation is destroyed. The communication therefore needs to be two-way and in touch with its audience (see also Chapter 5).

The third issue to consider is which *style* to use. Here it is a case of thinking carefully who the intended audience for the message is. For example, Oxford's Radcliffe Hospital produced a twelve-page supplement to the local newspaper (8 September 1995), with the aim of gaining a greater understanding of their work and commitment in the local community. The content could have been written from a variety of medical, managerial and technical points of view. However, the presentation was given a lively, local newspaper style accessible to most people in the Oxford area with an emphasis on the human interest story. Some of the same material was also used more formally in the various annual reports. The style suited the differing audiences even though the content was similar.

A fourth issue, that is often overlooked, is the *unintended communications* that are made by an organisation to the outside world. This includes incidental communications and non-verbal impressions that are made. For example, what impact is the organisation having on the local environment in its emissions from chimneys? What impression do the unit's surrounding grounds make on visitors? What impression are we giving in our job advertisements and recruitment practices to differing members of the community? What does this communicate about our attitudes to staff? Do we show the community our real work by allowing people to see what we do and by allowing visitors to comment? Again, there is no point in 'over-promising' on these fronts. But it clearly makes a nonsense of trying to be a considerate organisation and expecting people to regard you with trust and affection if you are harsh with staff and pollute the local community's air. Similarly, people will remember the reality of their visits to you long after they remember any glossy brochure. The advice is to look after the housekeeping as well as the PR.

Fifth, there is a need to decide *which medium* suits the purpose. Different media have their advantages and disadvantages. It is not the aim of this book to give details of professional communication and media services as others can do it better. But if you have something which you feel is particularly important or sensitive to convey it may be worth getting professional help about appropriate media, for example, asking the publicity or management services department.

Sixth, there are *hard and soft ways of communicating* with people outside the organisation. Hard ways are the formal mechanisms and bodies for people to get together. Soft methods are the more informal ways of making an impression and are more diffuse. Examples are given in Box 11.2.

ACTIVITY **11.4**

Try to collect some examples of organisations communicating with the outside; for example, prospectuses, annual reports, publicity material, videos, web sites. Think about the following questions in relation to this material.

- What are they trying to say?
- Are there any hidden meanings as well?
- How effective is this communication?
- Is there a better way?

Box 11.2
Hard and soft ways of communicating with those outside the organisation.

Hard	**Soft**
Advertisements	Public relations
Booklets and videos	Jamborees such as fêtes, parties and social events
Handling of social responsibility issues	Behaviour of staff to outsiders
Partnerships	Accessibility of staff and managers to queries and complaints
Contracts	
Being on mailing lists for legislation etc.	Attending seminars/conferences
Contributing to local forum, for example, TECs	Networking
Chambers of Commerce	
Sitting on regulatory bodies	

Conclusion

We have studied different ways of looking at the organisational context. This chapter has dealt with some of the received wisdom about organisations and some of the classical models. The rest of this part of the book is about organisations and some of the themes started in this chapter continue to be developed in the following three chapters. These will look at some of the more recent developments in organisations and the models that have been developed to understand them. The changing nature of organisations and the possibility of a virtual organisation will be dealt with, particularly in Chapters 14 and 15.

EXERCISE **11.1**

This can be done on your own or in a group. Box 11.3 gives the job titles of all those working in a secondary school. The higher the number on the pay scale the higher the salary.

- How would you arrange these jobs into an organisation structure?
- Can you think of another way of doing it?
- What were the difficulties of doing this?
- Can you find a place for everyone?
- What about those with dual roles?
- Do the salary scales bear any relation to the position you have given to the job titles in the hierarchy?

EXERCISE **11.2**

Get into groups of four to ten people.

1. Everyone should fill in Box 11.4 based on their individual likes and dislikes. Each contrasted pair of statements has a nine-point scale between them. Participants circle the appropriate number to suggest their opinion. For example:

   I like chocolate 1 2 ③ 4 5 6 7 8 9 I dislike chocolate

   would suggest a moderate liking of chocolate.
2. Everyone fills in Box 11.5 based on their perceptions of the methods prevailing in this organisation at the moment. 'This organisation' can mean the university or department. If people have recent or current employment they may prefer to look at that organisation.
3. Score both questionnaires by adding the numbers from each line together, in line with instructions given below – note that the order of the scales varies!
4. Add the scores for questions 1, 3, 4, 6 and 9 to give the consensus/conflict axis.
5. Add the scores for questions 2, 5, 7, 8 and 10 to give the control/autonomy axis.
6. Each person places a mark on Figure 11.5 to locate their combined scores on the grid; this shows their preferred management and organisation.
7. Each person also puts another mark to indicate their score for the organisation.
8. Discuss the following questions:
   - What do we each feel is ideal?
   - Are there differences between us?

Box 11.3
List of job titles for a secondary school.

Scale	Job title	Scale	Job title
T2	Integrated Curriculum/English	DH	Deputy Head/English
4	Head of Lower School/Head of Integrated Curriculum	1Supply	Special Needs (Part-time)
2	English/Library	4	Head of Humanities
2	Section 11	T2	Integrated Curriculum
H	Head	1	ACS/Art/Humanities
3T4(ACS)	Head of Art	3	Maths
3	On exchange (Head of Languages)	1	Science
3	Head of Drama	2	Section 11
2T4	Head of Science	DH	Deputy Head/Science
/	Languages	ST	Head of Middle School
2	Science/Control Technology		
1	Home Economics		Youth Tutor (On secondment)
2	Physical Education/Outdoor Pursuits		Youth Club Leader
1	Art		Registrar
2	Integrated Curriculum/Primary Liaison		Clerical Assistant
/	Research Associate/Centre for Research in Ethnic Relations (CRER)		Non-teaching Assistant
2	Integrated Curriculum		Technician
I3	Head of Music		Senior Lab Technician
4	Head of English/Acting Head of Languages		Lab Technician
1	Integrated Curriculum/English		Technician
2T3 (ACS)	Maths/Computers		Caretaker
3	Business Studies	T = Temporary	
ST	Head of Upper School/Humanities		
4	On secondment (Head of Science)		
2	Special Needs		
4	Section 11		
1	Languages		
2T3(ACS)	ACS Coordinator		
T2	Integrated Curriculum/Humanities		
1	Physical Education		
2	Science		
4	Coordinator for Special Needs		
3	Head of CDT		
3	Head of Home Economics		
4	Head of Mathematics		
2	Maths		

- Are there any differences between individuals in their view of the organisation?
- Can we explain any differences between our ideas and reality?
- When would the different quadrants be most appropriate?
- Have things changed?
- Are they changing?

Box 11.4
MOSS individual questionnaire.
(© Derek Torrington, Jane Weightman, Basil Blackwell Ltd, 1989.)

Circle the number that represents your opinion or preference

Tough competition between colleagues in an organisation may create distrust and hostility, but is needed to stimulate hard work.	9 8 7 6 5 4 3 2 1	A strong sense of teamwork and support in the organisation is most likely to produce good results.
People at work should have considerable freedom to decide their own activities, collaborating with colleagues in any way they wish.	1 2 3 4 5 6 7 8 9	Activities should be closely controlled from the centre, with little individual decision making and few personal initiatives.
It is a good idea to ask for help from colleagues, as they have resources to share.	1 2 3 4 5 6 7 8 9	One should be cautious about seeking help from colleagues, as they may take advantage.
There are a few colleagues with whom one could share hopes and discuss career plans.	9 8 7 6 5 4 3 2 1	One could feel confident about sharing hopes and career plans with most of one's colleagues.
Duties are precisely set down for me by someone else, with little scope for personal initiative.	9 8 7 6 5 4 3 2 1	As far as possible people plan their own work and take considerable personal initiative.
All members of the organisation should support, and agree with, the organisation's objectives.	1 2 3 4 5 6 7 8 9	It doesn't matter whether or not all members of the organisation agree with its objectives, as long as they do a good job.
Financial expenditure should be tightly controlled by top managers.	9 8 7 6 5 4 3 2 1	Financial controls should be loose enough for people to plan their own expenditure.
Policy and strategy for the organisation is decided by top managers only.	9 8 7 6 5 4 3 2 1	Policy and strategy for the organisation should be decided by extensive consultation with all members.
When there is a problem all should join in to find a solution.	1 2 3 4 5 6 7 8 9	When there is a problem, it should be resolved by the person responsible.
Arrangements for time off and other absence should be made according to strict rules.	9 8 7 6 5 4 3 2 1	There should be individual freedom to take time off work in a responsible way, according to personal needs.

Box 11.5
MOSS organisation questionnaire.
(© Derek Torrington, Jane Weightman, Basil Blackwell Ltd, 1989.)

Circle the number that represents your opinion or preference

There is much conflict of interest, creating distrust and hostility.	9 8 7 6 5 4 3 2 1	There is complete harmony of interest in the organisation, with a strong sense of teamwork and mutual support.
We all enjoy considerable freedom to decide our own activities, collaborating with colleagues in any way we wish.	1 2 3 4 5 6 7 8 9	We are closely controlled from the centre, with little scope for individual decision making and no encouragement to take initiatives with colleagues.
I can rely on colleagues to help me.	1 2 3 4 5 6 7 8 9	I am afraid to ask for help from my colleagues.
There are a number of my colleagues with whom I would not share my hopes and career plans.	9 8 7 6 5 4 3 2 1	I would feel confident about discussing my hopes and career plans with most of my colleagues
My duties are precisely set down for me by someone else, with little scope for personal initiative.	9 8 7 6 5 4 3 2 1	As far as possible people plan their own work and take considerable personal initiative.
We all agree with, and support, the organisation's objectives.	1 2 3 4 5 6 7 8 9	We have different ideas about what we are trying to do.
Financial expenditure is tightly controlled by top managers.	9 8 7 6 5 4 3 2 1	We all have some money to spend how we like.
Policy and strategy for the organisation is decided by top management only.	9 8 7 6 5 4 3 2 1	We have extensive consultation and participation in policy decisions.
When there is a problem we all join in to find a solution.	1 2 3 4 5 6 7 8 9	When there is a problem the people responsible resolve it.
Arrangements for time off and other absence are made according to strict rules.	9 8 7 6 5 4 3 2 1	We take time off work when we need it.

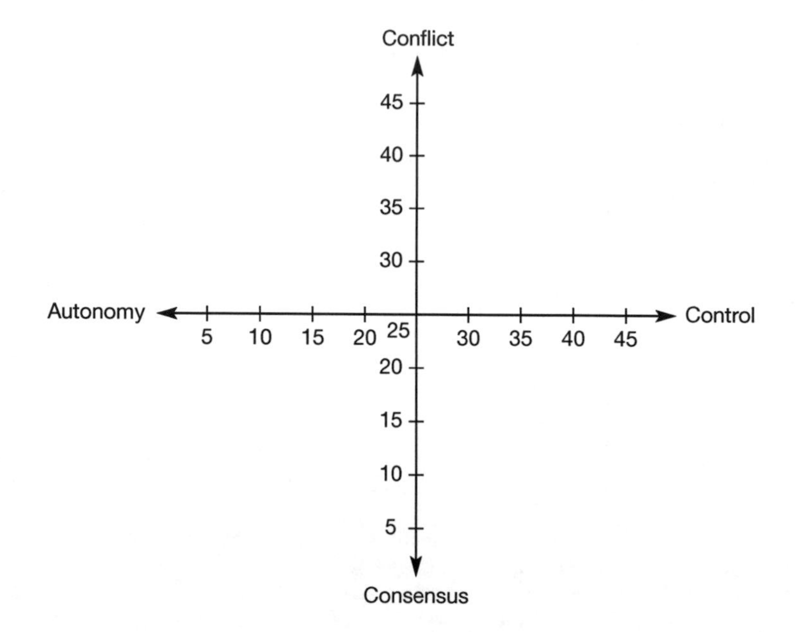

Figure 11.5
MOSS diagram – blank grid. (© Derek Torrington, Jane Weightman, Basil Blackwell Ltd, 1989.)

This model was developed after our (Torrington and Weightman (1989)) research in secondary schools. We concluded that dithering in the middle and going to the extremes had disadvantages, see Figure 11.6. We rarely came across a school in the top-left quartile, which we called anarchy. Prescription, schools with management and organisation described by the top-right quartile, is useful when consistency is important. Leadership, the bottom-right quartile, is helpful when there is uncertainty that can and should be dealt with quickly. Collegiality, the remaining bottom-left quartile, is useful when the full commitment of individuals is necessary. We found that all schools had all these in differing proportions at different times. The clever management art is to balance them appropriately.

Self-check questions

1. What are the various factors of organisations that classical theories consider?
2. What are Handy's four types of organisation?
3. What is organisation culture?
4. What are the primary and secondary mechanisms of culture change according to Schein?
5. What four forces, according to Porter, affect competition?
6. What are hard and soft ways of communicating with people outside the organisation?

Figure 11.6
Effective organisations can be found in any of the shaded areas. (© Derek Torrington, Jane Weightman, Basil Blackwell Ltd, 1989.)

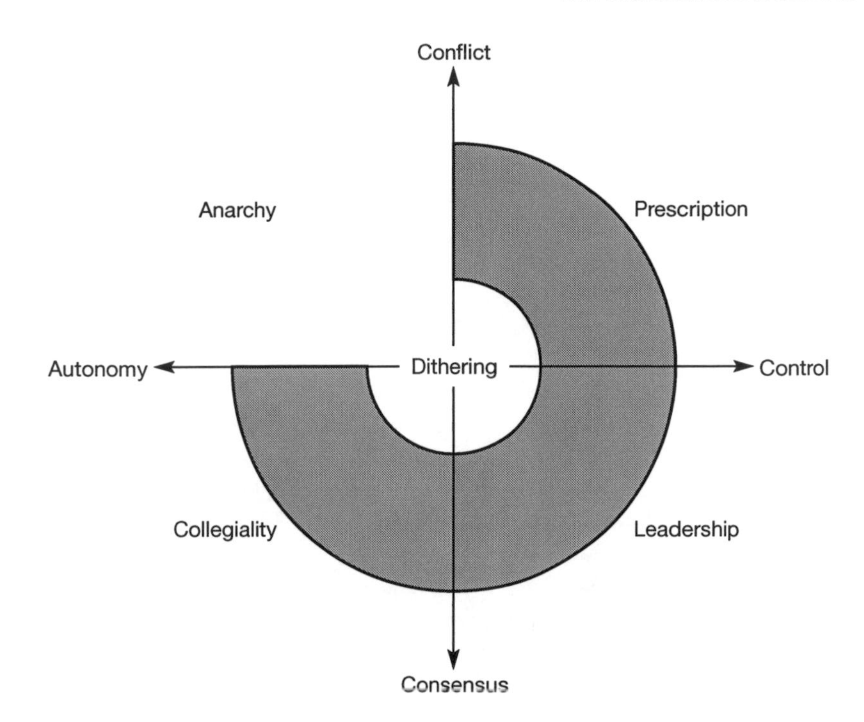

CASE STUDY **11.1** **An example of control and autonomy in an art department**

Ken (Head of Art) puts an emphasis on quality, both in the work of the children and that of his staff. In this he tries to lead from the front, spending considerable time each year preparing for the year to come. He regularly reviews the syllabus and changes elements from time-to-time to stimulate and motivate his staff, with whom he discusses the changes – 'I plant a lot of seeds and lay a lot of hints' – but he makes the decision in the end. He prides himself on being well organised and having a clear idea of what he wants. He produces policy documents, syllabuses and schemes of work which express a clear concern for quality in their content, style and presentation. There is a conscious department style he claims.

Tom, with an MA in fine art, says of Ken, 'He goads you, but he doesn't brutalise. When I started I really appreciated the amount of structure provided.' He finds Ken's thoughtful, well-presented policy documents very useful. 'It's much better than the back of the envelope approach.' Tom says that it is unusual to find that degree of structure in an art department. But he says that Ken emphasises the amount of flexibility that is possible within the structure. Tom thinks that he puts more of himself into the work now, and has gradually taken on more responsibilities. All members of the department were involved in drawing up a self-assessment questionnaire for the exams which Tom thinks is working very well. Ken has told him that he is more or less in charge of his own part of the department now. He orders his own materials and is responsible for a lot of the senior students' work. Tom talks of the advantages of being well prepared: 'It's a calm department. We don't rush for deadlines, it's all paced.'

Susan the pottery specialist has her own section at the far end of the building. Her expertise means she has a great deal of autonomy within Ken's overall scheme. She says that it compares well with her previous school.

1. How would you score Ken's management style on the model given in Exercise 11.2?
2. What sort of organisation would you describe this as in Handy's terms (see Figure 11.1)?
3. Do you think there would be difficulties if the department got very big?

References

Adair J. (1982) *Action Centred Leadership.* Gower, Aldershot.

Blauner R. (1963) *Alienation and Freedom.* University of Chicago Press, Chicago, IL.

Bourke K.J. (1994) Strengthening customer relationships and building customer service in a major bank. In *Successful Change Strategies: Chief Executives in Action,* Taylor B. (Ed.), Director Books, Hemel Hempstead.

Burns T. and Stalker G.M. (1966) *The Management of Innovation.* Tavistock Publications, London.

Drucker P.F. (1977) *Management.* Pan Books, London.

Fayol H. (1949) *General and Industrial Management.* Pitman, London.

Handy C. (1985) *Understanding Organisations.* Penguin, Harmondsworth.

Hofstede G. (1991) *Cultures and Organisations: Software of the Mind.* McGraw Hill, London.

Lawrence P.R. and Lorsch J.W. (1967) *Organization and Environment.* Harvard University Press, Cambridge, MA.

Mintzberg H. (1973) *The Nature of Managerial Work.* Prentice Hall, Englewoood Cliffs, NJ.

Morgan G. (1986) *Images of Organisation.* Sage, Beverly Hills, CA.

Pascale R. and Athos A. (1981) *The Art of Japanese Management.* Penguin, Harmondsworth.

Peters T.G. and Waterman R.H. (1982) *In Search of Excellence.* Harper and Row, London.

Porter M.E. (1980, 2nd edn 1985) *Competitive Strategy: Techniques for Analysing Industries and Competitors.* Free Press, New York, NY.

Schein E. (1985) *Organizational Culture and Leadership.* Jossey Bass, San Francisco, CA.

Smirchich L. (1983) Concepts of culture and organisation analysis. *Administrative Science Quarterly,* Vol. 28, 334–58.

Thompson A.A. and Strickland A.J. (1990) *Strategic Management Concept and Cases.* RD Irwin, Homewood, IL.

Torrington D. and Weightman J. (1989) *The Reality of School Management.* Blackwell, Oxford.

Trist E.L., Higgin G.W., Murray H. and Pollock S.B. (1963) *Organizational Choice.* Tavistock Publications, London.

Walker C.R. and Guest R.H. (1952) *The Man on the Assembly Line.* Harvard University Press, Cambridge, MA.

Weber M. (1964) *The Theory of Social and Economic Organization.* Collier Macmillan, London.

Yuet-Ha M. (1996) in *People Management* 25 July 96, p. 28.

Further reading

Classic books in this area are Handy (1985) and Schein (1985) mentioned above. They are both readable and accessible with lively examples and thought-provoking arguments. For more modern writing in this area look at the suggestions for Chapters 13 and 14.

CHAPTER **12**

Power, authority and influence

Objectives

When you have finished reading this chapter you should be able to:

- Discuss the importance of politics in the analysis of organisational behaviour.
- List different sources of power available to organisation members.
- Distinguish between 'in' authority and 'an' authority.
- Understand the relation between delegation, authority and responsibility.
- Understand different aspects of influencing.
- Understand how to organise meetings.

Introduction

As organisations depend more on less formal forms of influence it becomes increasingly important for understanding organisational behaviour to understand power and how it is used. Indeed, the very popularity of the phrase 'empowerment' in organisations shows the importance of this, see later in this chapter. Power is a property that exists in any organisation or system; politics is the way that power is put into action. Those who understand the subtleties of power in relationships are better able to get things done than those who ignore them. Or as the political theorist, Dahl, so trenchantly put it:

> The graveyards of history are strewn with the corpses of reformers who failed utterly to reform anything, of revolutionaries who failed to win power . . . of anti-revolutionaries who failed to prevent a revolution – men and women who failed not only because of the forces arrayed against them but because the pictures in their minds about power and influence were simplistic and inaccurate.
>
> (R.A. Dahl, *Power* (1970) p. 15)

Organisations have power as one of their crucial dimensions, and only by understanding how power is distributed and deployed can members get things done. The innovative idea or accurate diagnosis is insufficient without the means of implementation. The analysis of power is an important part of understanding how groups work and how leadership is exercised. These were discussed in Chapters 7 and 8 respectively. This chapter takes the ideas further.

Most of this book has relied on material from people with either a psychology or sociology training. This chapter is different in that most of the models are based on a political science perspective. This sort of analysis is often subsumed under a sociological perspective but I have tried to give you a flavour of some of the original political analysis that can then be applied to organisations.

ACTIVITY **12.1**

This chapter looks at various ways of analysing organisational behaviour associated with power and politics. The models used often come from political theorists and sociology but the discipline of psychology is represented when considering individual behaviour. Some theories were developed in the general context of society then applied to organisations. Some used general theories to analyse organisations and then develop specific models for organisational analysis. Can you discover which is which as you read this chapter? For example, would the model only work for organisations and not in the general social context? Would the model make more sense generally? Perhaps it is impossible to say and so it does not matter where the original ideas were developed. Perhaps developing ideas in one area and demonstrating their usefulness in another demonstrates the power of the model. See what you think.

DID YOU KNOW?

John Stuart Mill in his book On Liberty *(1859) said:*

> *The only purpose for which power can be rightly exercised over any member of a civilised community, against his will, is to prevent harm to others. His own good, either physical or moral, is not sufficient warrant.*

The place of politics in organisations

Dahl is one of the political theorists who help us to an understanding of organisational politics. As he points out this political behaviour comes from conflicting aims.

> If everyone were perfectly agreed on ends and means, no-one would ever need to change the way of another. Hence no relations of influence or power would arise. Hence no political system would exist. Let one person frustrate another in the pursuit of his goals and you already have the germ of a political system; conflict and politics are born inseparable twins.
>
> (Dahl (1970) p. 59)

PAUSE FOR THOUGHT *Can you think of three factors in organisations that lead to conflict that might lead to the development of organisational politics?*

Pfeffer (1981) suggests that the following elements produce conflict and the use of power in organisations:

- Interdependence – where what happens to one person affects another such as joint activities. My work affects your work.
- Inconsistent goals – where there are different aims. My aim might conflict with what you are trying to do.
- Technologies – differences will lead to conflict. For example, if you have one IT system and I have another who should pay to make them compatible? Incidently this is often an underestimated cost of joint ventures and amalgamation of organisations.

DID YOU KNOW?

Pfeffer (1981, pp. 67–8) uses the following story to illustrate the conditions when power is used. Two wounded soldiers are lying in a tent on the battlefield. Both need a pint of blood to save their lives. The orderly has only one pint left. One soldier will live, the other will die. Splitting the blood will mean both soldiers die. One is a captain, the other a corporal.

The captain argues he is entitled to the blood because of his rank. In addition he is important for planning and organising the fighting for his unit and so his recovery will affect many people whereas the soldier's, will only affect a single person. The corporal argues that the captain is just an overhead and part of the administration whereas he is part of the actual fighting. He also argues that as he is younger he has a greater life expectancy so the pint of blood might be expected to give more years of life if given to him. In addition they each claim family reasons for the blood – the captain has a wife and two small children, the corporal two aged, dependent parents.

How shall the orderly decide? Each soldier has raised legitimate, relevant and reasonable criteria. Suddenly the corporal reaches into his bag, draws a gun and shoots the captain. The decision is clear, the corporal gets the blood!

- Scarcity of resources – the greater the scarcity compared with demand, the more power and effort will be put into resolving the issue. If we both want to use the piece of equipment we will spend time trying to resolve a suitable rota of use.

Any organisation has limited resources for its members so they compete with each other for promotion and career development. On an everyday level they will be competing for a bigger budget, more space, newer equipment, more staff and a greater say over the direction of organisational policy. This competition causes the nature of political activity to vary according to the state of growth or decline of the organisation. With growth there is more opportunity for individuals than in a stagnant state so the politics is likely to have more winners in a state of growth than in periods of stability or stagnation.

Power, control and organisations

In the past management was seen as having to control what happened in the organisation with careful control of the minute detail of each individual worker, see, for example, the early scientific management work of Taylor discussed in Chapter 1. More recently the management task has taken into account some of the humanistic psychology approaches, also discussed in Chapter 1, to encourage staff to take more power and control of the details of their jobs. There is still central management control of budgets and objectives but less control over the how to achieve the desired results. Many theories of organisation structure, such as those given in Chapter 11, are also theories about who should control what. Power is the extent of influence that people in reality have in the organisation.

Etzioni (1975) compared a wide range of complex organisations and classified the nature of relationships within them based on the differences in power and involvement. Members of organisations differed in the way in which they complied with power:

- Coercive power relied on threats, sanctions and force – such as food and comfort.
- Remunerative power involved manipulating rewards such as wages.
- Normative power relied on manipulating symbolic rewards such as esteem and prestige.

Also, members of organisations varied in their degree of commitment and involvement:

- Alienative involvement occurs when individuals are there against their wishes.
- Calculative involvement is where attachment depends on extrinsic rewards such as cash.
- Moral involvement occurs where individuals believe in the goals of the organisation.

Etzioni suggests that a particular kind of power usually goes with a particular kind of involvement.

PAUSE FOR THOUGHT *Can you guess the appropriate power and involvements that Etzioni found?*

- *Coercive power with alienative involvement, for example, in prisons.*
- *Remunerative power with calculative involvement, for example, in many businesses and manufacturing.*
- *Normative power with moral involvement, for example, in charities and religious organisations, and organisations like Body Shop.*

Etzioni suggests that organisations which have matching power and involvement structures are more effective than those that are mismatched. This may account for some organisations' difficulties in implementing the current fashion for empowerment and facilitation. They may really be command and control organisations beneath the apparent new management style.

Sources of power available to organisation members

So far we have looked at the large-scale organisation-wide aspects of power. What about the individual working in an organisation who wants to influence events? There are four main sources of power available to individuals and groups to exercise political influence: position, expertise, personal qualities and political factors. The most obvious is the control of resources. Those who control what others need are in the position of relative power.

The bases of power were described classically by French and Raven (1958) as being:

- Reward – being able to give the other what they want.
- Coercive – forcing the other to do their bidding.
- Referent – having desirable attributes that make people wish to refer to the leader.
- Legitimate – as opposed to illegitimate in the eyes of the followers.
- Expert – having an expertise that others want.

They argue that all these depend on the belief of the followers, they are interrelated and a leader can operate from a multiple base of power.

Using French and Raven's list as a starting point the sources of power available to anyone in an organisation are listed in Box 12.1. Understanding these

Box 12.1
Sources of power. (Source: Torrington and Weightman (1989a).)

1 Position

Resources Control access to what others need; whether subordinates, peers or superiors. It includes the following: materials, information, rewards, finance, time, staff, promotion, references.

Delegation Whether jobs are pushed down the hierarchy; with rights of veto retained or not.

Gatekeeper Control information, relax or tighten rules, make life difficult or easy depending on loyalty of individuals.

2 Expertise

Skill Being an expert. Having a skill others need or desire.

Uncertainty Those who have expertise to deal with a crisis become powerful till it is over.

Indispensable Either through expertise or being an essential part of the administrative process.

3 Personal qualities

Motivation Some seek power more enthusiastically than others.

Physical prowess Being bigger or stronger than others ... . Not overtly used in management except as controller of resources. However, statistically leaders tend to be taller than the led.

Charisma Very rare indeed. Much discussed in early management literature as part of leadership qualities, but usually control of resources can account for claims of charismatic power.

Persuasion skills Bargaining and personal skills that enable one to make the most of one's other powers, such as resources.

4 Political factors

Debts Having others under obligation for past favours.

Contrast of agenda Coalition and other techniques for managing how the issues are, or are not, presented. Being present when important decisions are taken, control of minutes.

Dependence Where one side depends on the other for willing cooperation, the power of removal exists. Strikes, or threatening to resign *en bloc* are two examples.

and using them to change what is decided or done is part of working in an organisation. Power is sometimes felt to be a negative thing in organisations but access to resources and getting things done is after all what you are being paid to do. This does not necessarily mean putting others down but it does mean maximising the power available to you to influence events appropriately.

Examples of using one's power to influence things within an organisation are: trying to increase the section's allocation of the budget and so keep extra facilities open; increasing the profile of the department so that the service is used more; trying to get the security staff to help with unwanted visitors; attending the meeting and being prepared with clear slides to demonstrate why another action plan is more appropriate than the proposed one.

Trying to understand who has power and how it is used will also enable people to work better in their organisation as there is a constant shift of power as new partnerships develop. For example, joint ventures with other organisations shift the locus of power from the traditional hierarchy to those who can effectively influence the partners and represent the home organisation's strategic agenda. For example, an estate manager can suddenly rise in importance when land is being sold. Similar changes can happen when there is a change from having a central supplies department or agency to new supplier–customer partnerships. Instead of routine administration the purchasing department has to develop collaborative webs of relationships across the departments to negotiate appropriate supplies from a variety of suppliers.

All members of organisations need to understand the use of power to influence others, it is not just the prerogative of the mighty. With increased responsibility and accountability held at small section and individual level we all need to be able to influence what is going on. This is often summed up in the concept of 'empowerment'. Increasingly in organisations there is talk of empowering individuals to take initiatives and responsibility. Empowering must include granting the resources to carry out the initiative and having the power to say no. Otherwise it can often feel to the staff as if the bosses are just asking them to do more, for less. Those who feel most empowered are those who are confident that they can influence others and have the power to get things done.

ACTIVITY **12.2**

- Which of the sources of power in Box 12.1 have you used?
- Which others do you think you might use in the future?

Authority

Authority is an important concept for managers and is widely used in management literature. For example, Fayol (in Pugh (1971) p. 103):

> Authority is the right to give orders and the power to exact obedience.

Most examples show confusion between authority, legitimate power and gaining compliance. This is hardly surprising as the concept is widely discussed in political theory suggesting there is difficulty in finding a definition. Carter (1979, p. 1) says:

> Authority is a concept central to social and political thought, yet its precise nature remains remarkably elusive.

DID YOU KNOW?
Here are two anarchic views on authority:

- *Guerin (1970) sees authority as tyranny and incompatible with the natural order and social harmony.*
- *Wolff (1970) concludes that the legitimising of authority undermines the autonomy of the people.*

What do you think?

Interpretations of authority inevitably vary with the political persuasion of the writer. Conservative writers will tend to uphold existing forms of authority whereas liberal, socialist and anarchist writers will view authority with varying degrees of distrust, which, at its extremes, leads to the abandoning of authority altogether and the adoption of an anarchist framework.

Power made legitimate by position or expertise is called authority. Without the legitimising of the power in one of these ways the relationship is seen as coercive and unacceptable in societies based on democracy and ideas of personal freedom. See Carter (1979) for a full discussion of this political analysis. Carter suggests that we tend to distinguish two sorts of authority: 'in authority' and 'an authority'. It is an important distinction as the first relies on the position of authority as expressed through organisation charts and job titles. 'In authority' relies on control over resources to influence people, whereas 'an authority' is based on the personal attributes of credibility to influence people. Being in authority is a right to control and judge the actions of others. Leadership is the exercise of the power conferred by that right in such a way as to win a willing and positive, rather than grudging and negative response. Being an authority is often the basis of credibility, which is dealt with in Chapter 8.

How authority and its concomitant power is used in organisations is an important part of analysing organisational behaviour. Three related concepts or issues are delegation, networking and influencing. I will deal with each of them in turn.

Delegation

A closely related issue to authority and credibility is that of delegation. When, where and how do individuals delegate? Most books on management will have a chapter on delegation; in order to manage the work of another some sort of delegation is involved. Usually this means entrusting a degree of authority and responsibility to others. Normally this is perceived to apply more in the relationship of delegating power to those lower in the hierarchy, but this does not have to be exclusively so. For example, when someone 'acts up' to cover for an absent superior there is a delegation of powers and authority involved. Most cases of delegation in organisations are, however, from the top down.

Mullins (1996, p. 570) suggests that delegation is founded on the concepts of:

- Authority – the right to make decisions and take actions.
- Responsibility – the obligation to perform certain duties.
- Accountability (ultimate responsibility) – which cannot be delegated as the senior is ultimately responsible for the acts of the subordinates.

Most textbooks suggest that authority should be equivalent to responsibility. Responsibility without the authority to get things done is utterly frustrating for the people involved.

The advantages of delegation are:

- Training and developing people.
- Use of time.
- Diverse geography.
- Expertise and specialisms.
- Cheapness.

Some disadvantages of delegation are:

- Dependence on others.
- Fear of other doing better/worse than self.
- May not fit organisation culture.

Delegation is not giving people jobs to do, it is giving people scope, responsibility and authority. The questions to ask are: can the person try their own ideas, develop understanding and confidence? The more specific the instructions and terms of reference the less learning will be possible as a result of the activity. See also Chapter 10 about developing others in the organisation for further discussion of this and related areas.

Networking

A useful study of general managers was that of Kotter (1982). He concluded that the work of these senior managers could be analysed into the agendas of work that they set themselves and the network of contacts they maintained to implement these agendas. Having a network of contacts both inside and outside the organisation enabled people to consult about new projects effectively. A network also means they hear and understand when things begin to start going wrong rather than having to wait till they have gone wrong. People who rely on formal relationships will only be told what they expect to hear and when they have to be told.

Agenda setting is one way in which people impose their will on the situation around them. The other is by setting up and maintaining a network of contacts through which the agendas are implemented. Agendas and networks are independent as it is often through contact with people in the network that the agenda is kept up-to-date and appropriate. Networks are quite different from the formal structures, although no substitute for them, in large organisations. Networks are made up of a whole range of people both inside and outside the organisation who can help implement the agenda. They are also a source of information about what should be on the agenda. It is the people who can help things along by speeding up processes, providing information, jumping a queue, endorsing a proposal in a meeting, checking data, arranging for you to meet someone with relevant expertise and, of course, doing jobs. Networks are populated by people who work for you, people you have worked with in the past, useful experts, people who understand the system and a wide range of personal contacts. Expertise and personal charm are as important as position in the organisation for setting up and maintaining networks. There is usually some reciprocity implied in networks – 'you owe me one' is often heard (Figure 12.1).

Figure 12.1 **Networking.**

Some will claim that this networking can become too political. How can we judge whether we are becoming too political in our behaviour? A useful test is to distinguish between setting agendas for action and using networks to implement the agendas. Political behaviour is potentially useful when it is deployed to put agendas into action. It is counterproductive when it is deployed only to build and maintain networks.

Too much network and not enough agenda is associated with the type of person who is more concerned with their own promotion and position rather than getting on with the job. The person who under-emphasises networks and concentrates on agendas can be inward looking and fail to take power seriously and consequently fails to influence events sufficiently. Both these characters can be found in any organisation but the former is more likely to be in a managerial position. For example, June was the manager in the beauty and haberdashery department of a large department store. She was a friendly outgoing woman. She willingly went to meetings and conferences and everyone knew her. Her colleagues in the department felt that she never really had any view of what should happen and so always followed the latest fashions and management requests. Perhaps June would be better advised to use her obvious social skills for networking to inform her views and develop an agenda about the department. Another example is Paul who is the ward manager for the orthopaedic ward. He is passionate about the needs of people in traction and in hospital for relatively long periods of time. However, his style is rather brusque and intense so others tend to avoid him where possible. He might be advised to learn some of the influencing skills of networking.

ACTIVITY **12.3**

Make a list of all the individuals who can affect how effective you are in your studies but with whom you do not have a formal working relationship.

- Is there anyone not on your chart who should be?
- Are there any people on the chart who you need better communication with?
- What are you going to do about it?

Influencing

At the heart of working in an organisation is the desire to influence others in some decision or behaviour that would not otherwise have taken place. The main question is how can we do this when there are so many different personalities involved? We need to understand how these different people can be understood and influenced. Some of the answer may be found in social science. So a selection of the differing models which we explored in Part 1 of this book would be appropriate here to demonstrate that we are complex and that we all have a different point of view which needs to be appreciated if we want to influence each other's behaviours.

There are lots of reasons for trying to understand the differences between people. Among those we work with we are more likely to put requests, demands, expectations in a way that is appropriate to them. When we are experiencing difficulties in influencing someone it can be helpful to have a range of analytical models to understand their behaviour and suggest alternative approaches. When we have a difficult piece of information to give to those we work with we can think of different strategies and decide which is most likely to succeed with the particular individual if we have some sort of understanding of the person. Most of us do this instinctively, the social sciences can help to systematise our thoughts and perhaps suggest new approaches when everything else has failed. Three models, dealt with in Part 1 of this book, concerning individual differences in behaviour are psychoanalysis, behaviourism and humanistic psychology.

Also important are the questions of power, authority and delegation and the balance between the legitimate demands and claims made by the parties involved. Different organisation cultures will accept differing levels of influence from various members but when analysing organisational behaviour *how* people influence each other is an important issue. Questions to ask include:

- What are the formal methods of influence here? This would include meetings, memos, job appraisals, organisation charts, job descriptions, etc.
- What are the informal methods of influence here? This would include style of talking, where decisions are really taken rather than rubber stamped, who is 'in' and who 'out', which is not necessarily the same as the formal hierarchy.
- Who is most influential? What is the basis of this influence? Position, power, expertise, charm, length of service, ownership or just being there?

A special sort of influencing is the formal procedure of negotiating. This may be the business of negotiating a contract for supplying a service or products. It may be negotiating one's own terms and conditions of employment. It may be negotiating with the neighbouring hospital to share a consultant specialist. The important thing is that in most negotiations both sides expect to gain.

There are different sorts of negotiation problems. When there are just two players it is a situation of mutual dependence. Fifty:fifty sharing is a natural solution to the problem in these sorts of negotiation because it has an appearance of fairness. Getting there may take some time because of the element of ritual and face-saving required in some negotiations but the fairness principle does seem typical of British organisational behaviour.

Another sort of negotiation is where the number of potential parties on either side increases. Then the numbers and bargaining power of each member matter less. Here it becomes more useful in negotiation if the joint group can create a bigger pool to negotiate about. That is they try to find more customers, clients or users of the product/service so everyone can have a bit more. For example, when purchaser and providers are negotiating on a one-to-one basis it is reasonable to bargain about the fifty:fifty split. Whereas if there are several providers and purchasers negotiating together there may be more to be said in trying to generate more business than in exactly how it is split. This is certainly a lesson being taken up by conglomerates of leisure and tourist facilities in some towns who have found themselves in a stronger negotiating position by grouping and marketing the place generally to attract visitors.

ACTIVITY **12.4**

Imagine you are the tourist officer for your home town. Which facilities in the town would you try to influence to cooperate in making a joint marketing effort to attract tourists from out of the county? Can you imagine why they might resist?

Meetings

A particular form of power, authority and influence at work in organisations is seen in meetings (also discussed in Chapter 5). Many people in large organisations spend a lot of time attending, and complaining about, meetings. The usual question is 'what is the point of this meeting?' Meetings have both overt and covert reasons for taking place. Some of these reasons are given below.

Overt reasons for meetings include:

- *Making decisions.* The meeting may be the focus of the decision making with all the appropriate people present to enable the decision to be made. Or, as often happens, prior discussions have arrived at the decisions and the meeting merely ratifies them.
- *Making recommendations.* The assembled meeting has to agree what and to whom they wish to make recommendations, whether to individuals or groups. It might also only be a subsidiary meeting to recommend to a more senior meeting where the real decision will take place.
- *Training newcomers to the group.* It is often through attending meetings that managers learn about the wider implications of the work of their unit and the issues facing the organisation as a whole. It is also a source of learning about the politics and power play within the organisation.
- *Analysis and report.* Organising material for another group. This is particularly the function of working parties.
- *Information.* Exchanging information and asking for information which usually takes place under the 'any other business' or 'matters arising' sections in formal meetings.

Covert reasons for meetings, which on the whole are good reasons although hidden, include:

- *Cohesion.* Feeling part of the whole by chatting beforehand, catching someone's eye or joking. Some regular meetings try to engender this clubbiness by having regular breakfast meetings of the management team or an occasional 'away day' in a hotel.
- *Catharsis.* Sometimes it is useful to give vent to anger even when nothing can be done. At least people feel they 'have had their say'.
- *Manipulation.* This occurs when a particular decision or action is desired and the meeting is manoeuvred into agreeing to this as if it were their own decision. This is usually engineered by the more senior staff.

We (Torrington and Weightman (1989b)) developed a checklist to consider the arrangements for regular meetings. It was designed to assist in running them effectively so that the necessary communication and decision making can take place. The list of questions might also help when a regular meeting feels wrong as usually this means something on this list is not clear or agreed on. There are no right answers, it is just a list for you to consider if you are part of a meeting. See Box 12.2.

Conclusion

This chapter has looked at some of the political concepts that can be used to analyse behaviour in organisations. Using this sort of analysis alongside the psychology and sociology models gives us a fuller picture. It is like using different probes to come up with different evidence. In practice the different models can be used to analyse different problems. For example, if you are having problems with the boss you might use material in Part 1 of this book to understand their individuality or material from this chapter to analyse their use/abuse of power. The next two chapters are related to this one as they look at organisation design and change, both of which have a political component to them.

EXERCISE 12.1

Answer the questions below, already given above in the section on influencing, to look at an organisation you know. This could be your department/school within the university. Try to give specific examples of each.

1. What are the formal methods of influence here? This would include meetings, memos, job appraisals, organisation charts, job descriptions, etc.
2. What are the informal methods of influence here? This would include style of talking, where decisions are really taken rather than rubber stamped, who is 'in' and who 'out', which is not necessarily the same as the formal hierarchy.
3. Who is most influential? What is the basis of this influence? Position, power, expertise, charm, length of service, ownership or just being there?

Now list three ways you think would enable you to influence a change in this organisation.

If there is something you could change why not try it? Any luck?

Box 12.2

A meetings checklist.

Who should attend the meeting?

- A large group to represent wide interests?
- A small group to make discussion easier and more productive?
- Representative of each layer in the hierarchy?
- A variety of personalities to ensure a lively discussion?
- Only those with expertise in this area?

What is the brief or terms of reference of the meeting?

- Does this meeting have the power to take a decision?
- Can this meeting make a recommendation?
- How wide can the discussion usefully range?
- Has a decision relating to this topic already been made that cannot be changed?
- Are there some conclusions that would be unacceptable? To whom?

What should the agenda be?

- What do we need to consider and in what order?
- Is there too much to cope with?
- Who can include items on the agenda?
- Will matters arising and any other business take up a lot of time?

What about the physical location and arrangements?

- Does everyone know which room is to be used and is it the right size?
- Is the furniture arranged so that everyone can see everyone else and give them eye contact?
- Is it appropriate to have coffee served? Has it been arranged?
- Is it noisy, cold, likely to have interruptions?

How can contributions be stimulated and controlled?

- Who has something to say?
- How can I get them to say it?
- How can I keep the long-winded brief?
- When should I nudge the meeting towards a decision/the next item?

Minutes or report of the meeting

- Who writes these?
- Is it important to describe the discussion and issues or just the list of actions and who is responsible?
- Who gets a copy?
- What will be the effect of the minutes on those who did/did not attend?
- Who are we trying to influence with these minutes and in what way?

Implementation of proposals

- Who has agreed to do what?
- How can we help each other to get on with it?
- Who else can we involve?
- How can we monitor the implementation?
- Do we need a review date?
- What can I do to get things moving?

Self-check questions

1 Why is the use of power inevitable in organisations?
2 What are Etzioni's three sorts of power?
3 What are Etzioni's three sorts of involvement?
4 Name three sources of power open to people in organisations.
5 What is the difference between 'in' authority and 'an' authority?
6 Name Mullin's three aspects of delegation.
7 What are Kotter's two aspects of management?
8 What is the natural outcome of one-to-one negotiation?
9 Why do organisations have meetings?

CASE STUDY 12.1

In 1902 the Scottish dramatist J.M. Barrie wrote *The Admirable Crichton* in which an English aristocratic family is shipwrecked on a desert island. The authority of the head of the family rapidly disintegrates in this situation and the role of leader is gradually assumed by Crichton, the family butler. On the desert island his leadership is unchallenged. When the party is rescued the crew of the ship that rescue them immediately re-establish the norms and values of Edwardian England, so Crichton resumes his tailcoat and serves his master an excellent breakfast in bed.

What do you think might have been Crichton's sources of power on the island?

References

Carter A. (1979) *Authority and Democracy.* Routledge and Kegan Paul, London.

Dahl R.A. (1970) *Modern Political Analysis,* 2nd edn. Prentice Hall, Englewood Cliffs, NJ.

Etzioni A. (1975) *A Comparative Analysis of Complex Organizations: On Power, Involvement and their Correlates,* revised edn. Free Press, New York, NY.

French J. and Raven B. (1958) The bases of social power. In Cartwright D. (Ed.) *Studies in Social Power,* Institute of Social Research, Ann Arbor, MI.

Guerin D. (1970) *Anarchism: from Theory to Practice.* Monthly Review Press, London.

Kotter J. (1982) *The General Managers.* Free Press, New York, NY.

Mullins L.J. (1996) *Management and Organisational Behaviour.* Pitman, London.

Pfeffer J. (1981) *Power in Organizations.* Pitman, Marshfield, MA.

Pugh D.S. (1971) *Organisational Theory.* Penguin, Harmondsworth.

Torrington D. and Weightman J. (1989a) *The Reality of School Management.* Blackwell, Oxford.

Torrington D. and Weightman J. (1989b) *Management and Organisation in Secondary Schools: A Training Handbook.* Blackwell, Oxford.

Wolff R.P. (1970) *In Defence of Anarchism.* Harper and Row, London.

Further reading

Pfeffer J. (1981) *Power in Organizations* listed above is a classic discussion of this area.

Peter L.J. (1969) *The Peter Principle.* Morrow, New York, NY. This is a classic, humorous book, where the author suggests that people get promoted to the level of incompetence, the 'Peter principle'.

Mullins L.J. (1996) *Management and Organisational Behaviour* mentioned above has a good chapter (Chapter 16) on delegation.

I would also try some of the political theory books such as Carter (1979), just for a completely different flavour.

There are several novels that are well worth reading for their insights into power abuse in organisations. Michael Crichton's *Disclosure* (1992), which looks at sexual harassment and was also made into a film. *Primary Colours* by Anonymous (1996), about the rise of an obscure southern governor and his quest to become president of the USA.

Golratt E.M. (1997) *It's Not Luck,* Gower, on negotiation technique and lateral thinking is a light and humorous book.

CHAPTER 13

Organisation and job design

Objectives

When you have finished reading this chapter you should be able to:

- ➤ List the different influences on what people do at work.
- ➤ Understand the seven Ss organisations need.
- ➤ Know different ways of redesigning a job.
- ➤ Discuss advantages and disadvantages of 'flexibility'.
- ➤ Distinguish between 'diversity' and 'equal opportunities'.
- ➤ Understand the need to plan for staffing jobs.
- ➤ Know what job evaluation is used for.

Introduction

Chapter 11 dealt with structures and cultures of organisations, and Chapter 12 with the power and influence relationships within organisations. This chapter deals with some of the different ways people in organisations can consciously design the work that takes place to try to satisfy different ends. This particularly includes the rethinking that needs to take place after a reorganisation. The grand plans of reorganisation and organisation design are taken at the strategic level, whereas the redesigning within teams and sections takes place at the local level. For most of us this smaller sort of job design is where we start. The chapter finishes with a discussion on ways organisations can ensure that there are a suitable number of appropriate people to do all these beautifully designed jobs.

Organisation design

How the work of an organisation is done is affected by the variety of issues explored in this book, see, for example, Chapter 11 on structures and culture, and various others. A quick list of the factors that affect what and how the work is done might include:

- ➤ Demands from customers – particularly when these change.
- ➤ Legal requirements – affect what is done and the context in which it is done.
- ➤ Community pressures – such as pressure groups, ethics and cultural norms.
- ➤ Strategic decisions on goals and plans – what is the organisation trying to do?
- ➤ Technology – particularly where there is a major change.
- ➤ Labour market – changes in demography, transport and new employers in the area can change things.

These are the main factors outside the particular work team but internal pressures would include:

- Targets – which usually include budgets and due dates.
- Organisation structure and culture.
- Quality – standards, equipment and staff issues.
- Staff – competence and attitude of staff and management.

All these together influence the possible options for the way in which the work can be done, that is, the design of jobs and the organisation. How this might be achieved is linked to the organisation culture (see Chapter 11), performance management (see Chapter 9), the nature of the training that is done (see Chapter 10) and how the change is managed (see Chapter 14).

Let us first look at how organisation design might affect these decisions. One classic model for analysing organisations is the seven Ss model of Athos and Pascale (1981). The authors maintain that to succeed organisations must focus on all seven areas and that these areas must complement each other. The seven areas are:

1. Strategy – includes the plan or course of action. It is about allocating scarce resources over time to achieve specified goals.
2. Structure – the need to decide what type of organisation chart is appropriate, for example, decentralised, centralised or professional.
3. Systems – includes how we inform and coordinate our activities and is about such things as meeting formats, reports, formal communications, etc.
4. Staff – means ensuring a supply of suitably trained and motivated staff, with the right skill mix.
5. Style – is about how managers behave in achieving goals that assist rather than hinder.
6. Skills – what are the distinctive capabilities of key personnel?
7. Shared values – the meanings and guiding concepts used by members of the organisation to ensure they belong.

Athos and Pascale's work was based on comparing Japanese and American manufacturing companies and they felt that the Americans were devoting less time than the Japanese to the four soft Ss – staff, style, skills and shared values. Since then much management writing has concentrated on these four soft Ss. Indeed this book has too.

Although British organisations are in many ways different from the companies studied by Athos and Pascale the same argument can certainly be made that these four soft Ss need careful consideration (and are often neglected) if the organisations are to work. Without attention to some of these softer aspects of organisation it may lead to people feeling estranged, uninvolved, aggressive, anxious and lacking commitment or low staff morale. These feelings, summarised in the sociological term 'alienation', described in Chapter 3, are worth re-emphasising here, and are summarised by Seeman (1959) as being composed of the following aspects:

- Powerlessness – the sense of low control over events.
- Meaninglessness – the sense of incomprehensibility of personal and social affairs.

Figure 13.1 **Super organisations.**

- Normlessness – lack of high commitment to socially approved goals.
- Cultural estrangement – individual rejection of commonly held values.
- Self-estrangement – where activities are undertaken that are not intrinsically rewarding.
- Social isolation – feelings of exclusion or rejection are sensed.

This term is rather less used now as the emphasis in management writing and discussions is on the other side of the same coin, we hear about job satisfaction, motivation, commitment and job involvement. However, any particular worker can only be as motivated, satisfied and committed as both the job and they allow themselves to be.

If this model of emphasising the softer aspects of management is used it is then logical that jobs need to be designed so that people have a suitable chunk of work to call their own and that they can liaise with others to contribute to the whole in a meaningful way.

Designing jobs and structures

Many organisations are reorganising departments and teams by changing the number, skill mix and organisation of staff including increasingly using contract or part-time staff. It is very important in all this that someone knows what work needs doing. The work to be done needs organising into coherent jobs, into a suitable structure for communicating and liaising with each other.

In general terms there are five main steps that need thinking about:

1. Purpose. What purpose in the organisation will the department, section or team serve? Does it provide a service to others in the organisation? Deal directly with customers? Coordinate other's activities? Some other purpose?
2. Activities. What activities are needed to fulfill the purpose? What are the essential things to be done? This is not necessarily everything that is currently being done and may include new tasks.
3. Job design. How are the activities best grouped into jobs? Which of the above activities are best done by one person because of the expertise or access to others required? Are some jobs best done by everyone because they keep everyone in touch? Chapter 10 has something on job rotation and job design.

4 Authority. What formal authority do the job holders need to have delegated to them?
5 Connections. How can the activities of the job holders be connected through information systems and reporting?

The above questions are the starting points for considering what people are asked to do at work. Having a clear view of the task to be done is important, see, for example, Chapter 9 on performance management. But there are other issues to be considered.

Job design

Ensuring that everyone has a suitable job has been one of the enduring themes of management thought and writing. This is usually called job design although more commonly it is job redesign. It is the process of getting the optimum fit between the organisational requirements of the individual employee and the individual's need for satisfaction in the job. This can either be done by 'dumbing down' jobs so that anyone can do them and then using a carrot and stick method or it can be a 'holistic' approach of trying to motivate people to develop themselves and the job.

Hackman (1987) suggests there are various dimensions in jobs associated with good performance by the job holder. Box 13.1 lists five characteristics noted by Hackman. We might want to add the following based on the human relations models:

- Dealing with others. How much staff have to deal with other people will vary and different amounts suit different people.
- Friendship opportunities. Establishing informal relationships at work is again of varying importance to different people.

These dimensions give meaning to work, responsibility to the job holders and knowledge of how they are doing. By taking various actions, see Box 13.2, motivation and performance can be improved in the Hackman model.

As an example of how these characteristics work, many of the ideas have been incorporated in the concept of individual team members having their own customers. For example, in hospitals patients having a named nurse – not only does the patient know who is their carer but the nurses get some of the above characteristics in their working day.

Box 13.1
Job characteristics likely to motivate people in their work. (Based on Hackman (1987).)

1 **Skill variety**. Having a range of competencies needed to carry out work.
2 **Task identity**. Completing a whole or identifiable piece of work.
3 **Task significance**. The work needs to have a significant impact on other people.
4 **Autonomy**. Individuals need a degree of freedom, independence and discretion in when and how things are done.
5 **Job feedback**. The tasks are more easily achieved if the work itself gives direct and clear information about how it has gone.

Box 13.2
Ways of getting good results on the five job dimensions.
(Based on Hackman (1987).)

	Action	Job dimension affected
1	*Forming natural work units* so that the work to be done has a logic and makes sense to the job holder.	2, 3
2	*Combining tasks* so that a number of natural work units may be put together to make a bigger and more coherent job.	1, 2
3	*Establishing links with clients* so that the job holder has contact with the people using the service or product the job holder is supplying.	1, 4, 5
4	*Vertical loading* so that job holders take on more of the management of their jobs in deciding what to do, organising their own time, solving their own problems and controlling their own costs.	4
5	*Opening feedback channels* so that job holders can discover more about how they are doing and whether their performance is improving or deteriorating.	5

Several different ways of improving job satisfaction through redesign have been tried. The major ways of redesigning, or designing, jobs that have been described are:

- Job rotation. This involves moving from one job to another to reduce boredom and increase skills. For example, in one chemical factory the operators are moved around from receiving goods from suppliers, checking the process, running the process, and packing the final product ready for transport to their customers.
- Job enlargement. This increases the number of tasks done by an individual. For example, the waiting staff at TGI Fridays, a restaurant chain, are expected to entertain and 'host' the customers at their tables. The job is larger than just taking orders, serving meals and clearing dishes.
- Job enrichment. This broadens the responsibilities and increases autonomy for decision making. For example, hotel reception staff can negotiate the price charged for a room that night and work out a suitable package rather than having to keep to a set price and lose the customer.
- Autonomous work teams. Here the team decides how, when and for how much the work is done. This requires a skilled team and for management to be prepared to let go. It has been less common in Britain than in the USA and Scandinavia.
- Leadership models. Here the vision of the leader is sufficient to give meaning and significance to everyone, jobs can feel more worthwhile. It is, however, difficult to achieve most of this (see Chapter 8).

- Quality movement. This concentrates on the process of the work rather than the people but assumes people will be challenged by the need for constant improvement (see Chapter 1).
- Flexibility. This is where people work non-traditional hours. This is discussed in detail later in this chapter.

All of these can be used successfully at team, section or departmental level. However, they can also all feel very manipulative if staff are suspicious, feeling aggrieved over pay and conditions or are left feeling uncertain about their personal futures. Like all change it needs careful managing and implementation.

None of the above will be terribly effective if the department, section or unit is poorly organised and has poor structures. Box 13.3 gives a checklist for reviewing the organisation of a team, section or department, that we (Torrington and Weightman (1989)) developed.

PAUSE FOR THOUGHT

If one asked the players of Manchester United football team to appoint a new striker they are most likely to appoint someone adequate but not startling – otherwise they would each lose their place in the hierarchy. Only a manager will appoint the star to come in above the existing team. This reminds us that there are different perspectives that cannot all be represented by the same person and that organisations sometimes need to pay people to represent the different interests necessary for an effective performance.

Competency approaches to job design

There has been considerable interest in designing jobs around competencies following the national initiatives on competencies and NVQs. The design of jobs in this approach is based on analysing exactly what is required in terms of performance and then specifying the competencies required to achieve this performance and the level/standard required.

The advantages claimed for this sort of approach are that it is:

- Employment led – it is about what people actually need to do.
- Based on job analysis – that is, on the skills needed.
- Outcome led – it is expressed in terms of things achieved.
- Linked to national qualifications – for work-based competencies.

The difficulties can be:

- Outcomes – these are not always easy to specify in these terms.
- Standards – it can be difficult to keep low enough and not over-specify jobs.
- Competency analysis – it becomes a complex system that is an end in itself.
- Checking – how often should the competencies be measured?

Box 13.3
Checklist for reviewing the organisation of a department, section or team.

Step 1 The *purpose* of the department or section

(a) Does it meet a basic business need, like purchasing or providing, or is it intended to make things run more smoothly, like personnel? Is it necessary?
(b) Is it set up on the basis of output, like business objectives to be achieved, or on the basis of inputs, like people and problems? Are the outputs already being produced elsewhere?
(c) Does the department exist to deal with matters that other managers find uninteresting or unattractive? If 'yes', are the reasons good enough?

Step 2 The *activities* to meet the purpose

(a) Does the section bring together those who share a particular skill or those with a particular responsibility?
(b) What activities have to be carried out to meet the purpose?
(c) How many people with what experience and qualifications are needed for those activities?
(d) How many ancillary staff are needed? How can that number be reduced? How can that number be reduced further?
(e) Are all the identified activities needed? Is there any duplication with other sections and departments? Is there a better way?

Step 3 *Grouping* the activities

(a) How much specialisation is needed? How will this specialisation affect job satisfaction, commitment and efficiency?
(b) Are boundaries between jobs clearly defined and in the right place?
(c) Will job holders have the amount of discretion needed to be effective?

Step 4 The *authority* of job holders

(a) Do job titles and other 'labels' indicate satisfactorily what authority the job holder has?
(b) Do all job holders have the necessary equipment – like keys, computer codes, and information – for their duties?
(c) Do all job holders have the required authorisations – like authorisation to sign documents – that are needed?
(d) Is the authority of any job holder unreasonably restricted?

Step 5 *Connecting* the activities of job holders

(a) Do job holders know what they need to know about the activities of their colleagues?
(b) Are there enough meetings of staff, too few, or too many?
(c) Are there enough copies of memoranda circulated for information, too few, or too many?
(d) Are job holders physically located in relation to one another in a way that assists communication between those who need frequently to exchange information?

Flexibility

Flexibility has become a major redesign tool for organisations and has various meanings and implications:

- It usually refers to the hours worked, which is discussed later.
- It can also mean functional flexibility where people can be moved around through increased training and relaxation of job demarcations.
- Numerical flexibility allows the numbers employed to fluctuate.
- Financial flexibility where the employment costs reflect the demand and supply of people and so vary the pay given to people.

One way of giving people greater freedom and control over their work is flexible working hours or flexitime. This usually means that there is a core time when everyone must be at work and then an agreed minimum hours per month to be achieved. Technological changes have meant this can be extended to include people working at home, so-called 'teleworking'. This in turn has led to the use of flexibility by employers to develop core and periphery staff. The core staff are full time and the periphery are called in when required, see Chapter 3. For example, most retail organisations have part-time staff to cover busy times, indeed many shops only have part-time staff.

Here are two examples of companies using flexibility in an attempt to meet both the staff and the organisations needs:

- British Airways have 33 per cent and 50 per cent contracts for their cabin staff as well as full-time posts. This means they work one month in three or one month in two, respectively, with the normal rota of off and on days. This allows the staff to have whole months on and off, it also allows those managing the rotas to treat everyone equally within the month.
- Lilly Industries have a 'Worklife Programme' which includes the following options:

  Part-time working – of varying lengths.
  Job shares – for two people to share the same full-time job.
  Teleworking – people work from home.
  Term-time working – people work only when their children are at school.
  Paid paternity leave – for fathers in the first year of their child's life.
  Career breaks – for parental care.
  Sabbaticals – for a variety of reasons.
  Periods of reduced hours – again for a variety of personal reasons.

  Part of the options for staff also include health insurance, share options and pensions. The aim is to retain skilled staff who the organisation has invested in through training and experience, to deal with skill shortages, lower sickness rates and reduce burn out and enhance recruitment.

ACTIVITY 13.1

What difficulties do you think it would create for the full-time workers if there are a lot of part-timers?

These examples show how flexibility in job design, and particularly job hours can benefit both employers and employees. However, not all such schemes are so equally balanced. Flexibility is too often a one-sided bargain with intolerable insecurity for individuals who are having to take all the risks of the organisations. For example, zero hours contracts where there is no guaranteed work or income; full-time staff who are compulsorily made part time; imposed self-employed status where unfair dismissal and redundancy rights are removed. All these have been common practice in British organisations in the 1990s. These practices may help short-term survival of the organisation and profits but do little to engender commitment over the long term.

Diversity

One aspect of job design that has attracted attention over the years is how to ensure fair treatment for different people. This has also included legislation on equal opportunities and discrimination about gender and race. In many management books and particularly personnel or human resource management there is increasing use of the term 'managing diversity'. This is used where in the past the phrase 'equal opportunity' was used. There is a different emphasis as well as a change of vocabulary.

Box 13.4 gives a list of the legislation which to some extent protects people from discrimination. This is known as the Equal Opportunities legislation.

Box 13.4
Equal opportunities legislation.

Sex discrimination
Sex Discrimination Acts 1975 and 1986
Employment Protection Act 1978
Equal Pay Act 1970
Employment Rights Act 1996

Racial equality
Race Relations Act 1976

Disabled people
Disability Discrimination Act 1995

Part timers
European Court of Justice rulings.

Ex-offenders
Rehabilitation of Offenders Act 1974

Northern Ireland
Fair Employment (Northern Ireland) 1989

Figure 13.2 **Diversity cake.**

Managing diversity, however, is less about helping different groups cope with a dominant male, white, able-bodied culture which was the concern of the earlier equal opportunities movements and legislation. Managing diversity is more about valuing the differences which people have and using and celebrating these differences. This might include diversity of:

- qualifications
- accent
- sexual orientation
- caring responsibilities
- learning difficulties
- political affiliation
- spent convictions
- Trade union membership
- gender
- ethnic origin
- age.

For many well-established organisations managing diversity is still a novelty and far from achieved. For newer, small organisations, particularly in the so-called 'gorgeous' industries of fashion, hospitality and performance, there are more examples of the celebration of diversity.

The personnel or human resource management approach

Organisation and job design is really part of the whole planning process. A development of the classic approach to planning has been to integrate the need for people with the planning of the goals and objectives of the organisation. This planning is done at a senior level. Once the strategic plan or initiative is decided it will certainly involve line managers in trying to propose possible ways of putting the plan into practice. The strategy may include ideas of improving services for the customers, reducing staffing costs, improving the quality or innovations of products.

> ***DID YOU KNOW?***
> *Approaches to planning questions can be on a sectional or team basis as well as organisation-wide. For example, the common target of reducing staffing costs could be done by:*
>
> - *Improving recruitment techniques so that there are better employees and less turnover.*
> - *Reducing absenteeism.*
> - *Using the skills and time of individuals better.*
> - *Rewarding people more effectively.*
> - *Having annual hours rather than paying for overtime.*
>
> *Any of these might be effective at reducing staffing costs on a unit, section or team.*

This chapter is about the various aspects of planning that try to ensure that the jobs are designed appropriately. There is also a need to ensure that there is adequate staffing for the work to be done in the section or department. At the strategic, whole organisation level, this would be a major aspect of the personnel department and top management's function. There is also an increasing expectation that the line manager is involved in 'human resource management', as it is only at this level that particular decisions about what is needed can be integrated with the development of the particular activities, or business, of the section and department. The team leader or department manager is best placed to do all the prior analysis about the workloads, work methods and practices which will affect the number and expertise of staff required.

Planning to have the right people to do the job

One classic approach to these issues has been Human Resource Planning where an attempt is made to see whether there is likely to be a mismatch between the future needs of the organisation and the supply of suitably qualified and experienced staff. This is usually done by:

- *Scanning the horizon* to see what likely changes are coming up and what the implications are for staffing. This involves looking at the organisation's plans, government action, trends in techniques, technologies and approaches to the task involved. Any of these might affect the nature of the work to be done in the department and consequently the number and nature of the staff required. For example, in hospitals the rise of less intrusive surgery has led to more and more day cases and fewer overnight stays with the obvious changes in staffing required on the wards at night.
- These changes need to be put alongside the *demand for labour* within the organisation due to current practice and future plans for contraction or expansion of the service.
- The *supply of labour* within the organisation needs to be examined in terms of age, experience, qualifications, pay and conditions and performance of existing staff. The external supply of labour will vary depending on changes in the population, competition for workers from other organisations and the education and training available for people to qualify in particular areas.
- A comparison is made between the demand and supply of staff. This *forecast* is the basis for planning for the future. Matching supply and demand can be done manually or by computer. Except for the simplest cases the personnel department should have access to some sophisticated information systems using payroll and personnel information.
- The figures forecast are not an absolute, nor are the outcomes, as they can be influenced by interdepartmental relations, organisational politics and the empire building of senior managers. The figures will also be affected by artificial restraints from the top management, as Rothwell (1995, p. 171) points out. For example, the board may have put a cost limit or a headcount limit for the organisation. This will affect estimates of labour demand. There will also be arguments about how these costs are counted. Does labour include only the salary or the total employment costs? Are heads counted as actual numbers or full-time equivalents?

Once there are plans and a human resource forecast, Bramham (1989, p. 155) suggests that the forecast allows plans to be made. Some of the areas, in alphabetical order, to ask questions about and plan for are:

- Accommodation. Is there a need for more or fewer rooms, desks etc?
- Costs. Where is there a need for additional/less resources?
- Culture. How are the changes going to affect the way people interact?
- Development. Will there be different opportunities for staff development?
- Industrial relations. How will the unions react to the changes?
- Organisation development. Do reporting relationships need to be changed or reorganised?
- Outplacements. Will some people need to find new jobs?
- Promotion. What opportunities for promotion will there be?
- Productivity. Will these changes affect the amount of work each person can sensibly do?
- Recruitment. What sort of people will need to be recruited?
- Redundancy. Which groups are likely to face redundancy and how is this going to be handled?
- Retirement. Is there a need to change the ages at which retirement is offered?
- Reward systems. Should the salary structures change?
- Training and retraining. Which areas need to develop new skills?
- Transfer. Should the transfer of staff be voluntary or compulsory?
- Working practices. Is there a need to rethink the way of working?

Decisions and practice about all of these can affect the utilisation of people at work. Decisions about each will also affect how much work gets done, how well the work is done and how many people are needed to do it. For example, if you have a section which is spread across a variety of different buildings you are going to need more staff than if you are all together. But there may be important aspects of the service which require you to be spread out. While every attempt to keep costs of staff down is to be praised, it can at times seem absurd when this becomes the prime decision factor at the expense of providing a suitable quality of service.

DID YOU KNOW?

Here are some examples of the need for planning staff use from a Healthcare Trust I was associated with:

- *The use of theatres and the need to get a precise costing of them. Some consultants were overrunning their time in the theatres and the question was who pays for the overtime of the porters and nurses? One way round this has been to get consultants to manage their lists by having whole days rather than half-days in the theatre.*
- *The maternity unit was getting regional manpower figures on the future number of midwives needed and the number of projected deliveries. The question was how typical was the Trust's catchment area compared with these regional figures?*
- *One directorate was looking at the workload activities of the staff and the dependency of individual patients. The higher the dependency of patients the more staff are needed to look after them. This was to enable them to forward plan what sorts of staff they needed and how many.*
- *Another directorate was obtaining information on waiting lists so they could draw up plans for various initiatives such as operating at weekends and evenings. This had obvious implications for staffing and who was to pay for it.*
- *Looking at the case mix, including care profiles, allowed one group to manage their resources better. By having different mixes of routine and difficult cases the specialist technical staff required for the assessment stage could be better used.*

Matching the supply and demand for staff

Related to this analysis of what people are needed is the issue of the supply and demand for staff. If they are more or less in balance there is no real problem, at the moment. If there is a mismatch between the supply and demand for staff various strategies can be used.

If there are *too many staff* the number can be decreased by organisations using such methods as early retirement, assisted career changes, encouraging people to seek other employment, sending people on secondment, asking people to work part time or do less overtime, voluntary and compulsory redundancy. Organisations have also discouraged people from committing themselves to the organisation by giving short-term contracts and flexible working. All of these are better done as an organisation-wide initiative rather than at the local department level as there may be other parts of the organisation who are desperate for staff or who could certainly use them effectively. An alternative strategy to reducing staff is to increase the demand for the services by offering it to more people and developing new services.

If there are *too few staff* organisations can try recruiting differently. This means trying to attract different people from the usual, advertising in different places, offering assistance in transport or childcare, improving the terms and conditions of employment. Organisations could also redeploy, train and promote existing staff. Encouraging existing staff to take on new work through changes to the terms and conditions, changes in management style and communication, promotion, recognition, training and development have all been tried successfully. Organisations can also reduce the demand for more staff by redesigning the work, subcontracting the work or using staff differently, such as on overtime.

Job evaluation

Many of the pressures for job redesign and the change in the number of people doing the work become focused in the organisation on job evaluation. When all the jobs have been decided the question that inevitably rises is: what are we going to be paid for doing these new, redesigned jobs? This is usually to establish fair pay. Income Data Services (1979) also give the following reasons why organisations start job evaluation.

- Demands for rational grading structures.
- Union recognition.
- Move to greater employee participation.
- Single status.
- Sex discrimination and equal pay.
- Decay or disrepute of old systems.
- Changes in technology and job content.
- Relocation and mobility.
- Multinationals: transferring staff between countries.
- Allowing for future expansion.
- Changes in personnel staff.

The most common evaluation scheme is that of points rating. Each benchmark job has a job description written by the job holder, by the manager of the job holder or the job analyst. A small group then considers each description in turn. Each factor has a different weighting and each job is awarded points for each factor. The total gives the relative worth of each job. The International Labour Organisation has produced the following lists of factors most frequently used.

Accountability
Accuracy
Analysis
Complexity
Contact and diplomacy
Creativity
Decision making
Dexterity
Education
Effect of errors
Effort
Initiative
Judgement
Know how
Knowledge and skills
Mental effort
Mental fatigue
Physical demand
Physical skills
Planning
Problem solving
Resources control
Social skill
Stress
Supervision
Task completion
Training and experience
Work conditions

Responsibility for cash/materials/confidential information/equipment/process/records/reports

The main difficulty of implementing job evaluation is that it is time consuming and expensive. In addition it can upset long-established differentials and vested interests.

Conclusion

Organisation and job design is intertwined with the nature of the organisation structure and culture (see Chapter 11). The issue of performance management (see Chapter 9) is where the effectiveness of the jobs people have is measured and rewarded. The particular choices about which sort of structure, culture, job design and performance management is required vary enormously. The analysis of these organisation behaviours and trying to judge their effectiveness keeps us all intrigued, thrilled and frustrated with working life. The aim of a more systematic approach is to learn from this variety.

EXERCISE 13.1

1. List five things that an employer might want from a person doing the job(s) below. Think about different areas such as knowledge, skill, social skills, personal attributes and efficiency.
2. List five things that an employee might want from doing the job.
3. Now try to write a simple job description to meet both these people's needs.
4. Try one of the following jobs or one you know:
   A school leaver starting hairdressing.
   A management trainee in a retail chain.
   A GP in a suburban practice.
   A clerical assistant in a charity office.

Self-check questions

1. What factors might affect what work is done? Try to give at least six.
2. What are the 7 Ss of organisation?
3. What is: (a) job rotation; (b) job enlargement; (c) job enrichment; (d) job evaluation?
4. What is flexibility? Give three different ways this is achieved.
5. Name four areas where there has been equal opportunities legislation. Six were given.
6. What are the main stages of Human Resource Planning?

CASE STUDY **13.1**

In 1998 the Lord Chancellor's Department asked all Magistrates Courts to reorganise to match the equivalent local police authority. In the Greater Manchester area this meant matching the area covered by the Greater Manchester Police Authority. Incidentally, they also wanted the Probation service to reorganise into this geographical setting. Originally there were separate courts with their own management, training, budgets and staff in the following areas:

Manchester City	Bury
Salford	Bolton
Stockport	Oldham
Trafford	Rochdale
Thameside	Wigan

What do you think will need considering in the new design for the organisation? Use one of the models given to help you, for example the seven Ss or five steps.

There are no absolute answers!

References

Athos A. and Pascale R. (1981) *The Art of Japanese Management: Applications for American Executives*. Simon and Schuster, New York, NY.

Bramham J. (1989) *Human Resource Planning*. IPM, London.

Hackman J.R. (1987) Work design. In *Motivation and Work Behaviour*, 4th edn, Steers R.M. and Porter L.W. (Eds), McGraw Hill, London.

Income Data Services (1979) *Guide to Job Evaluation*. IDS, London.

International Labour Organisation (1986) *Job Evaluation*. ILO, Geneva.

Rothwell S. (1995) Human resource planning. In *Human Resource Management: A Critical Text,* Storey J. (Ed.), Routledge, London.

Seeman M. (1959) On the meaning of alienation. *American Sociological Review,* Vol. 24, 783–91.

Torrington D.P. and Weightman J.B. (1989) *Effective Management,* 2nd edn. Prentice Hall, Hemel Hempstead.

Further reading

Child J. (1984) *Organization: A Guide to Problems and Practice,* 2nd edn, Harper and Row, is a standard reference in this area and gives good solid material.

Handy C. (1997) *Understanding Organisations*, 3rd edn, Penguin, is by far the most readable and accessible standard text for British readers in this area.

CHAPTER 14

Dealing with change

Objectives

When you have finished reading this chapter you should be able to:

- Describe what OD includes.
- Work out a plan for change.
- Understand what is meant by the learning organisation.
- Distinguish between innovation and creativity.
- Discuss ways of coping with change at an individual level.
- Describe the psychological contract.

Introduction

It has become a recurring theme in studies of organisational behaviour to emphasise that dealing with change is the norm. These changes can be such things as small alterations in procedures because of a new IT system, or major changes because of legislation or reorganisation in the face of increased competition from overseas. This chapter looks at the process of dealing with change at the organisation level and the individual level. The chapter uses material from elsewhere in the book to show how understanding organisational behaviour is an important part of dealing with change. The chapter starts by looking at some of the models which analyse how organisations deal with change. The latter part of the chapter looks at the impact of change on individuals, including a section on those who are particularly creative and contribute to the changes organisations make.

Organisation development

Organisation development is a generic term used to describe a wide range of tactics used to try to develop the individuals, groups and whole organisation as a total system. In Chapter 11 I emphasised that organisations cannot develop, behave or learn; to say so is to reify the concept of organisation. It is the people who make up the organisation who do these things. In a general sense organisation development, or OD as it is known, is about trying to improve the overall performance and effectiveness of the organisation by analysing what changes in the behaviour of individuals and groups could bring about the desired change. OD has very much been the arena

DID YOU KNOW?
Change cannot take place successfully when the whiff of hypocrisy is in the air.

for management consultants with a behavioural orientation. It is where the analysis of organisational behaviour is used to effect change. The areas which are covered by OD would include an analysis of:

- Organisational culture – the characteristic beliefs and values of the organisation that we talked about in Chapter 11 on organisational settings.
- Organisational climate – similar to culture but reflecting more the morale of the people in the organisation, which we covered in Chapter 8 on leadership and autonomy.
- Employee commitment – the level of trust and motivation of people to the organisation and those they work with that was discussed in Chapters 3 and 7 on motivation and group working.
- Organisational conflict – looking at the differences between various people and groups within the organisation and how they influence each other and which we discussed in Chapter 12 on power, authority and influence.
- The management of change – looking at various strategies for change (the subject of this chapter).
- Management development – this particularly includes developing personal and people skills so managers can deal with emotions and feelings as well as tasks and functions that we dealt with in Chapter 10 on development.
- Organisational effectiveness – this includes the quality movement and the structures and systems of organisations as well as the softer people skills, see, for example, Chapter 9 on performance management.

These are all traditional areas of study for the analysis of organisational behaviour so any particular OD could use models from a variety of perspectives. This can be very useful as each organisation is different and so needs different changes. To encourage a better fit between the organisation and the proposed OD most consultants try to take an action-orientated approach. Various methods are used such as:

- Surveys to determine the attitudes of people working in the organisation.
- Team building exercises to improve communication and trust.
- Management training in people skills.

By using these and other methods, it is hoped to open people's attitudes to change and permit different levels of discussion to take place. Two particular developments of OD are the approaches of managing change and the concept of the learning organisation.

DID YOU KNOW?

Samuel Johnson (1709–1784) said:

> *Change is not made without inconvenience, even from worse to better.*

Managing change

A great deal of management training and consultancy time has been spent on trying to find ways of managing change effectively. The main issues are deciding on what, if any, are the appropriate changes for a particular group and how to ensure that change is carried out with the minimum of difficulty. These changes can be dramatic reorientations of the organisation away from their traditional product or service or smaller internal changes to reduce the costs of providing that product or service. For most organisations changes associated with IT developments have also been made. So what models of managing change have been used?

The sequence given for managing change in most management textbooks and courses goes along the following lines:

- Scan the horizon. This is where the necessity for change is evaluated. It involves looking at influences inside and outside the organisation. It would probably include some of the OD list as well.
- Establish the project. What are we going to do?
- Set goals. What should be done by when?
- Identify a solution. How are we going to get there?
- Prepare for implementation. What resources do we need? How do we get the commitment of people involved? Whose power do we need? Who needs to know?
- Implement the project. How do we influence people and deal with the unexpected?
- Review progress. How are we doing?
- Maintain the project. Are there any problems?

This sort of list is useful as a checklist to prepare for change. However, too much planning can mean that you never get on to the action. The important point is that, like trust and commitment, ownership of a project by the people builds and develops over time. It comes through actually working to improve something. So it makes sense for the initiator to give a firm push at the beginning of a project so it really gets started. It is also important to offer lots of help and support to those affected by the change and this help is better done after the initial planning. For many it is helping them deal with the fear of change so they can trust the proposed action. A later section of this chapter deals with this.

ACTIVITY **14.1**

Think of a change in your environment you would like to implement. Now use the above list to prepare for this.

If you cannot think of a change try planning for a change to the cleaning/cooking arrangements in your house/flat.

A simple model of change that is commonly used in organisations for talking about small changes is that of force field analysis, based on Lewin's (1952) field theory which we described briefly in Chapter 3 on motivation. This device looks at the driving forces for change by representing them as arrows. Those on the left represent the forces for change and those on the right the restraining forces for no change. For example, Figure 14.1 might represent the field of a proposed change in work procedures for a waste disposal site. This device can be used for looking at those for and against a proposed change to see where the power lies. The value of force field analysis is in seeing where other stakeholders are positioned and what needs to be tackled if a proposed change is to be implemented or resisted.

Driving forces →	← Restraining forces
Legislation	Established routines
Local community	Cost
Senior management	Workgroup

Figure 14.1
Force field analysis for change.

ACTIVITY **14.2**

Now use the same change as you used in Activity 14.1 and draw a force field analysis of the problem.

Which method of analysing change do you find easier to use?

There is plenty of advice available about how to manage change, see, for example, McCalman and Paton (1992), and it is not my intention to deal in any more detail with managing change here as this book is about various ways of analysing organisational behaviour not about specific areas of management.

ACTIVITY **14.3**

Think about some changes you have experienced in organisations. For example, a change of teacher, a change of the way a team is organised, a change of timetable or rooms for working in. Now think about the following questions.

- What changes, large and small, have you experienced at work/college/club in the last three months?
- Which of these were successfully achieved?
- Does anything distinguish the successful changes from the more problematic?

The learning organisation

Dealing with change has attracted a lot of attention from managerial writers and they tend to describe organisations that cope well as 'learning organisations'. The idea of a learning organisation was first articulated by Argyris and Schon (1978) and developed by people such as Morgan (1986) and Pedlar, Burgoyne and Boydell (1991). The last group are influential British writers on various aspects of training and development. Various lists, probably not quite well established enough yet to call models, have been developed to describe these 'learning organisations'.

Building an organisation's capacity to learn according to Marquand and Reynolds (1994) is based on the following:

- Transforming the individual and organisation's image of learning. The aim is to encourage life-long learning and a desire for continuous improvement.
- Create knowledge-based partnerships with people inside and outside the organisation to share ideas and information so a real understanding develops.
- Develop and expand team-learning activities to encourage people to share questions, information, ideas, solutions and approaches.
- Change the role of managers to facilitators rather than controllers.

- Encourage experiments and risk taking so that new possibilities emerge rather than everyone playing things safe.
- Create structures and systems with time to extract learning. This suggests some 'soft' time for people to talk and develop rather than always being busy.
- Build opportunities and mechanisms to disseminate learning both formally and informally.
- Empower people to take decisions and actions.
- Push information through the organisation and to external associates.
- Develop the discipline of system thinking, what are the implications for others?
- Create a culture of continuous improvement.
- Develop a powerful vision of organisational excellence and individual fulfilment.
- Root out bureaucracy.

Pedlar, Burgoyne and Boydell (1991) suggest that the following features are indicative of a learning organisation (although they prefer the term 'learning company' to 'learning organisation'):

- Learning approach to strategy – so that risks are taken and new opportunities are tried so people learn about the new as well as the well-established.
- Participative policy making, with consultation and participation by people from all parts of the organisation.
- Open information systems – nothing is hidden from members of the organisation unless it is imperative.
- Formative, that is encouraging people, accounting and control rather than restrictive methods.
- Internal exchange of ideas and information.
- Flexibility of rewards so people can work to their own best way.
- Enabling structures for individual contributions.
- Boundary workers act as boundary scanners.
- Inter-worker learning.
- Learning climate for all.
- Self-development opportunities for all.

Some of these ideas are frankly rather idealistic and these lists can become 'wishlists' rather than a practical guide to the reality of most organisations. Many would feel that not only are they unworkable but they could damage the viability of the organisation. However, the advantages of these criteria for a learning organisation are that they can form a useful checklist for raising questions about an existing organisation. It is rather difficult though to see how you could set out with such a checklist as an indication of how to transform an organisation. However, by taking each of the concepts as a question we can ask how a particular organisation does things.

The concept of the learning organisation has obvious similarities with some of the underpinning ideas of Total Quality Management (TQM) and Business Process Reengineering (BPR) with their emphasis on continuous improvement, breaking down barriers, customer supply chains and empowerment.

Hammer is probably the best known exponent of BPR, although his view changes over the years, see, for example, Hammer and Champy (1993). He suggests that BPR is carried out in the following stages.

- Map the existing work process. For example, what happens to a patient when they come to hospital. Often this demonstrates a lack of concentration on the main process and more emphasis on the departments and functions of individuals.
- Dismantle the existing functional departments, such as admissions, imaging, wards, theatres, pharmacy in the hospital example and create process teams where the focus is the main activity. For example, everyone necessary for a team to deal with hip replacements.
- Every customer, patient or client is given a case manager or champion, for example, a named nurse.
- Empower individuals and enrich jobs so that individuals can take responsibility and carry out the necessary work without constantly referring to others.
- Train and develop, and retrain individuals to meet the new tasks.
- Flatten the management and supervision levels as individuals practise more self-management.
- Measure results not activity.
- Promote on ability, not 'one of us' or some other criteria.
- Develop leaders.

The two main criticisms of this approach, which was very popular in the late 1980s and early 1990s, are first, that it is too mechanistic and does not take into consideration the softer aspects of organisational behaviours, and second, it led to too much job insecurity to get the best from people, as well as the consequences for society of large numbers of unemployed people. A more theoretical criticism is that it is not really a new approach but very much carries on the socio-technical and operational management approach developed in the 1960s (see Chapters 1 and 7 for details of this sort of research).

The useful aspect of this view is that it looks at the organisation as a whole and how the various functions and specialisms relate to each other. Many of the concepts listed have already been written about elsewhere in this book. One way of looking at the learning organisation models, indeed the OD movement generally, is to see them as integrating models of organisational behaviour.

ACTIVITY **14.4**

If you want to do some research try to find the answer to the following using either of the learning organisation lists given above. (To do this you will have to decide who will be the best people to ask the following questions, how you are going to approach them and how you are going to phrase the questions. These decisions about gaining access to the appropriate people are at the heart of a lot of social research. Those who can charm their way into organisations often get much more open responses!)

- How does your university decide on policy?
- Who participates in this?
- Does it differ depending on what the policy is about?

Creativity and innovation

So far we have been discussing change in organisations that are led by senior staff and their understanding of the environment in which the organisation operates. Another important aspect of change in organisations is the drive for innovation and creativity by individuals. These are not terms to describe dark forces disturbing the ordered calm but interesting activities undertaken by people at work that keep their organisations lively by exploring possible new activities and changed methods of doing things. As Steiner (1965 p. 4) says:

> Innovation and creativity have to do with development, proposal and implementation of *new* and *better* solutions.

Proposals have to meet the criteria of being both new and better. When colleagues are reluctant to support innovations, it may be because of lethargy and lack of imagination but it may also be because the proposed innovation is not a very good one. Examples of proposed innovations that had to be revoked were a proposal to replace the London Underground map, a masterpiece of design, and the disastrous marketing of 'new' Coca Cola. The public did not like the new Coca Cola so the original was reintroduced as 'Classic Coke'. Hill and O' Sullivan (1996) in the companion volume, *Marketing*, suggest (p. 171) that:

> ... *a new product is simply a product that is perceived as new by the customer.* It may be a brand new technology for which its inventor won a Nobel prize, or simply a reworking of an age old concept which by virtue of its new design, offers new benefits to the customer.

Innovation is the whole process from invention to practice; creativity is the initial phase of generating the new idea, product or approach. Pavitt (1979) pointed out that technical innovation and industrial development are increasingly important for the following reasons:

- There is growing competition from developing countries that produce an expanding range of standard goods as their industrialisation progresses.
- The taste of consumers and their expenditure level are constantly changing in the more advanced countries.
- We have to consider ways of reducing the consumption of energy and the environment if we are to have a sustainable lifestyle.
- The possibilities of emerging technologies.

A continuing academic discussion considers whether the demand for a new or revised product is the push of innovation or whether it is new inventions that provide the pull. The dilemma for organisations is whether they should look for innovation by being sensitive to the market or whether should they invest in speculative research. The answer is they do both, but different markets put a different emphasis on either end of the continuum. For example, teenage fashion is more likely to be driven by the market than a pharmaceutical company that will be more driven by scientific breakthroughs.

DID YOU KNOW?

Brainstorming is frequently used in organisations to generate ideas. This can be for new products, services or ways of working.

- *To start you need a flip chart, blackboard or overhead projector and someone who can write quickly and legibly. (Another way, in a small group, is to use 'post-its' which make the classification process later on quicker.)*
- *Decide on the purpose of the session beforehand and make a note of your own ideas.*
- *Appoint the note taker.*
- *Ask group members to call out ideas that come into their heads.*
- *Write these down so all can see.*
- *Encourage participation.*
- *Do not allow any judgement at this stage*
- *Keep things fast.*
- *Reach a target number, say 50 in 15 minutes.*
- *Now classify the ideas into groups.*
- *Ask the group to rank them for newness/ relevance/feasibility.*
- *Decide on the action to be taken about the preferred ideas.*

The exercise at the end of this chapter suggests you use this method.

Whatever the reasons for the demand for innovation there is always a small number of people in organisations who produce a large proportion of the initial ideas which trigger the innovation process. Psychologists have tried to distinguish the characteristics of individuals associated with high levels of creativity. Steiner (1965, pp. 7–8) summarises these as:

- Conceptual fluency – the ability to generate a large number of ideas rapidly.
- Conceptual flexibility – the ability to discard one frame of reference for another.
- Originality – the tendency to give unusual, atypical answers.
- Preference for complexity over simplicity – looking for new challenges of knotty problems.
- Independence of judgement – being different from peers and seeing superiors as conventional or arbitrary.

If this list is accurate then creative individuals are in need of nurturing as these qualities are unlikely to make them easy colleagues. When there is great emphasis on the organisation culture and the team, the odd personality who sees things differently may be crushed. Torrance (1970) in a classic study of creative children suggested how one might provide for the highly creative. His advice seems appropriate for adults within the conforming organisation. He suggests we should:

- Provide a refuge.
- Become their sponsor or patron.
- Help them understand their divergence.
- Let them communicate their ideas.
- See that their creative talent is recognised.
- Help others to understand them.

People respond differently to change

Changes in organisations and in the technical aspects of work have meant most people have experienced change in their working practice. To some these changes mean excitement and the thrill of being part of the action. For others it feels like a threatening dismantling of the stable order of things. Although there is actually less change generally in society and industry in Britain now

Figure 14.2 **People respond to change.**

than at the end of the nineteenth century, we all feel as if change is an everyday part of our lives.

There are several different kinds of change which can be put into four broad types of change experience.

1 Imposition, where the initiative comes from someone else and we have to alter our ways of doing things to comply with outside requirements. This undermines our sense of being able to handle things and we worry about the implications. New rules and laws are the obvious examples.
2 Adaptation, where we have to change our behaviour or attitudes at the behest of others. This can be very difficult and leads to people leaving and retiring. Examples are changes in attitudes about race and gender or taking on a business orientation rather than a public service one.
3 Growth, where we are responding to opportunities for developing competence, poise and achievement. Examples would be 'acting up' or job changes.
4 Creativity, where we are the instigator and in control of the process. Examples would be introducing new standards at work, developing a new technique or trying something new to see whether it will work.

Most of us resist the first, are uncertain about the second, delighted with the third and excited by the fourth kind of change. As a member of an organisation you will undoubtedly experience all of these and have to sustain yourself and maybe others as well through periods of change. How can we manage this?

Keep something stable in a period of change

For a satisfactory life we all need a balance of novel experiences and experiences that give us comfort or stability. How each of us wishes to balance these will obviously vary from individual to individual. In addition how we interpret novelty and comfort depends upon our experience – your comfort may be my novelty. The stimulation of novelty and change usually means we will put effort into something. However, if the stimulation becomes too great we become less able to make a contribution, see Figure 14.3. It is at this point that stress is experienced with all the associated feelings of increased ambiguity and the possibility of failure.

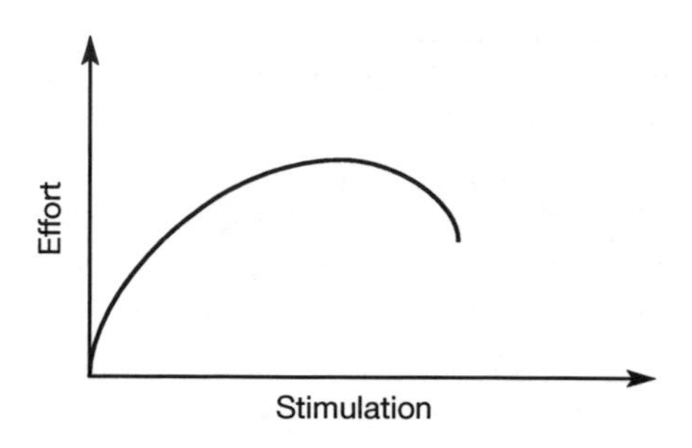

Figure 14.3
Effect of stimulation and effort.

Toffler (1970) recognised that we can cope with a lot of change, pressure, complexity and confusion if at least one area of our lives is relatively stable. We can rely on this stable part of our lives and so risk change elsewhere. If we have nothing stable everything becomes turmoil. He suggested that stability zones were all-important but that each of us had different ones. The main stability zones described by Toffler are:

- Ideas – moral, religious, political beliefs.
- Places – home, town, pub, place of work – that we know well.
- People – spouse, partner, parents, old friends who we share our life with.
- Organisations – church, employer, clubs that we belong to.
- Things and habits – routines, possessions, cars that are familiar.

We all need at least one of these to be secure. Working out where our stability zones are and maintaining them helps us to cope with stress in other areas.

Schein (1978) developed this idea of stability zones for the workplace. He coined the phrase 'career anchors' to suggest that there are distinct categories of stability zones at work that individuals evaluate themselves with. Each of us will have one of these as most important in our working lives:

- Managerial competence – seeking out opportunities to manage and take responsibility.
- Technical competence – enjoying the technical activity of engineering, cooking or medicine, for example.
- Security – job security, income and pension are foremost considerations here.
- Creativity – important for those who want to build something of their own such as a new process, theory, technique or product.
- Autonomy and independence – where valuing freedom from constraints and having your own lifestyle is the most important thing at work.

ACTIVITY **14.5**

- What are your stability zones?
- What are those of the people who work with you?
- What about your career anchors?
- Have any of the people who work with you got unreasonable career anchors?
- Who could you go to for advice and succour with problems at work?

There are various other strategies for keeping one's balance when there is a period of rapid and unsettling change. In addition to the long-term strategy of trying to keep something stable, such as the stability zones or career anchors listed above, there are the smaller strategies such as trying to calm the pace at which you work by breathing slowly for a second or two. You might also try to remember that you do not have to deal with something on your own. Asking for help can bring new insights, companionship and learning. Even just unloading your fears and frustration can make it easier to cope. But beware the danger of becoming a real advice junkie!

Sometimes we also need to consider other people's reaction to a change we propose. There are several questions you need to ask when trying to persuade people to change. Such as:

- What is in it for them? If the person can see that the new behaviour, procedure or technology will make their work more satisfying they are likely to be enthusiastic. If they cannot see any benefit they are likely to be resistant.
- Have they had a say in the change? If people help to create a new scheme they are more committed to trying to make it work. This needs to be a genuine opportunity to participate in the introduction, design, execution and feedback of the new programme. If people are not involved at all, or the consultation is sham, their innovative and creative behaviours will often be used to demonstrate just why something will not work.
- Is it clear what change is envisaged? We need a clear vision of what we are trying to achieve if we are to persuade others to get involved. It needs to be put into terms that others will understand, not everyone speaks in management terms!

The psychological contract

The balance between the organisation and the individual has been summed up in the phrase psychological contract. This phrase was first used by Mumford (1972) and has since been frequently used by writers on personnel management and human resource management. The psychological contract between employers and the employed in the past was a job for life in return for your effort. The new style contract is lifelong employability in exchange for your effort. The employer is offering development, experience and maintaining a currency with modern events and methods. All of which are invaluable when seeking employment.

As Herriot and Pemberton (1995) point out, the concept of a contract requires two people and in reality the employers are usually bullying the employees to accept what is on offer. Their model of the balance between organisations and individuals suggests there are various dimensions where the contract between the individual and an organisation can be negotiated. See, for example, Figure 14.4, which I have based on some of these ideas.

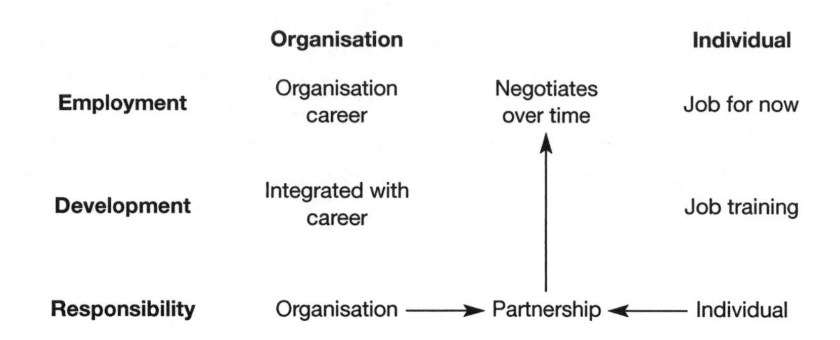

Figure 14.4
The psychological contract.

Conclusion

Change is part of life for all of us and most organisations change. In many ways the nature of humans is that they seek novelty as well as comfort. Many writers discussing organisational behaviour have used this aspect of organisational life as a central organising device to develop an integrated theory about organisation behaviour. Whether called OD, managing change or the learning organisation these writers include insights about the behaviour of individuals, groups and the whole organisation. So far they are rather idealistic but who knows what the next change in the models or organisations might show! An elegant solution?

EXERCISE **14.1**

Using the description of brainstorming described in the 'Did you know' section on page 240, have a go with a group on one of the following. (An ideal group is six to ten people.)

1 Uses for a matchbox.
2 Uses for plastic that can conduct electricity.
3 Markets for blue food colouring.
4 How to develop partnerships with other years of your course.
5 How to reduce the cost of textbooks in a modular course.
6 Ways to celebrate a 21st birthday.

Self-check questions

1 What might OD include?
2 What is force field analysis?
3 What is a learning organisation?
4 What are Steiner's five characteristics of creative individuals?
5 What are the five main stability zones of Toffler?
6 What is the psychological contract?

CASE STUDY **14.1**

The Scottish Office in Glasgow experimented with a variety of 'new' ways of working. (Reported in *People Management,* 9 October 1997, p. 44.)

They had a staff of seventy, in four teams, in a third of the space previously occupied. The aim was to create an efficient, effective and creative workplace. They used office design, technology, changes in working practices and the workplace culture to try to achieve this.

They set up the following:

- Virtual telephone numbers that followed the individual at home/commuting/office.
- Plug-ins for laptops all over the office.
- Video conferencing facilities.
- Wire-free workplaces for quiet work.
- Shared space so no one had their own spot.
- Hot workspace/desks/worktops/cubicles/offices which were all bookable.
- Soft areas for discussions, such as a café.
- Meeting areas for more formal discussions.

This led to a status free, creative, productive, knowledge-sharing output culture rather than an input culture. The emphasis changed from what people did to what they achieved.

When the scheme was assessed they found the following:

- Productivity – was increased and not dominated by presenteeism.
- Creativity – less successful, as only those who were previously known got involved, this environment was difficult for newcomers to become known in.
- Communication – a similar problem to creativity.
- Esteem – it was liked by the participants but resisted by others in the organisation.

Now, draw a force field analysis to suggest the forces for and against such a change, and answer the following:

1. Why do you think the participants were keen but not the other members of the organisation?
2. What would you do to ensure that newcomers could be as equally involved as the established members?

References

Argyris C. and Schon D. (1978) *Organizational Learning: A Theory in Action Perspective.* Addison-Wesley, New York, NY.

Hammer M. and Champy J. (1993) *Reengineering the Corporation.* Brearly, London.

Herriot P. and Pemberton C. (1995) *New Deals.* Wiley, Chichester.

Hill E. and O'Sullivan T. (1996) *Marketing.* Addison Wesley Longman, Harlow.

Lewin K. (1952) *Field Theory in Social Science.* Cartwright D. (Ed.), Tavistock, London.

McCalman J. and Paton R.A. (1992) *Change Management: A Guide to Effective Implementation.* Paul Chapman, London.

Marquand M. and Reynolds A. (1994) *The Global Learning Organisation.* Irwin, London.

Morgan G. (1986) *Images of Organization.* Sage, Newbury Park.

Mumford E. (1972) Job satisfaction a method of analysis, *Personnel Review,* Summer.

Pavitt K. (1979) Innovation and industrial development, *Futures,* p. 458.

Pedlar M., Burgoyne J. and Boydell T. (1991) *The Learning Company: A Strategy for Sustained Development.* McGraw Hill, London.

Schein E. (1978) *Career Dynamics: Matching Individual and Organisational Needs.* Addison-Wesley, Reading, MA.

Steiner G.A. (1965) *The Creative Organisation* University of Chicago Press, Chicago, IL.

Toffler A. (1970) *Future Shock.* Pan, London.

Torrance E.P. (1970) Causes for concern in creativity. In Vernon P.E. (Ed.), Penguin, Harmondsworth.

Vernon P.E. (Ed.) (1970) *Creativity: Selected Readings.* Penguin, Harmondsworth.

Further reading

There are innumerable books about the change process in organisations.

Pedlar, Burgoyne and Boydell (1991), mentioned above, is particularly well-regarded in the UK.

McCalman and Paton (1992), also mentioned above, is a very useful survey of all the relevant theories and with a practical slant on how to do it. It includes some case studies as well.

Casey D. (1993) *Managing Learning in Organizations,* Open University Press, Buckingham, is a readable book on how to support people while they change the way they work, from a consultant's perspective.

It is also worth looking at the IPD publication *People Management* for up-to-date stories of real organisations to see what and how people are changing.

Vernon (1970), mentioned above, is a useful book about the psychology of creativity.

Most textbooks on psychology also have a section on creativity.

CHAPTER 15

What next?

Objectives

When you have read this book you should:

- Be able to use different models for analysing a variety of organisational behaviours.
- Have experienced some practical exercises in using these analytical tools.
- Have a better understanding of the variety of ways there are of understanding the behaviour of people in organisations and the different factors that might affect this behaviour.

Introduction

This book has given you an introduction to the various ways that organisational behaviour can be analysed. As I said in the first chapter there is a variety of academic traditions which all have contributions to make to this analysis. This book has also shown some of the applied and practical uses of this sort of analysis, as many people using this book will be on courses that are mostly concerned with acquiring knowledge and skills not directly concerned with social sciences and management. So what should come next? This chapter tries to answer that question from various perspectives. What comes next for the academic social science analysis of organisations? What comes next for the organisations and their behaviours that need analysing? What comes next if you want to pursue the academic analysis of organisational behaviour, and, finally, what should you do if you want to apply some of the skills you have learnt?

What next for the analysis of organisational behaviour?

Throughout this book we have looked at a variety of models to analyse organisational behaviour. I have organised the material under various specific kinds of behaviour to be found in organisations, for example, the individual's behaviour, the group and the whole organisation make up Parts 1, 2 and 3 respectively.

The attraction of looking at behaviours in organisations continues and new ideas and models appear regularly. Some become popular and some stand up better to the scrutiny of academic questioning. However, they can appear contradictory and confusing. Some way of organising the material is needed. One way, traditionally, has been to organise the theory around particular topics, as this book does. Others organise it around the specific ideological point of view of the authors, such as positivist versus phenomenology, see, for example, Burrell and Morgan (1979). From these different models gradually a body of accepted views are developed that become organisation theory.

One very influential academic book in the study of organisational behaviour is *Images of Organization* by Gareth Morgan. He argues that there are seven quite distinct ways of looking at organisations, see Box 15.1. Each is a different sort of probe into a complex area, and each is appropriate for giving us an insight into some aspect of an organisation's working. An organisation is all these things at the same time, it is like examining different sides of the same mountain, they are quite different from each other but all ultimately belonging together. Only by having a variety of strategies for investigating or reading the situation can we have a true understanding of the organisation or indeed be effective members of an organisation. The importance of accepting that there are different ways of looking at the same thing and that they can all be valid gets away from the linear view of academic progress. It is particularly useful in a multi-disciplinary subject like organisational behaviour.

Box 15.1
Some ways of looking at organisations. (Based on Morgan (1986).)

1 *Organisations as machines*
With orderly relationships
clearly defined parts
determined order

2 *Organisations as organisms*
With adapting to the environment
life cycles
dealing with survival

3 *Organisations as cultures*
With patterns of belief
daily rituals
own language

4 *Organisations as political systems*
With authority
power
right to manage or individual rights

5 *Organisations as brains*
With think tanks
strategy formulation
corporate planning teams

6 *Organisations as psychic prisons*
With the trap of one way of thinking

7 *Organisations as instruments of domination*
With some having influence over others
work hazards

ACTIVITY **15.1**

Look at the following examples of the ways different schools organise things and decide which of Morgan's images (Box 15.1) would be the most suitable probe to investigate each issue. Clearly, any of them could be used but see if you can distribute each of the seven views against one of the seven examples.

(a) Two schools amalgamating into one.
(b) A school with a very strong headteacher where the phrase 'The PS (the head's initials) Show' was often used.
(c) A school with a very detailed staff handbook.
(d A school which makes a lot of contact with local people and parents.
(e) A school with a much higher staff sickness record than comparable schools.
(f) A school where the emphasis is on the role of the senior management group's corporate plan.
(g) A school that seems to be in a time warp; 'we are a good school' they say, but this in reality refers to a few years ago.

In contrast to Morgan's pluralist view of theories and models at the academic level there are continuing debates between academics about suitable methods of research and content of study. Arguments rage over not accepting that other viewpoints could be legitimate. For example, many have a managerialist viewpoint implicit in their work; for others this is anathema. Differences in the use of words and viewpoints is part of the tradition of social science and continues to generate strong language. For further understanding of this I refer the reader to Morgan (1997), Burrell and Morgan (1979) and Alvesson and Wilmots (1996). They each give a good overview of the technical models in this area of study. They also all outline some of the debates and differences between different schools of thought covering organisational behaviour. None of them are particularly easy to read but they are worth the effort for those interested in the academic study of behaviour in organisations and who want a disciplined approach.

What next for organisations and employment?

The only sensible answer to this question is 'Who knows?' There has been a long history of trying to predict the next step in society and there has certainly been a great rush of futurologists talking about organisations. One of the more popular ones in Britain has been Charles Handy. He argues (1997) that in an ever-changing environment for social, business, and political organisations we will increasingly need to decide what we are about before we decide what we have to do. He argues that these values will have to be more sustaining than the values of the free market. He includes such issues as:

- Personal autonomy.
- Responsible individualism.
- Self-discovery.
- The need for others.
- Citizenship.
- Education.

Like all predictions for the future they become something of a statement of ideals with less attention on how we are likely to get there.

In contrast to the futurology type of predictions about organisations are the studies of specific organisations that have changed dramatically and which may show the way in which others will follow. For example, some people are now working in what have come to be called 'virtual organisations'. These are temporary networks of otherwise independent organisations who come together for a specific purpose. An obvious example is in the building trade where, when there is a big project, the hoarding will list all sorts of engineers and surveyors and suppliers who are brought together for the project.

DID YOU KNOW?
Many book publishers use contract writers, editors, proof readers, indexers and printers and finishers to produce the book which is then marketed and supplied by separate contracted agencies. A virtual organisation to publish a book.

Miller *et al* (1996) point out that the main issues in dealing with virtual organisations for global teams are:

- Objective – the content or task needs to be clear as the process by which people work is more problematic when people do not work in the same organisation.
- Technology – the problem of incompatible computers, e-mails and telecommunications should never be underestimated when working across organisations. It is amazing how many updates are forgotten about when trying to synchronise different elements. A common understanding of procedures and computers is useful.
- Motivation is difficult to judge if people are very distant from each other.
- Power between people becomes more egalitarian in virtual organisations as it is the contribution of each that matters.

To these we might add:

- The importance of having the right members to work with so that there is a suitable standard across the members.
- Each member needs to gain from the project otherwise their commitment is likely to be different.

Hale and Whitham (1997) provide further reading on virtual organisations.

A further influence on what might be happening to organisational behaviour in the future is the pressure from outside for organisations to consider the effect they have on both their physical and social environment. This is called governance in management circles. The extent and potential of socially responsible action by managers are considerable, and their behaviour is shaped by a number of factors: legal regulation, public pressure, labour market forces, competitive threats, the personal values of individual decision makers and considerations of company image. Most significant is probably the organisation culture.

DID YOU KNOW?
Harry Ramsden's give pre-interview training to long-term unemployed people because they found that in Manchester this group were very committed if they were taken on. The five-day course involved food hygiene, customer care and confidence building with job interviews at the local college. When the real interviews were held the managers were not told which applicants had come through which route.

These ideas are increasingly being talked of as 'stakeholding' and using this responsible individualism as a model for organisations. See, for example, Handy (1997) and Plender (1997).

Another view of what will happen to organisational behaviour is to be found in the material which looks at successful organisations or effective organisations. Since Peters and Waterman's study of excellent companies, many have sought to find what makes some organisations better than their contemporaries. If we can find that then we can hope to improve the less good organisations. Almost every year another version of these lists appears.

A recent list that has some prestige, as it comes from a government department, is included in DTI/DFEE research of successful companies, both large and small, reported in *People Management* 24 July 1997, p. 13, which has led to a model of successful organisations. They found that successful organisations:

- Shared goals – the business planning was shared with all the staff.
- Shared culture – felt fair policies with high expectations and celebrating success was common.
- Shared learning – continuous development of people.
- Shared effort – teams cooperate inside and outside of the organisation.
- Shared information – communicating in 360 degrees.

What next for your further study?

If you have become intrigued with the study of organisational behaviour you can follow up in various ways. You could start by reading some of the recommended books and references. If you find the development of models and the analysis to your taste you could carry on studying some of the pure social sciences such as psychology and sociology. In the specifically organisational context most universities have higher level courses in organisational behaviour. There are also more serious textbooks on the subject; Mullins (1996) is probably the most widely read in the UK.

Figure 15.1 **Take your cake and eat it.**

If on the other hand it is the application of some of these ideas that has most intrigued you then courses with a more specifically management bent will probably interest you. For example, anything with personnel or human resource management in the title will cover some of the applied material in this book in more detail. A post-graduate qualification on one of the Institute of Personnel and Development courses would certainly do so. A widely read textbook for this would be Marchington and Wilkinson (1996).

I hope you might also have leant some survival skills for your own employability. The technical skills you develop with experience and the transferable personal, social skills you acquire make up the package of your employability. Continuing to develop these and keeping them up-to-date gives you the opportunity to indulge in some organisational behaviour of your own!

What next for the practical application of all this?

Perhaps you do not have the time now or the desire to do any further study of the subject but would like to use some of the things you have learnt. Working in any organisation will give you the opportunity to use some of these materials to analyse what is going on. I think this will be of most use when everything else you have tried has not worked, so why not refresh your outlook by trying a new model? You might also use some of the models at an individual level to help you appraise your own behaviour and career choices, as we discussed in Chapter 6.

What I hope you have learnt now we have reached the end of this book is that there is a wide range of views on how to interpret organisational behaviour, that it is fascinating in its own right to some of us, and that it is practically useful for anyone trying to operate in society, particularly those who are trying to influence events within an organisation.

References

Alvesson M. and Wilmotts H. (1996) *Critical Management Studies*. Sage, Newbury Park.

Burrell G. and Morgan G. (1979) *Sociological Paradigms and Organisational Analysis*. Heinemann, London.

Hale R. and Whitham P. (1997) *Towards the Virtual Organisation*, McGraw Hill, London.

Handy C. (1997) *The Hungry Spirit*. Hutchinson, London.

Marchington M. and Wilkinson A. (1996) *Core Personnel and Development*. IPD, London.

Miller P., Pons J.M. and Naude P. (1996) Global teams, *Financial Times*, 14 June, p. 12.

Morgan G. (1986) *Images of Organization*. Sage, Newbury Park.

Morgan G. (1997) *Images of Organization*, 2nd edn. Sage, Newbury Park.

Mullins L.J. (1996) *Management and Organisational Behaviour*, 4th edn. Pitman, London.

Plender J. (1997) *A Stake in the Future*. Brearly, London.

Answers to Activities, Self-check questions and Case studies

Not all the activities and exercises have answers that I can give. They are things for you to do that generate your original material, so obviously there are no answers to those questions here.

Chapter 1

Activity 1.1

1. Psychology.
2. Sociology.
3. Psychology.
4. Sociology/psychology.
5. Sociology.
6. Psychology.

There are no absolute right answers which is the nature of the study of organisational behaviour. Although there is a tendency to use one for preference. Often one uses both in research and particularly in consultancy. Frankly, if it works use it!

Activity 1.2

Some examples might be:

- The effectiveness of a meeting.
- How people report to each other.
- About the meaning of the work people do.
- On what people think about the culture and effectiveness of the new organisation.

Exercise 1.1

It is up to you to generate some original material.

Exercise 1.2

Again, you have to do it.

Self-check questions

1 Behaviour.
2 Social groups.
3 Advice on the use of power.
4 Productivity.
5 Role definition.
   Hierarchy.
   Rules and procedures.
   Qualifications.
   Impartiality.
6 People enjoying the effect of attention of researchers so messing up the results of the research.
7 It depends on the particular circumstances.
8 Excellence.
9 Hard is seen in quality and competence.
   Soft is seen in development models.

Case study 1.1

(a) = 1
(b) = 2
(c) = 1
(d) = probably 3
(e) = 4

But you may have good reasons for disagreeing. In social science justifying the reasons for your conclusions and the evidence for these conclusions is important. As I give rather sketchy pictures you may have imagined a different example from the one I had in mind!

Chapter 2

Activity 2.2

Extroverts	*Introverts*
Bar person	Long distance truck driver
Trader	Research chemist
Hotel receptionist	Nature reserve warden
Museum guide	Computer programmer
Leisure centre manager	Teleworker

But it would depend on the details of the job. Also, someone can make a job work in a different way through their own style.

Self-check questions

1 Nature and nurture
2 Psychoanalytic models remind us that some behaviours are due to deep-seated conflicts of desires and socially acceptable behaviour. Behaviourist models give us a technology for human learning. Humanistic psychology advocates that mature adults can be trusted to take responsibility.
3 Physical sensitivity.
Selective attention.
Categorise.
Limit.
Context.
Attitudes.
4 Can lead to prejudice and discrimination.

Case study 2.1

1 Try to explore differences in personality.
Emphasise ego to explore difference.
Different levels of energy and drive might be explored.
2 Would explore different experiences of the two brothers.
Were there different parental expectations of them?
Emphasis on the learning of each to account for the difference.
3 Would want to know to what extent each of them feels fulfilled, and satisfied with their careers.
Questions about the level of conformity to other people's views or doing something for themselves would be asked.

Chapter 3

Exercise 3.1

Establishing a staffroom is often suggested

(b) 1 Eye contact; talk to them; thank them where appropriate; include them.
2 Decent surroundings.
3 Clean and suitable coffee-making facilities. Preferably free.
4, 5 and 6 are up to you.

Self-check questions

1 See Figure 3.1.
2 See Box 3.1.
3 Their own belief, circumstances and the nature and organisation of their work.
4 See pages 48–9.
5 Because it is an internal state.

Case study 3.1

1 You should be able to find examples in all three areas.
2 Cooperative.
3 Someone who wants to switch off and just be told.
4 Not necessarily. It needs the will of everyone and the leadership of someone to get it going.
5 Large ones would need to break into smaller sections.
6 Think up some that would work easily this way and others that might be difficult and use your judgement.

Chapter 4

Activity 4.3

Procedural.
Comprehension.
Comprehension.
Procedural.

Exercise 4.1

Use Kolb's cycle to answer this (Figure 4.1).

Self-check questions

1 Classical is stimulus response whereas operant involves rewarding the response to establish the conditioning.
2 Recognition and recall.
3 Figure 4.1.
4 Figure 4.2.
5 Comprehension.
Reflex learning.
Attitude development.
Memory training.
Procedural learning.
6 The effect of social learning and expectations.
7 Becoming part of the group.
8 Because of changes in the employment world.

Case study 4.1

Socialisation at law firm – clothes style, coffee and lunch routines, start/finish rituals.
Technical – content of report.
Publication skills – collating material for a particular audience, public relations and publication skills.

Chapter 5

Activity 5.4

1. Encoding important.
2. Encoding and transmitting important.
3. Decoding critical.
4. Environment paramount.
5. Transmitting and receiving in balance.
6. Feedback.
7. In balance.
8. Encoding important.

These are my answers but it is important to remember that all communication involves all stages and this activity is merely to show there is a difference in emphasis and you may well have different answers.

Self-check questions

1. See Box 5.1.
2. See Figure 5.1.
3. Different ways grown-ups communicate and behave towards each other.

Case study 5.1

1. Sort letters into priority.
2. Emphasise they are different audiences and what they need.
3. Emphasise their usefulness or destructiveness effect on the school.

For example:

- Letter 5.1, Mr and Mrs Heaven – ignore or brief thanks.
- Letter 5.2, Miss Steak – emphasise cannot promise, but remind the children of behaviour. Possibly go and find out more about why and what happened near shop.
- Letter 5.3, Mrs... – No reply as undecipherable. Inform class teachers and ask if they recognise the writing.
- Letter 5.4, J. Campbell – Ask her to discuss. Set recruitment process in train by informing chair of governors.
- Letter 5.5, The Minister – Fill in and return if possible. If difficult consult LEA and/or other headteachers.
- Letter 5.6, June Blunt – Arrange a meeting with her and chair of governors.
- Letter 5.7, Arthur Capp – brief letter of apology stating problems of getting school into baths quickly and orderly.

Chapter 6

Activity 6.1

Strategic jobs would include:

vice chancellor
managing director
chief executive

Operational jobs would include:

store manager
front of house manager
ward manager
head of department

Administration jobs would include:

publicity officer
central registry
wages and pensions officer

Self-check questions

1. Accountability and empowerment.
2. Strategic jobs scan the horizon and operations jobs cover the day-to-day.
3. Doing things for different employment and organisations.
4. Core are central, full-time permanent staff. Periphery staff are temporary, contracted staff.
5. Demands, constraints and choices.
6. Ideas are drawn over the page as they connect to each other.
7. Emotionally, physically, problem solving, hobbies and social.

Case study 6.1

1. Set the style. Make things happen. Manages all the other waiters. Central core man looking after the interests of the owner.
2. The cost of the staff can be kept down by using a lot of periphery staff while ensuring standards are maintained by keeping Charlie well-rewarded.
3. Vulnerable to losing Charlie through sickness or poaching by another restaurant. To say nothing of the high trust put in Charlie.

Chapter 7

Activity 7.3

Most are either two-player games such as tennis and squash or 8–12, such as football and hockey. They are stable groups. Why are there so few with 3–8? Because of stability problems?

Activity 7.4

1 Get AB, CD and EF to agree the travel budget by 10 Feburary.
2 Visit customers X, Y and Z by 31 June.
3 Hold a team briefing meeting every Friday at 9 o'clock to talk about objectives.

Self-check questions

1 They allow the exchange of information and understanding which is not given formally.
2 See Table 7.1.
3 See Box 7.1.
4 Socially accepted ways of behaving in the particular group.
5 Completely connected network.
6 Company worker, chair, shaper, ideas, resource investigator, monitor/evaluator, completer/finisher.
7 Look at the section called group environment.
8 The exaggeration of the irrational.

Case Study 7.1

Informal networks.
Tuckman's stages for cohesiveness.

Chapter 8

Self-check questions

1 Enabling others to perform well.
2 Various, see Krech.
3 See Figure 8.1.
4 See Figure 8.2.
5 Tells, sells, consults, joins.
6 It depends on the situation.
7 Ability to get things done based on authority rather than position and formality.
8 Consideration, feedback, delegation and participation.
9 Responsible for own action.

Case study 8. 1

By being there every morning before surgery started, everyone knew they could pass on information and requests and develop things without having to waste time in meetings or more formal methods. By being available to everyone Sid picked up on problems more quickly than he might have done otherwise. By treating everyone as an important individual, regardless of rank, he was liked and trusted by nearly everyone. All this meant Sid was able to make the resources of the directorate stretch just that little bit further so that everyone had the satisfaction of attending to the patients more efficiently. A lot of Sid's job was working with people on all sorts of long- and short-term issues. The great strength of his method of doing this was acknowledging individual differences and trying to meet them half-way to get things done.

Chapter 9

Self-check questions

1. Implicit contract.
2. No.
3. Management by objectives.
4. See stimulating improved performance section.
5. No, some is for time and some for commitment.
6. Self, peers, boss, others.
7. As part of performance management and for the reasons given in the performance review section.

Case study 9.1

She has considered various approaches: staff meeting, individual talks, informal discussion in her office and asking the personnel department to do something. In the end she has decided to introduce a developmental appraisal scheme for all the staff with nurses on G and H grade and the chief technologist being responsible for conducting the appraisal interviews. She wants the appraisal scheme to include some objective setting and discussion of personal development plans.

She and I have spent two days running an appraisal workshop for all the senior nurses and technicians, in two groups as, obviously, the critical care still has to go on despite management training! At the end of the two days an action plan has been agreed about how to set up the appraisal interviews. Everyone still claimed they were nervous of the process but said they felt less threatened as they could see how such a system could be separated from pay by keeping the reporting forms confidential and 'owned' by the individual rather than the manager and with the staff being able to nominate two senior staff they would be prepared to be appraised by. So far, it all seems to be going well.

Chapter 10

Activity 10.3

	Less than 6 mths	Longer-term goals	Everyone	Self-confident	Low cost	High cost
Acting up	X	X		X	X	
Action learning		X		X		X
Audio-visual	X		X		X	
Case study	X	X	X	X	X	X
Coaching	X	X	X	X	X	X
Delegation	X	X	X	X	X	X
Discussion	X	X		X		X
Distance learning		X		X	X	X
Exercise	X		X		X	X
Group		X		X		X
Job rotation		X	X	X	X	
Learning contract		X	X	X	X	
Learning opport.	X	X		X	X	
Lecture	X	X	X	X	X	
On the job	X	X	X	X	X	
Programmed	X	X	X	X	X	X
Project		X		X		X
Role play		X		X		X
Secondment		X		X		X
Simulation		X		X		X
Skill instruction	X	X	X	X	X	X
Talk	X	X	X	X	X	

Exercise 10.1

The reasons I would give are:

- Learn each other's strengths and weaknesses.
- Learn what a challenge feels like.
- Improve their fitness and general well being.
- Discover their credibility and role is contingent on what they are doing, such as airport, piste and bar may change the leader.

Exercise 10.2

Acting up	Kolb	CA
Action learning	Kolb	CA
Audiovisual		CRP
Case study	Kolb	CP
Coaching	Kolb	CRP
Delegation	Kolb	CA
Discussion		CP
Distance learning		MP
Exercise		MP

Group	Kolb	CA
Job rotation	Kolb	CRAMP
Learning contract		CRAMP
Learning opport.		CRAMP
Lecture		C
On the job	Kolb	CRAMP
Programmed		RMP
Project	Kolb	CRAMP
Role play	Kolb	CA
Secondment	Kolb	CA
Simulation	Kolb	CRAMP
Skill instruction		RMP
Talk		C

Self-check questions

1 National vocational qualifications.
2 Elitism, voluntarism, centralism, conformism, humanism, co-development.
3 Ability to do something.
4 At appraisal, changes, instigation of individual, induction, recovery of poor performance.
5 Learning by doing:
agreed targets
audio-visual, computer and book materials that do not rely on a teacher
do different tasks
acting out problems and jobs
6 Continuing professional development.
Investors in people.

Case study 10.1

Helen. Helen has gone from a low timetable and lots of systematic support in her probationary year to a full timetable and no systematic support. She is left alone to sort out the demands and requests on her time and skills. She has become overloaded and now feels a failure. Yet her only failure is appearing so confident, competent and keen that more and more was expected of her. No one helped her make sense of this.

Gary. If someone had either used his skills to aid the introduction of computing into the administration or explained why he was not included perhaps his energies would still be organisationally functional whereas they are in danger of becoming dysfunctional.

Doreen. Doreen's teaching role requires her to give consistent, continuous attention to 30 or so pupils in her classroom. This role has become particularly demanding with the investigative and discussion types of teaching. Yet her constant interruptions can only be coped with in the more traditional, formal styles of teaching that are considered old fashioned and out of date at this school. No one is helping her make sense of her two incompatible roles.

Chapter 11

Self-check questions

1 Structure including
   task efficiency
   technology
   structure
   people
   management
   context
2 Power, role, task and person.
3 The characteristic spirit and beliefs that are taken for granted. Also Schein's three levels.
4 The primary are about informal methods, the secondary are the more formal methods.
5 The threat of new entrants and substitute products; the bargaining power of buyers and suppliers.
6 See Box 11.1.

Case study 11.1

1 Collegiality.
2 Role culture.
3 Knowing everyone sufficiently well to trust and communicate appropriately.

Chapter 12

Self-check questions

1 Because of conflict over resources, decisions etc.
2 Coercive, renumerative and normative.
3 Alienative, calculative, moral.
4 See Box 12.1.
5 'In' is position, 'An' is expertise.
6 Authority, responsibility and accountability.
7 Setting agendas and developing networks.
8 Fifty:fifty.
9 Making decisions, recommending, training newcomers, analysis of reports, innovation, cohesion, catharsis, manipulation.

Case study 12.1

His ability and resourcefulness.
He is the only one with skills and experience of funding, making and doing practical things.
In other words, his experience.

Chapter 13

Activity 13.1

Additional work of informing of changes.
Core to keep control.
Jealous of freedom.
Feel ignored if too much attention is given to the part-timers.

Self-check questions

1 Ten factors are given at the beginning of the chapter – have a look.
2 Strategy; Structure; Systems; Staff; Style; Skills; Shared values.
3 (a) Moving from one job to another
(b) Increasing the number of tasks done by an individual
(c) Broadening responsibilities and autonomy
(d) Comparing the worth of jobs with one another systematically.
4 Flexible hours of working. Three out of:
job share
teleworking
term-time working
variable contracts
zero hour contracts.
5 See Box 13.4.
6 New and established demand for labour.
Supply of labour.
Forecast.
Implementation plans.

Case study 13.1

Strategy – how are we to do it?
Structure – carry on as discrete units except for top management or should all be integrated?
Systems – should have joint meetings for all things or only at the top?
Staff – career progression across courts or within one?
Style – carry on quite local differences or move to a corporate whole?
Skills – need to develop some senior staff able to take an overview.
Shared values – how to stop Manchester City court, by far the largest, dominating.
As yet nothing has been decided but these questions are currently (1998) being asked.

Chapter 14

Activity 14.1

Try to analyse whether success was because of:

Clear plans.
Clear communication.
Everyone knew what was needed.
Good leadership.
A consequence of a previous initiative.
Or something else.

Self-check questions

1. Organisational culture.
   Organisational climate.
   Employee commitment.
   Organisational conflict.
   Management of change.
   Management development.
   Organisational effectiveness.
2. A device for comparing the forces for change and the restraining forces for no change.
3. These are models of how organisations ought to be effective that include ideals of how individuals and groups behave.
4. Conceptual fluency, flexibility, originality, complexity, independence of judgement.
5. Ideas, places, people, organisations, things and habits.

Case study 14.1

Force field analysis:

For change	*Against change*
Cost of buildings	Traditions of working
Reduce staff costs	Cost of re-equipping
Flexible hours for staff	Fear

1. 'Hawthorne' effect as well as the new equipment.
2. Weekly/monthly compulsory lunch meetings?

Index

Note: A page reference in **bold** indicates a definition